MEDIEVAL EUROPEAN SOCIETY, 1000–1450

Consulting Editor:

EUGENE RICE

Columbia University

MEDIEVAL EUROPEAN SOCIETY, 1000-1450

Margaret Hastings

DOUGLASS COLLEGE

Rutgers, The State University of New Jersey

Random House   New York

Library of Congress Catalog Card Number: 72–128048

Standard Book Number: 394–30329–6

Manufactured in the United States of America. Composed by Cherry Hill Composition, Inc. Printed and bound by Halliday Lithograph Corporation, West Hanover, Mass.

Designed by Ronald Farber

First Edition

9876543

Acknowledgements

The author wishes to express gratitude to the following publishers and individuals for copyright permission to publish selections from the works designated:

Selections from *The Portable Medieval Reader*, edited by James Bruce Ross and Mary McLaughlin. Copyright 1949 by the Viking Press, Inc. Reprinted by permission of the Viking Press, Inc.

Selection from *The Basic Writings of St. Thomas Aquinas*, edited by Anton C. Pegis. Copyright 1945 by Random House, Inc. Reprinted by permission of Random House, Inc.

Selections from *The Statesman's Book of John of Salisbury*, Translated and edited by John Dickinson. Copyright 1927, 1955. All rights reserved. Reprinted by permission of Appleton-Century-Crofts, Educational Division, Meredith Corporation.

Selection from Sidney Painter, *William Marshal*, Copyright 1933 by The Johns Hopkins Press. Reprinted by permission of the Johns Hopkins Press.

Selection from W. A. Nitze, "The So-Called Twelfth Century Renaissance," *Speculum*, vol. XXIII (July, 1948). Copyright *Speculum*. Reprinted by permission of *Speculum*.

Selection from *Lord Hastings' Indentured Retainers, 1461–1483*, by William H. Dunham. Copyright William H. Dunham, Jr. Reprinted by permission of William H. Dunham, Jr.

Selections from *The Crusades: A Documentary Survey*, by J. A. Brundage. Copyright 1962 by the Marquette University Press. Reprinted by permission of the Marquette University Press.

Selection from *The Art of Courtly Love*, by André le Chapelain, edited and translated by J. J. Perry. Copyright 1941, by Columbia University Press. Reprinted by permission of the Columbia University Press.

Selections from *Medieval Trade in the Mediterranean World,* by R. S. Lopez and I. W. Raymond. Copyright 1955, by Columbia University Press. Reprinted by permission of Columbia University Press.

Selection from *University Records and Life in the Middle Ages,* compiled and edited by Lynn Thorndike. Copyright 1944 by Columbia University Press. Reprinted by permission of Columbia University Press.

Selection from *De Profectione Ludovici VII in Orientem,* by Odo of Deuil, translated and edited by V. G. Berry. Copyright 1948 by Columbia University Press. Reprinted by permission of Columbia University Press.

Selection from *Life in the Middle Ages,* by G. G. Coulton. Copyright 1928 and 1954 by Cambridge University Press. Reprinted by permission of Cambridge University Press.

Selection from *Bracton on the Laws and Customs of England,* Vol. II, translated by S. E. Thorne, Cambridge, Mass.: The Belknap Press of Harvard University Press. Copyright 1968 by the President and Fellows of Harvard College. Reprinted by permission of the publishers.

Selection from *Western Views of Islam in the Middle Ages,* by R. W. Southern, Cambridge, Mass. Copyright 1962 by the President and Fellows of Harvard College. Reprinted by permission of the publishers.

Selection from *The City of God* by Saint Augustine, translated by John Healy, revised by R. V. G. Tasker. Everyman's Library edition. Used by permission of E. P. Dutton & Co., Inc.

Selection from *Rural Economy and Country Life in the Medieval West,* by Georges Duby, translated by Cynthia Postan. Copyright 1968 by Edward Arnold Ltd. Reprinted by permission of University of South Carolina Press.

Selection from *The Fifteenth Century,* by Margaret Aston. Copyright 1968 by Thames and Hudson, London. Reprinted by permission of Harcourt, Brace & World, Inc.

Selections from *Abbot Suger on the Abbey Church of St. Denis and Its Art Treasures,* edited, translated, and annotated by Erwin Panofsky. Copyright 1946 by Princeton University Press. Reprinted by permission of Princeton University Press.

Selection from *Medieval People,* by Eileen Power. Copyright 1924 Methuen and Co. Reprinted by permission of A B P International.

Selections from *The Mongol Mission,* by Christopher Dawson. Copyright 1955 Sheed and Ward. Reprinted by permission of Sheed and Ward.

Selection from *The Origins of Modern Germany,* by G. Barraclough. Copyright 1946 by Basil Blackwell. Reprinted by permission of Basil Blackwell and Mott, Ltd.

Selection from *Social Theories of the Middle Ages,* by B. Jarrett. Copyright 1926 by Ernest Benn, Ltd. Reprinted by permission of Ernest Benn, Ltd.

Selections from *Feudalism,* By Joseph R. Strayer, Copyright 1965 by Joseph R. Strayer. Reprinted by permission of Van Nostrand Reinhold Company.

Selection from *Chronicles of the Crusades,* by Joinville and Villehardouin, translated by M. R. B. Shaw. Copyright 1963 by M. R. B. Shaw. Reprinted by permission of Penguin Books, Inc., Harmondsworth, Middlesex.

The second stanza from Daisy Aldan's translation of "Can vei la Lauzeta mover," in *An Anthology of Medieval Lyrics,* edited by Angel Flores. Copyright 1962 by Angel Flores. Published by Random House, Inc. Reprinted by permission of Daisy Aldan.

To the students in
The History of Western Civilization
at Douglass College,
for whom this book was written

Preface

Human history is tragedy in the Greek sense. This is true because man is mortal. We know neither where we came from nor whither we are going. Homer's gods can be ineffably comic because they are larger-than-life-size men who will never die. For them there is no judgment day. They have no ultimate responsibility. Men, even heroes, are born; they live; they experience joy and sorrow; but, in the end they die, and we do not know what death is. About the body we know a lot but not enough; about the indefinable spirit that makes one person different from another we know even less. Shakespeare, a modern man, or perhaps just a timeless one, put it that:

> We are such stuff as dreams are made on
> And our little life is rounded with a sleep.

Medieval men in western Europe like many others in other times and places thought they had an answer to the question where men come from and whither we are going. Derived from Judaic-classical origins as it was, it said that God, a being outside and beyond the scientifically examinable world, created us for purposes beyond our knowledge or comprehension and that, in a hereafter that we cannot rationally predict or describe, God will punish us for the evil that we do and reward us for the good. A barbarian chieftain of the early seventh century, when presented with a choice whether to adopt Christianity, argued for it in these terms:

The present life of man, O king, seems to me, in comparison of that time which is unknown to us, like the swift flight of a sparrow through the room wherein you sit at supper in winter, with your commanders and ministers and a good fire in the midst, whilst the storms of rain and snow prevail abroad; the sparrow, I say, flying in at one door, and immediately out at another, whilst he is within, is safe from the wintry storm; but after a short space of fair weather, he immediately vanishes out of your sight, into the dark

xi

winter from which he emerged. So this life of man appears for a
short space, but of what went before, or what is to follow, we are
utterly ignorant. If, therefore, this new doctrine contains something more certain, it seems justly to deserve to be followed.

Bede, *Ecclesiastical History*, Dent ed. pp. 90–93.

The certainty accepted by this man and others is said to have
given to medieval men a kind of stability in their lives that we
lack today. Perhaps some medieval men, in certain times and
places, did find some stability in their lives. The question is
whether a fifth-century inhabitant of Gaul, or an eighth-century
inhabitant of Spain, or a tenth-century inhabitant of Britain, or
a fourteenth-century inhabitant of Italy would have known that
he lived in a period generally characterized by stability. The
more historians learn about the medieval period, the more they
impress us with the diversity and insecurity of human existence
in those times. Between 450 and 1450 lie a thousand years of
human activity, and nothing is more clear from the evidence
than that the Western world of 1450 was unimaginably different from the same part of the world in 450. Significant changes
must have occurred in the intervening thousand years, changes
worthy of the attention of historians.

Modern historians tend to think that medievalists in their
unending study of the Middle Ages are simply moving piles of
dust from one part of a room to another. There are at least
two misconceptions here. One is that all the dust of the period
has not yet been exposed or examined. Literary sources are far
fewer than for modern times and are no less fallible than your
daily paper, or your favorite commentator, or your favorite
poet. Documents, also fewer than for modern times, have not
yet all been read and analyzed. Even if they had, they must
constantly be reinterpreted in relation to new discoveries and
new insights into old materials. Rapidly increasing knowledge
and technique in archeology, anthropology, and psychology
force historians into ever new interpretations.

In the end, all historians, medieval or modern, must face the
fact that they are as much poets as they are scientists. They try

as scientists to get at all the basic facts and to interpret them intelligibly. But they do not succeed. It is doubtful whether a committee including the top-level historians of the United States could establish beyond a shadow of reasonable doubt all the significant facts about what happened in Dallas, Texas, on November 22, 1963, or that they could agree with one another in their interpretation of the meaning of John Kennedy's death. What is certain is that historians will have to try to get the facts straight and the meaning clear, and that, if they do not abdicate their function, there will be a great deal of historical writing with many interpretations based essentially on the same facts. What the experts write will all be valuable even though they disagree with one another. Disagreements about relative importance of particular facts and about the significance of the whole episode will depend on each historian's view of life, and that is a matter not of science but of art.

The book I present here does not pretend to be a new scientific exploration of the Middle Ages. I have attempted not an original scholarly interpretation, not a summary of all the latest scholarship, not a comprehensive synthesis, but merely an introduction to a long period of history, the study of which is at present in relative eclipse in the United States. What I hope that the student will get from the book is not just a few clichés that he can encapsulate or learn for a test but an understanding that human beings lived in the medieval thousand years, interacted and tried to solve the problems of human existence, not knowing all that they needed to know nor what the outcome of their actions would be.

I have had great help from colleagues in the History Department at Douglass College in Rutgers University and from students who have been kind enough and serious enough to express their complaints and their appreciation. I have written the book for students who know next to nothing about the Middle Ages. Professional medievalists will find much to criticize or reject. Students will, I hope, go on to find out more about the people of a period that is formative for the world we live in.

M. H.

New Brunswick, N.J.
December 1969

Contents

Maps

MEDIEVAL EUROPEAN SOCIETY, 1000–1450

I

The Formation
of Europe

The Middle Ages was the formative period in European history. From the ruins of Mediterranean civilization in the area north of the Mediterranean Sea and west of the Carpathian Mountains there grew up between the fifth and the fifteenth centuries that new European civilization that was to become dominant throughout the world by the nineteenth century. Its essential characteristics were beginning to be identifiable in the tenth century, and there has been no real break in continuity since that time.

Chronology of the Middle Ages

The so-called Dark Ages with which the Middle Ages began, that is, the centuries between A.D. 400 and 800, are "dark" because we neither know nor understand enough about them. During these 400 years Germanic peoples migrated en masse into the old Roman Empire. The one great vital force they encountered was the Christian religion, and in the four "dark" centuries there was worked out a viable association between Christian teachings and traditions and Germanic concepts and customs. Roman law, imperfectly understood and applied, played a part, but its impact had a reverse relation to the proximity to the old centers of civilization. Greek ideas and ideals influenced the West chiefly in the form in which they had become part of Christianity. Christianity and Germanic culture interacted profoundly, but the essential contradiction between a doctrine of

3

brotherly love, humility, peace, and self-abnegation, on the one hand, and of individual courage, fierce loyalty, and honor, on the other, remained to produce in the twelfth century the kind of strong, polarized tension that is so often a condition of human creativity.

The twelfth and thirteenth centuries—the great centuries of the Middle Ages—are usually designated the High Middle Ages. In these centuries the conflict and interaction of values and ideas from Europe's mixed heritage produced the excitement of early scholastic thought, of reviving scientific curiosity, of chivalric and romantic literature, and of Gothic sculpture and architecture as well as the tragic warfare of the Crusades. The Crusades are the most dramatic expression of the union of Christian and Germanic values, and the Crusader knight has rightly become a familiar symbol of the age. The Christian West, in the name of the Prince of Peace, and carrying the cross and lamb on its banners, waged a long series of wars against the Muslims. The Crusaders meant to recover the original centers of Christianity, to reunite Christendom under the leadership of Christian Rome, and to convert or conquer the "infidel," so that all men might live in Christian peace. They failed ultimately, and their failure brought a reorientation of values. Europe turned inward and put its energies into internal wars and a search for new sources of inspiration.

The last two centuries of the medieval period, from 1300 to 1500, were centuries of crisis and change, so much so that some historians have described these years as the period of death of medieval civilization. It is the contention of this book that these were centuries of *growth* rather than of death. To be sure, no new peoples were added to the melting pot and no new ideas and principles were introduced, but there was a more articulate demand from the common people for a share in the rewards of society, and among the intellectual aristocracy there was a more fervent study of the classical past. Rulers of society became more literate. They became patrons of the philosophers, poets, and painters. The Church and the papacy declined, but there was more lay piety, suggesting that the Christian message had reached the common people and become more meaningful to them. There was steady progress in technology, in matters such as navigation, measurements of time and space, the use of artillery in battle, and the development of business instruments and methods. Polarization of inherent conflicts became more extended. There was more diversity and way-out lunacy, but no really revolutionary tendency or principle was put forth. Men of the late medieval and early modern period broke less with the past than did men of the eighteenth century.

Europe: Terminology and Geography

The term Europe has been used freely in the discussion thus far. It was a term scarcely used by medieval men, although it had been applied by the Greeks as early as the fifth century B.C. to one of the three great land masses of the earth they knew. They had used the word rather more for propagandist than for scientific purposes, and it crops up occasionally in Roman and medieval writing used in the same way. Aristotle had expressed the Greek prejudice in these terms:

> Those who live in a cold climate and in Europe are full of spirit, but wanting in intelligence and skill; and therefore they keep their freedom, but have no political organization, and are incapable of ruling over others. Whereas the natives of Asia are intelligent and inventive, but are wanting in spirit, and therefore they are always in a state of subjection and slavery. But the Hellenic race, which is situated between them, is likewise intermediate in character, being high-spirited and also intelligent.[1]

In other words, Greece, though in Europe, was near enough to Asia to reap the benefits of both worlds. The Greek prejudice against Asiatics has had a long life as part of Western thought.

Christendom, a more common word than Europe in medieval writing, only occasionally refers to a geographically definable territory. It meant those people converted to the faith—or, more ambitiously and loosely, all mankind. In the fifteenth and six-teenth centuries "Europe" and "Christendom" achieved some sort of territorial definition and began to be used interchangeably. The ultimate victory of the term Europe in the eighteenth century is no concern here. What is pertinent is that the word itself as well as the concept and the actuality it represented have a long history and that an important part of the process by which the word acquired precise meaning occurred in the medieval period. By the end of the period "Europe" identified a culture, though not yet a "continent."

Western civilization until the Middle Ages had been Mediterranean-centered. It had been started on the eastern shores of the Mediterranean Sea and had spread westward around the sea. Rome, from its vantage point in the center of this sea-centered world, brought unity and some sort of peace to the whole area surrounded by the wall of Roman legions defending an extravagantly extended frontier. The Romans were a restless and ambitious people. In their greatest days they constantly sought new conquests. Defense of frontiers meant subduing aggressive peoples beyond the frontiers. Reputations in Rome (like Julius Caesar's, for example) were made by military conquests. Military conquest added northwest Europe to the Mediterranean Roman Empire as far northwest as the Irish Sea, lowland Scotland, and the North Sea and as far east as the Rhine and the Danube rivers. The Romans successfully established their power in western Europe and maintained it for something like 400 years. Beyond the Rhine-Danube frontier, their renown, the allure of the land they ruled, and their trade exerted great attraction, but they never successfully established or maintained governmental power there. Medieval civilization grew up in the area dominated by Rome. By A.D. 1000 it had begun to spread to parts of the world which had never been ruled by the emperor in Rome and which were Christianized without having been civilized in the Greco-Roman sense, that is, without having created cities and the civic spirit that develops in cities. The decisively formative developments had already taken place in western Europe, the part which, in varying degree, had been Romanized.

An important part of the story of the Middle Ages is the conquest of the west European physical environment, a conquest more complete and enduring than that which had occurred in Roman times and one involving a transfer of the centers of power from the shores of the Mediterranean to the north. Europe, even just western Europe, has a great diversity of geographical characteristics. Yet there are certain general points of contrast with the Mediterranean world. The whole scale of the landscape is more expansive. Plains are broader and flatter than the little pockets of fertile valley running down to the sea that characterize the northern shores of the Mediterranean. River valleys are longer and wider. Hills and mountains north of the line drawn by the Pyrenees, the Massif Central in southern France, and the Alps are more gently sloping. Heavy, damp, and less easily cultivated soils extend over considerable areas. Large and deciduous trees take the place of the relatively smaller evergreens and subtropical trees of the Mediterranean shores. The sea is far distant and difficult of access from many parts. The climate is more extreme. Winters are longer and colder than in the Mediterranean region, and the rainfall is heavier and less predictable, coming in the summer as well as in the winter. The land is more difficult to settle and to till. In the Mediterranean region both soil and climate had been favorable to early development of human society and to its continued existence without extravagant effort. Light soils with a high lime content, predictable and adequate rainfall, and alluvial deposits flowing down from the wooded slopes of the mountains had been favorable for the growth of wheat, the most nutritious of all the grains, and of the grape vine. In many parts of northern Europe it was possible to cultivate only the poorer grains—barley, oats, or rye—and the growing of grapes for wine was impossible. In the Mediterranean region the slopes of river valleys could be used to cultivate olive and other fruit trees. Relatively small holdings of arable land could, with proper irrigation and crop rotation, support a man's household. Diminishing productivity set in only when men cut down too much of the mountain woodland and so reduced the natural water storage as to denude and erode the land. North of the Alps, heavier plows, more animal draft power (ox power rather than horse power in this era), and more cooperation were required to clear heavily wooded land and to plow its heavy soil.

Central Europe, beyond the Rhine-Danube frontier, was even less hospitable to human takeover than western Europe. The cold and snowy winters there make for a short growing season. Summers are cool and rainy. Lakes and marshes break up the sandy plains in the north, and the rivers flow northward into the turbulent North Sea or into the enclosed Baltic Sea, from which access to the ocean is difficult. The Baltic is, in any case, ice-blocked for a considerable part of the year. In the north, the heavy-timbered deciduous trees of the southern mountains give way to pine, birch, and other short-lived trees that grow in cold climate and sandy soil. The Germans, who inhabited this region in the great days of the Roman Empire, lived by hunting, by war, and by raising some grain crops in the inhospitable soil. Their livelihood was supplemented by trade with the Romans. The Germans were continually drawn toward the warmer climate and richer land to the west and south of them. The Rhine, Rhone, and Danube valleys and the penetrable passes of the Alps provided routes to these more gracious parts of the world.

The Coming of the Germans

The Romans constantly had to defend themselves against raids or more massive attacks by the Germans on their eastern frontier. In A.D. 9 a Roman army of three legions (perhaps 13,000 men) was caught in ambush and destroyed when, on a punitive expedition against raiders, it ventured beyond the Rhine into the German forests. After that disaster the Romans fell back to the Rhine. This frontier was then accepted as permanent and was strengthened. However, Germans continued to infiltrate in small war bands, and many found service with the Roman army. In the middle of the second century the Romans, because of increasing shortages of manpower for agriculture, for the trades, and for the army, began deliberately to recruit Germans as soldiers. This led to a gradual Germanization of the army and eventually even to a preponderance of the German element in the officer ranks, including commanding generals. Whole colonies of Germans were given land to settle on under "guest rights" in Roman law. These peoples did not assimilate into the Romanized population of Gaul or the other provinces where they settled. In 376 occurred the first mass invasion of Germans into Roman territory. Terror-stricken by a sudden attack by the Huns (a nomadic oriental people probably of Mongol origin), the Visigoths had petitioned the emperor to let them cross the Danube and settle under Roman protection. He granted them "asylum." Inevitably conflicts arose between these refugees and the local inhabitants and Roman imperial officials who supervised their settlements. The Visigoths revolted, defeated a hastily collected imperial army, and even killed the emperor.

The Germanic victory was a signal for a general movement of Germans from east to west. They settled mainly in the western provinces of the Empire. The routes of their incursions into western Europe can be followed best by reference to Map 1 on pages 10 and 11. The Visigoths moved on into Italy, then in the century after the death of their leader Alaric (410), through southern France into Spain, where they established a Visigothic kingdom. The Franks, beginning in the fourth century, moved at a slower pace across the Rhine and down into the area of modern France. The Vandals, in less than two generations, fought their way across France, then down through Spain and across the Strait of Gibraltar, from west to east across northern Africa, and then back across the Mediterranean to attack Rome from the south (409–455). Everywhere they left behind them the kind of destruction that has immortalized their name.

Angles, Saxons, and Jutes settled in Britain, pushing the Celtic inhabitants into the rugged mountainous areas of the west and northwest (450–550). The Roman legions had been

NORTH SEA

Elbe R.

Thames R.

Rhine R.

ENGLISH CHANNEL

ATLANTIC OCEAN

Seine R.

Loire R.

Garonne R.

Rhône R.

Po R.

Ebro R.

Tagus R.

Invasion routes

- ·········· Anglo-Saxons, 367-550
- •••••• Burgundians
- – – – – Franks, 358-498
- ——— Huns, 375-451
- ——— Lombards
- – – – Ostrogoths, 150; 200-375; 375-489
- ——— Vandals, 409-455
- –·–·– Visigoths, 376-410; 412-507

Map 1. The Germanic Invasions

withdrawn from Britain early in the fifth century, and the Roman commander of the imperial army in Gaul was deaf to the pleas of the Britons for help against the invaders. Burgundians descended from the upper Rhine valley into the area east of the Rhone River in the latter half of the fifth century. Ostrogoths established a strong kingdom in Italy after Odovacer, an Ostrogothic chieftain, in 476 had deposed Romulus Augustulus, a twelve-year-old boy and the last Roman emperor in the west, who was living in retreat from Rome at Ravenna. Finally, the Lombards, the most savage of the invaders, attacked and occupied northern Italy in the latter part of the sixth century. This takeover of the west by the Germans had been briefly interrupted in the middle of the fifth century by a breakthrough of the Huns under their ablest king, Attila. They burst across the Rhine into northern Gaul and were only turned back with difficulty in a fierce battle near Châlons (451) by an army that was made up largely of Visigoths but commanded by a Roman general.

German success in taking over the western Roman Empire would have been impossible if Roman institutions had not been disintegrating from within. Many explanations have been offered in answer to the question why the Roman Empire of the West fell apart as it did. Edward Gibbon, in a historical classic *The Decline and Fall of the Roman Empire,* written in the late eighteenth century, expressed the view that it "was the natural and inevitable effect of immoderate greatness." The Romans had too much prosperity, too much success, and too much ease, and they, therefore, failed to take essential measures against threats to their power. Others have seen "causes" in the unsoundness of an economy involving an unfavorable balance of trade between a western part of the Empire producing largely foodstuffs and raw materials and a more complex industrial and commercial East. Poor technology, ascribed by economic historians to the use of slave labor, declining manpower and agricultural productivity, racial mongrelization, an overrigid governmental structure, political confusion, overregulation of the economy and society, oversimplification of culture resulting from the gradual absorption of the educated classes by the masses, the influx of the Germans, and the spread of the Christian religion, all these have been suggested as major causes for the weakening of the internal structure of the western Empire. There is some merit to each hypothesis except for "racial mongrelization," defined by its author, Tenney Frank, as an admixture of Asiatic elements with Roman culture through the importation and ultimate integration of slaves from the eastern Mediterranean.[2] This seems to be just a perpetuation of the kind of prejudice that Aristotle had expressed. The decisive factors were probably a decline in population and productivity that made it impossible for the citizens of the Empire to bear the ever increasing costs of military defense and government. The transfer of the main seat of the emperor to the new city of Constantinople on the Bosporus in 330 and the acceptance of Christianity as the exclusive religion of the Empire were critical decisions for the Empire. The first meant that the emperor paid closer attention to the problems of defending the southeastern frontier and less to the northeastern and western frontiers. The other gave to the leaders of the Christian Church in the West (the bishops and monks) an authority that they could not have exercised otherwise.

The Germans by their onslaught completed the destruction of the Empire, although their intent was not necessarily to destroy. Some of their leaders appreciated the grandeur of Roman political institutions and would have preferred to preserve rather than to destroy them. Ataulf, successor to Alaric as leader of the Visigoths, put the problem in these terms:

> I have found by experience that my Goths are too savage to pay obedience to law, but I have also found that without laws a State is never a State; and so I have chosen the glory of seeking to restore and to increase by Gothic strength the name of Rome. Wherefore I avoid war and strive for peace.[3]

In the same spirit, Theodoric the Great, Ostrogothic king of Italy (496–526), attempted to enforce a policy of religious toleration and of *civilitas,* that is, of the civic virtue of the citizen, on which Rome's political strength had rested. But the Germans were not city dwellers and understood little or nothing of Roman civil government. Roman cities and the spirit behind the words "citizen" and "civilization" had already fallen into decay before the mass migrations of the Germans began. The "barbarians" completed the destruction by taking over the land and by-passing or destroying the cities. The terror that they inspired as they overran the countryside was expressed by a fifth-century poet as follows:

> In village, villa, cross-roads, district, field
>   down every roadway, and at every turning,
>   death, grief, destruction, arson are revealed.
> In one great conflagration Gaul is burning.
> Why tell the deathroll of a falling world
>   which goes the accustomed way of endless fear?
> Why count how many unto death are hurled
>   when you may see your own day hurrying near?[4]

Germanic Culture

German society was tribal and rural rather than urban. It is difficult to obtain an understanding of a people so important in the history of the West, for there are relatively few sources about their early history and culture. They "originated" in the area around the Baltic Sea. Their home before they reached the Baltic area is not known. The main Roman sources for their culture are Julius Caesar, writing about 55 B.C., and Tacitus, writing about A.D. 100. To learn about their society one must turn to epic poems like *Beowulf,* written down several centuries after its original composition, the laws and customs gathered and written down by German rulers after contact with Roman administrators and Roman Christian clergy, and a few narrative histories written long years, even centuries, after the events they relate—for example, Bede's history of the victory of Christianity in Britain or Gregory of Tours' *History of the Franks.* There was a wide diversity in German customs and a wide range in the degree of Romanization depending on the proximity to Rome and the extent of the exposure to the Roman world. Some Germans were still nomadic or seminomadic and depended mainly on hunting and war for their living. Others, such as the inhabitants of the Rhine valley, had a settled agriculture that was technically not very different from that of their Roman neighbors.

German political organization was simple compared to the state organization of the Roman Empire. The *folk,* or group of related tribes, was led by a king chosen from a royal family. His "election" depended on his ability to lead in war and to command loyalty from the nobility. He ruled people rather than land, and it was only gradually, as the Germans settled down, that government became at all territorialized. The Germans did not understand taxation in the Roman sense. Their kings supported their households and armies from plunder and from lands won from their enemies. They kept for their own use "gifts" contributed by their followers. As kings, they reciprocated with "rings," feasts, and other gifts exemplifying their generosity and wealth. Their followers owed them nothing. In fact the freeborn German owed nothing to anyone except what he chose to give.

Kings were assisted in their task of leadership by tribal leaders from noble families, probably also chosen for leadership and lordship. According to Tacitus, German folk groups, or "nations," held periodic assemblies to consider such matters as peace and war:

> About minor matters the chiefs deliberate, about the more important, the whole tribe. Yet even when the final decision rests with the people, the affair is always thoroughly discussed by the chiefs. . . . When the multitude think proper, they sit down armed. Silence is proclaimed by the priests, who have on these occasions the right of keeping order. Then the king or the chief, according to age, birth, distinction in war, or eloquence, is heard, more because he has influence to persuade than because he has power to command. If his sentiments displease them, they reject them with murmurs; if they are satisfied, they brandish their spears. The most complimentary form of assent is to express approbation with their weapons.[5]

Evidently these assemblies, like the assemblies of the Greeks encamped before Troy, consisted of the fighting men only, and the men of noble rank dominated the proceedings.

Tacitus speaks of magistrates "who administer law in the cantons and the towns." This probably applies only to those Germans who had established fairly permanent settlements. Justice among the Germans consisted in enforcing through popular courts the law and custom of the tribe. Until contact with the Romans, the law and custom was carried in the minds of the freemen participating in the courts, and its application to individual cases was decided by them under the presidency of the magistrate. From a study of Germanic codes written down after German settlement within the Empire, certain principles emerge. No distinction was made between criminal and civil matters. The law was mainly concerned with the enforcement of the individual's "peace," from the king down to the lowest freeman. Individuals, of whatever rank (except for slaves), were entitled to compensation for attacks on themselves, their families, their guests, or their slaves within their houses and environs. The amount to be paid for the breach of a man's peace depended on his rank in society. The master of a slave must be compensated for an attack on his slave. Injuries, including murder, could be paid for under an elaborate tariff of compensations: so much for a nose, so much for an eye, for a right thumb, for a big toe, and so forth; so much for a free Frank, for a Frank "in the service of the king" (three times as much), for a Roman "who eats in the king's palace," for a tribute-paying Roman (just over one-fifth as much).[6] Money compensation for murder was called *wergeld,* the money worth of a man, and it obviously varied according to the man's rank in society. Despite efforts of kings and chieftains to enforce the principle of compensation, the older blood feud and *lex talionis* (eye for eye, tooth for tooth) persisted. Theft and robbery, as well as personal injury, were subject to compensation—so much for a stud boar, so much for a breed sow, so much for a suckling pig. Cattle, sheep, and pigs were important in Germanic society; values were expressed in terms of them, and elaborate arrangements were provided for recovery of stolen cattle.

The law was personal, not territorial. That is, a man accused had to prove his innocence according to the law of his particular folk, not, like the Roman citizen, according to a law of the land applying equally to all "citizens." Bishop Agobard of Lyons, writing about 850, stated that very often when five people met in a case for judgment, each followed a different law.[7]

The first stage in Germanic legal proceedings was accusation by a plaintiff. Defendants were expected to deny the accusation under oath and to support their oaths with a specified number of oath-helpers, depending on their rank. An ordinary freeman needed twelve; a king or a bishop needed none. Those who could not produce oath-helpers, either because they were untrustworthy or were strangers among the people where the injury occurred, had to submit to trial. The popular, or *volk,* court decided whether there should be a trial and, if trial was to be held, what method of trial was to be used. The commonest methods were ordeals: the hot-water, the hot-iron, and the cold-water ordeals. In the first, the accused was expected to plunge his arm to a specified depth into boiling water to pick up an object at the bottom. Afterward, his hand and arm were sealed in a bandage. If, after three days, his wound showed signs of suppuration, he was guilty; otherwise he was not guilty. The ordeal of the hot iron was a variation. In trial by the cold-water ordeal, the accused was trussed up with a rope, knees to chest, and thrown into a pond. If he sank, he was innocent and was pulled out and revived (one hopes). If he floated, he was thought to be in league with the devil and, therefore, guilty. In these methods of trial, resort was to divine judgment. God, it was assumed, would save the innocent and let the guilty perish. The Christian priesthood, who presided over these trials until they were forbidden to do so by the Fourth Lateran Council of 1215, probably exercised some degree of personal judgment that mitigated the rigor of the ordeals for the innocent.

A common method of trial among northern people (although, for unknown reasons, not among the Anglo-Saxons) was trial by battle. Here an elaborate set of rules prevailed. Combat was with wooden cudgels, and that party won who first drew blood from his opponent's head. Priests, children, and women were permitted to choose champions to represent them. The most popular trials for women in medieval Europe were trial by cold water for commoners and trial by battle of champions for aristocratic women. This may have been a little hard on women of the lower orders. Women float better than men, and men often think that women are permanently in league with the devil.

Kinship ties were presumably strong among the Germans before their major migrations, and they survived into the tenth century in relation to the blood feud and the payment of *wergelds*. Yet the migrations tended to weaken them. As was inevitable in a time when war bands went off in search of loot and places to settle, relationships among fighting men, particularly the relationship between fighting companions and their leader, or lord, grew stronger. Tacitus had described such war bands, and in the lyric and narrative poetry of early medieval centuries, of *The Wanderer*, for example, the lost feeling of the lordless man is movingly expressed:

> And he dreams of the hall-men
> The dealing of treasure, the days of his youth,
> When his lord bade welcome to wassail and feast.
> But gone is that gladness, and never again
> Shall come the loved counsel of comrade and king.
> Even in slumber his sorrow assaileth,
> And, dreaming he claspeth his dear lord again,
> Head on knee, hand on knee, loyally laying,
> Pledging his liege as in days long past.[8]

In battle narratives, both the passion of loyalty and the shame of desertion were vigorously voiced. Aethelstan, King of England (925–937), enforced by law the responsibility of kin to find a lord for a man who had none on pain of the man's outlawry.

The virtues most valued among the Germans were evidently courage, loyalty, and leadership, and the vices most severely punished were cowardice and treachery. A man's honor, that is, his reputation for bravery and loyalty, were his most important possessions. Unwarranted attacks on his honor, such as calling him a "fox" or his wife a "harlot," entailed heavy penalties. The free fighting man among the Germans was an only partially tamed savage, and he was very much an individual. He had no civic virtues.

The Origins and Victory of Christianity in the Mediterranean World

The victory of Christianity as the official and only tolerated religion of the Empire coincided chronologically with the beginning of the mass invasions of the Germans into the western Empire. In fact, many of the Germans had been "converted" to Christianity before their invasion of western Europe. However, mere conversion had not effected any marked transformation of Germanic cultural values. For that a long process of education would be necessary. For example, Clovis, the first Christian king of the Franks, successfully liquidated by savage force and ruse all possible challengers to his throne. He persuaded the son of a fellow king to assassinate his father, then arranged the brutal murder of the son. Denying all knowledge of the plot, he persuaded the people to choose him as king in place of the murdered father and son. The Christian bishop who tells us this story comments:

He received Sigibert's kingdom with his treasures, and placed the people, too, under his rule. For God was laying his enemies low every day under his hand, and was increasing his kingdom, because he walked with an upright heart before him, and did what was pleasing in his eyes.[9]

Clovis and his bishop biographer were a long way in spirit from Jesus, the teacher and healer of Nazareth, who had taught a doctrine of brotherly love and peace. It is not surprising, however, that Germans, educated to their own system of values, should have failed to grasp the full Christian message. Clovis, in becoming a Christian, meant to enlist for his designs the protection and support of a god more powerful than those he had hitherto worshipped. Gregory, bishop of Tours, the historian of Clovis' reign, commended all that Clovis did because the king had espoused Roman doctrine in preference to the Arian heresy accepted by many of the Germanic invaders. Neither of them is likely to have thought of trying to practice Christian ethics in the warlike society of the Franks.

Christianity itself had changed since the time of its founder. Any major religion takes its shape from a complex set of factors: the teachings of the founder, the interpretation of these teachings by successors, the organization set up for worship and for maintenance of the doctrines and of religious discipline, the mental attitudes and traditions of the converts, and the conditions under which the religion spreads. In the case of Christianity, a simple narrative of "what happened" is virtually impossible. Jesus gave his message to Jews, a civilized people living in a highly complex society created by interaction among Greeks, Romans, and oriental peoples on one of the strategic highways of the world. The message was carried to speculative and argumentative Greeks, to disciplined and civilized or enslaved and impoverished Romans, to partially Romanized and civilized Celts in Gaul and Britain, to the "wild Irish," and to other barbarians outside the boundaries of the "civilized world."

Let us begin our tracing of the development of Christianity with the fact that Jesus was a Jew and taught a way of life and faith grounded in a long-established prophetic tradition of Judaism. He emphasized the love and mercy of God, the love and brotherhood of men of good will, the unimportance of worldly wealth and power, and the comfort and promise of redemption and happiness in a blessed hereafter. Some authorities contend that Jesus may have been influenced in his rejection of success in the world by the Essenes, an ascetic sect of

Jews who were in conflict with the Jewish establishment and had withdrawn to retreats in the desert near the Dead Sea, where they practiced an extreme asceticism and a rigid adherence to the ancient law. They lived in hope of an apocalyptic deliverance from the world of the flesh and the devil. These practices and concepts derived ultimately from Persian religious ideas of the sixth and fifth centuries B.C. Jesus, in contrast, did not withdraw from the society but went out to teach and preach among the humble and poor, to help and heal the sick and the destitute, in other words, to change conditions in the world as well as to give men hope for a hereafter. He taught the observance of ancient Jewish law but said that the law was made for man—not man for the law. On the whole, the connection with the Essenes is inadequately proved.

Most of the Jews did not accept Jesus as the promised Messiah (or in Greek, *Christos*) who would bring "justice and righteousness from this time forth and for evermore." There were those who thought he was an imposter and a subverter of the social order. There seems little in his teaching to threaten either the Jewish or the Roman establishment. Yet, he was arrested and crucified, a common Roman penalty for criminal activities. Then, from the brief, tragic story of his life and mission, his followers created that powerful and enduring myth that became the center and core of Christianity as it spread through the Mediterranean world.

Peter, one of the twelve whom Jesus chose as his disciples, and Paul, a convert who had been a persecutor of Christians, made the crucial decision to preach and teach the faith among Gentiles as well as Jews and not to require circumcision or Jewish observances other than the basic ethical teachings of the ancient Hebrews. The carrying out of this decision led to the spread of the religion throughout the Roman Empire and beyond its boundaries in the first great experiment in mass education the world had yet seen. Ancient religions had been public, that is, participated in by all the inhabitants of a city-state or the members of a nation, or they had been "mystery" religions, participated in only by an initiated few who had been properly inducted into the celebration of the rites. Christianity became the greatest of the mystery religions in the sense that baptism and instruction were necessary for introduction to its rites. It kept its social character, speaking a message of hope and comfort for mankind. Moreover it became also an explanation of man's existence and purpose in the world that challenged the best minds of the period.

Changes in Christianity occurred, no doubt, because men brought to the religion what they had to give and took from it what they were able to take on the basis of their past experience. Paul, for example, brought to the faith a vast knowledge of Jewish Scripture and rabbinical tradition as well as of Greek philosophy. He brought also the ardency of spirit that had made him a great persecutor of Christians, and he brought the testimony of his own conversion. It was he who created a comprehensive theology in which the death and resurrection of Christ, the son of God, given by God for the redemption of mankind, became the culminating event in the world's history. And it was he, in the many pastoral letters he wrote to congregations that he had formed, who introduced the emphasis on the rejection of the world of the flesh and the devil and on the experience of conversion as the highest experience of the Christian.

But the disputatious Greeks, Jews, and other oriental converts of the eastern Roman Empire could not accept any one exegesis of the theology of Christianity, particularly not of the difficult problem of Christ's relation to God. How could Christ, being God, be born like any other human baby from the womb of a human mother, and did this in some way affect his divinity? Was God, the Father, superior to the Son, did He exist before the Son, and what was the nature of the Holy Ghost by whom Mary was supposed to have been impregnated? The controversy over the nature of Christ rose to such a pitch in the early fourth century that Emperor Constantine decided to call a general council of leaders of the Church at Nicaea to settle the violent dispute initiated by the teaching of Arius, a priest of the great Egyptian city of Alexandria. He taught that Christ, having been born of woman, was of a nature subordinate (though still divine) to God. The formula adopted at Nicaea is the basis of the creed as recited in many Christian churches today:

> We believe in one God the Father All-sovereign, maker of heaven and earth, and of all things visible and invisible; And in one Lord Jesus Christ, the only-begotten Son of God, Begotten of the Father before all the ages, Light of Light, true God of true God, begotten not made, of one substance with the Father, through whom all things were made; who for us men and for our salvation came down from the heavens, and was made flesh of the Holy Spirit and the Virgin Mary, and became man, and was crucified for us under Pontius Pilate, and suffered and was buried, and rose again on the third day according to the Scriptures, and ascended into the heavens, and sitteth on the right hand of the Father, and cometh again with glory to judge living and dead, of whose kingdom there shall be no end:
>
> And in the Holy Spirit, the Lord and the Life-giver, that proceedeth from the Father, who with Father and Son is worshiped together and glorified together, who spake through the prophets:
>
> In one Holy Catholic and Apostolic Church:
>
> We acknowledge one baptism unto remission of sins. We look for a resurrection of the dead, and the life of the age to come.[10]

This formula did not, as hoped, settle the question. The followers of Arius continued to teach their heretical doctrine and even took it to the Germans beyond the Roman frontiers, thus creating for Church authorities a doctrinal problem in the education of the Germans to add to the already difficult problem of Christianizing their savage behavior.

Paul was not the only highly educated man to become converted to the Christian faith during its early history. As men trained in the schools of Athens, Alexandria, and other great centers of learning became converts, they brought into the faith their knowledge and their methods of disputation acquired in these schools. The first four centuries of the Christian era were the age of the so-called Fathers of the Church, the scholars who elaborated a Christian theology in answer to challenges from their former colleagues and who created a Christian literature that became the heritage of medieval men in search of wisdom. The greatest of these were Ambrose, bishop of Milan (?340–

397), Jerome (?347–419), and Augustine of Hippo (354–430). The first became a great statesman of the new religion and wrote a treatise on Christian morality based on classical models, mainly Cicero. Jerome, a man learned in Latin, Greek, and Hebrew, translated the Bible into Latin, increasingly the only language of learning in the West. Augustine, a simple and charming man equipped with a powerful mind and imagination, came to Christianity only after a long and, to him, painful flirtation with the major philosophical and religious traditions of his day. In treatises on Christian doctrine, in voluminous letters and polemical tracts, he explained for other educated and sophisticated Christians the major problems of the faith with such success that his works became the main source for study in later medieval schools of Christian theology. One of his major contributions was the doctrine of original sin—that is, that all men are involved in the sin of Adam, the first man, who broke the contractual condition of his existence in Eden and so forfeited God's gift of grace to him. But God did not permanently reject man. He sent his only begotten son for man's redemption. Redemption is a great gift of God, not broadcast at large but only to those who can open their hearts to receive it, submitting their human will to God's will. Augustine himself, like Paul and many others in these centuries in which Christianity was fighting for acceptance, had had the experience of conversion, of suddenly feeling himself charged with a power that lifted him beyond and above his petty human capacities.

During these early centuries also a Christian church came into being, that is, a public institution with an apparatus for spreading the faith, for maintaining its purity, for ordering its worship, and for protecting the faithful against hostile external power. From the beginning when the disciples were left frightened and confused by the sudden loss and departing injunctions of their leader, the central part of remembrance and worship had been the celebration of the mystery of Christ's death and resurrection in a ceremony in which participants partook of bread and wine thought by miraculous transformation to be the body and blood of Christ. The ceremony was thus a communion with the resurrected Christ by consuming the flesh and blood of His incarnation. It was thus a kind of incarnation for the communicants and a highly sacred ritual. Only initiates, that is, those instructed and baptized in the faith, could be admitted. Someone was needed to preside over the ceremony. In response to this and also to the need for caretakers to control the common funds contributed by converts to the congregations, there emerged officers of the faith: on the one hand, priests and bishops to lead in spiritual matters, on the other, deacons to take care of the money and other common property of the congregations. Quite naturally there developed a doctrine of Apostolic Succession. All properly constituted priests were expected to be able to trace their authority back to the disciples, those whom Christ Himself had constituted the propagators of the faith. Bishops were the chief among these. They had their seats in the principal cities of the Mediterranean world and, eventually, the west European world. The churches in which they presided were called cathedrals to differentiate them as the higher seats of authority.

In the East there were many great cities, the greatest of them Alexandria, Antioch, Jerusalem, and from the time of Constantine, his new city, Constantinople. In the West there was the one great city, Rome, the dominant city of the Mediterranean world during the first crucial centuries of Christianity. Not unnaturally, bishops of Rome claimed from early times a preeminent power in the Church. Scriptural justification was found in the words of Christ to Peter, the traditional first bishop of Rome:

> Thou art Peter, and upon this rock I will build my church; and the gates of hell shall not prevail against it. And I will give unto thee the keys of the kingdom of heaven: and whatsoever thou shalt bind on earth shall be bound in heaven and whatsoever thou shalt loose on earth shall be loosed in heaven.[11]

Bishops of Rome did not always find it easy to enforce this doctrine of the Petrine Succession on a vast and rapidly growing church. But there was a historical logic in it which could be a source of strength to bishops of Rome like Leo I in the fifth century or Gregory I at the end of the sixth.

Persecution of Christians by the Roman authorities encouraged the spread of the faith and a change in its emphasis. "The blood of the martyrs was the seed of the Church." The example of the many who died bravely calling on Christ as their Savior was now added to the verbal teaching and preaching as a method of propagation. Not everyone could understand the preaching of Paul or the treatises of Augustine, but anyone could understand the fortitude in her faith of a Blandina who endured the terrors of the arena inspiring her fellow sufferers:

> . . . she, the little, the weak, the contemptible, who had put on Christ, the great and invincible athlete, and worsted in many bouts the adversary and through conflict crowned herself with the crown of immortality.[12]

A cult of these martyrs developed, and even those who had not the heart for martyrdom themselves revered local martyrs, and believed in the miracles reported of them in their lives and of their relics after death. For simple and uneducated people, these martyr saints supplied the place of older deities who had been credited with magical powers and gave them something closer than a remote majestic God and his crucified Son with which to meet the terrors and trials of the world.

Roman persecutions were not just haphazard and irresponsible, although they were certainly atrocious. The crux of the problem as it became clear in the early second century, in the reign of Trajan (98–117), was that the Christians were uncivic in spirit. They intolerantly refused to take part in the public worship of the old gods that was part of the civic duty of Roman citizens. And, owing to the secrecy of their central rites, open only to initiates, wild charges could be made against them of sacrificing children, drinking their blood, and the like. A harassed Roman provincial governor wrote to Trajan, the emperor, to ask for an official policy in dealing with what he termed "a depraved and extravagant superstition." The answer was sober and moderate although it made no concession with regard to the main requirement of participation in public worship:

You have taken the right line, my dear Pliny, in examining the cases of those denounced to you as Christians, for no hard and fast rule can be laid down, of universal application. They are not to be sought out; if they are informed against, and the charge is proved, they are to be punished, with this reservation—that if anyone denies that he is a Christian, and actually proves it, that is, by worshiping our gods, he shall be pardoned as a result of his recantation, however suspect he may have been with respect to the past. Pamphlets published anonymously should carry no weight in any charge whatsoever. They constitute a very bad precedent, and are also out of keeping with this age.[13]

However, the moderate Trajan-Pliny policy did not prevail in Rome. Persecutions continued with increasing severity until at the end of the reign of Diocletian (303–305) a last all-out effort was made to exterminate the Christians and destroy the Church. This failed, and Diocletian's successors then embarked on a policy of toleration. In the Edict of Milan (313) they declared:

. . . we decided that of the things that are of profit to all mankind, the worship of God ought rightly to be our first and chiefest care, and that it was right that Christians and all others should have freedom to follow the kind of religion they favored; so that the God who dwells in heaven might be propitious to us and to all under our rule.[14]

By the end of the fourth century, the triumph of Christianity was so complete that Emperor Theodosius (379–395) adopted Christianity as the exclusive religion of the Empire by issuing an edict requiring:

. . . that all the various nations which are subject to our Clemency and Moderation, should continue in the profession of that religion which was delivered to the Romans by the divine Apostle Peter, as it hath been preserved by faithful tradition . . . According to the apostolic teaching and the doctrine of the Gospel, let us believe the one deity of the Father, the Son and the Holy Spirit, in equal majesty and in a holy Trinity. We authorize the followers of this law to assume the title of Catholic Christians; but as for the others, since, in our judgment, they are foolish madmen, we decree that they shall be branded with the ignominious name of heretics . . .[15]

With the end of persecution there emerges a new type of Christian leader and a new mode of Christian life. The kudos that had formerly gone to the martyr saints was transferred to the hermits and monks, who, having withdrawn to the solitude of the desert or wilderness, had succeeded in conquering the temptations of the world, the flesh, and the devil by self-imposed austerities and constant prayer. Monasticism had started in the third century in the eastern Mediterranean region as a movement of individuals in flight from the corruption of the cities to the peace of the desert. Notable hermits like St. Anthony (?250–?350) were sought out by imitators. The large number who desired to emulate these first hermits necessitated the organization of communities in order to maintain discipline. The monastic movement became more social in character. Monks and nuns lived in community apart from the world, but they prayed together and practiced the Christian virtues of love, humility, and obedience in their relations with one another. St. Benedict (480–543), who formulated the monastic rule that became the model for all others in the West, did not reject life or social values. He thought of the monastery as a school for the teaching of the true Christian life:

> We have, therefore, to establish a school of the Lord's service, in the institution of which we hope we are going to establish nothing harsh, nothing burdensome. . . . For it is by progressing in the life of conversion and faith that, with heart enlarged and in ineffable sweetness of love, one runs in the way of God's commandments, so that never deserting His discipleship but persevering until death in His doctrine within the monastery, we may partake by patience in the suffering of Christ and become worthy inheritors of His kingdom.[16]

An abbot was to be chosen by the monks themselves, the older and wiser heads carrying the greatest weight. Once chosen, he was to have an absolute paternal power. Yet he was to exercise this power with humanity, sanity, and humility before God. The novice, or candidate for the monastic life, had to give up the pleasures and pains of sexual love, taking a vow of chastity before entering the community. He was to have no personal property, not so much as a knife or pen, and he was to obey the abbot and senior brothers in all humility. Eating and sleeping were restricted to limits balanced between the body's subordination to the spirit and its natural animal needs. The monk was to divide his time among prayer, labor for the community, study, and meditation. The monastery became his home and his family, and he was not to leave except on permission or order of the abbot. In relation to earlier laxities and other rules, St. Benedict's was moderate, sensible, and deservedly triumphant in western Europe. St. Benedict did not directly enjoin study as a necessary part of monastic life, although he did encourage reading for his monks. Yet, inevitably, because the monasteries were sanctuaries from the hazards of the world and because many who became abbots were learned men, the copying and reading of books became part of the monastic life.

A First Flowering of European Culture

By A.D. 600 the main cultural constituents of the brew that created Europe were already there. The Germans had moved in and settled down in the areas that they continued to dominate until modern times, and they had begun to develop the particularities that became the bases of later European "nations." Christianity had conquered and been conquered by the West. Relics of the Greco-Roman world lay everywhere to be wondered at and used to the extent of the capacity of their users. The times seemed ripe for the emergence of something new and creative. In fact, something new and creative did emerge.

The first flowering of a new European culture occurred, not as might be expected in one of the old centers of Mediterranean culture, but in the remote north of England. The first impetus came from Ireland, beyond the boundaries of the old Roman world, as a Christian-Celtic movement that swept back into northern England in the sixth century to encounter and join

with a Christian-Germanic movement in the south of England
initiated by a mission from Rome. Ireland had been converted
by a mission from the continental mainland, traditionally by
St. Patrick in the middle of the fifth century. Irish Christianity
had developed its own peculiarities in the absence of close
supervision from Rome. Monks rather than bishops provided
the leadership, and monasteries rather than cathedrals and
bishops' palaces were the centers of intellectual and spiritual
activity. Irish monks were freer to move about than those held
to the strict Benedictine rule. Great saint missionaries flourished among them and went out to plant monasteries in the
north of England and on the continent, even as far east and
south as Burgundy. In 595 Pope Gregory I (590–604) sent a
mission to Britain to convert the Anglo-Saxons and reconquer
the land for the Church. Inevitably this Germano-Roman and
Celtic Christianity met and came into conflict in the north of
England. The problem was essentially one of authority and was
resolved by synods or councils to which clergy of both parties
were invited. The details are unimportant. The main point is
that out of this intermingling and conflict of religion and general culture developed a creative literature and scholarship
that makes late Roman work seem sterile by comparison. The
dynamics of the movement carried it to the continent in religious and scholarly missions. The excitement of the poetry
stimulated by the encounter between two cultures lies in the
attempt of the poets to bring together the two lines of their
Germanic past on the one hand and Christian classical tradition on the other. Constantine in their poetry becomes a Germanic king, "battle-lord and leader in war," "protector of
princes," and "giver of gifts." Satan is the treacherous retainer
companion of the "All-Ruling God." And in the *Dream of the
Rood*, this is how the poet sees Christ:

> Then the young Warrior, God, the All-Wielder,
> Put off His raiment, steadfast and strong;
> With lordly mood in the sight of many
> He mounted the Cross to redeem mankind.[17]

The greatest figure in scholarship was Bede, a monk of the twin monasteries of Wearmouth and Jarrow. The founder of these monasteries had brought back from Rome a remarkable collection of books, Latin, Greek, and Hebrew. Bede mastered these books, wrote works of theology, of science, and of history, and taught students. For historians his invaluable contribution is the *Ecclesiastical History of the English Nation*. A man of humble Christianity and considerable critical intelligence, he based his history as far as was possible on documents and firsthand reports. He was concerned mainly with the triumph of the Church in Britain, but he gives us incidentally invaluable material about the German conquest of Britain and about the subsequent political history of the various nations after they had settled in the island. Bede's pupil, Egbert, founded a school at York. Charlemagne, the greatest of Frankish rulers in early medieval times, chose Alcuin, Egbert's pupil, as the teacher for the palace school that he founded. Anglo-Saxon missionaries joined the Celtic monks in traveling to continental Europe to convert the heathen and to restore the purity of the faith in Francia.

Meanwhile, in this same period—the eighth century—the Frankish kings of the Carolingian dynasty created a vast though ephemeral Christian empire. Charlemagne (768–814), the greatest of them, eventually ruled all the land from the Spanish Marches to an Elbe-Danube frontier. (See Map 2, page 32.) He conquered the heathen Saxons and offered them the choice of conversion or death. He fought the Muslims in Spain in the name of Christianity and established the Spanish March (that is, a frontier state). He and his father before him established a protective relationship with the popes defending them against the Lombard kings and eventually taking the iron crown of Lombardy. In return, they received the Church's sanctification of their royal power. And on Christmas Day, 800, Charlemagne was crowned "Emperor and Augustus" by the pope in Rome, a title not conceded by the emperors of the eastern Roman Empire. Historians have debated endlessly the significance of

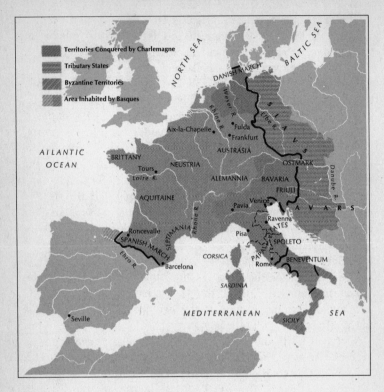

Map 2. Charlemagne's Empire

this event, but there is no doubt that it was conceived as a revival of Roman imperial power in the West and that it was fraught with momentous consequences for the future. (See Chapter V.)

Charlemagne was a great and able ruler, but he ruled as a German-Christian king, not as a Roman emperor. He and his courtiers adopted classical and biblical nicknames and some-times wore Roman dress, but the organization of the empire was Germanic rather than Roman. Counts, margraves, and dukes (vassals of the king-emperor with delegated royal power held on a personal basis) ruled the various parts of the empire in cooperation with bishops and archbishops whom the king-emperor appointed. To check their activities and other local matters, Charlemagne periodically sent out members of his royal household, both lay and ecclesiastical representatives, the *missi dominici*. He himself traveled from one royal estate to another to collect the income in terms of produce. His household consumed this income on the spot. At his favorite residence at Aachen (Aix-la-Chapelle), situated at the angle of the Meuse and Rhine rivers, he founded a palace school to educate his nobility and the clergy. From this center, scholars like Alcuin directed a revival of learning in monastic schools established throughout the Holy Roman Empire. The learning was indiscriminately Greek, Roman, and Christian. Though he earnestly tried, Charlemagne never learned to write. Through his secretaries he corresponded in a tone of equality with eastern Roman emperors and even with Harun-al Raschid, the caliph of the eastern Muslims. Charlemagne's government was essentially personal, and his empire collapsed under his son and grandsons.

Attacks from Muslims, Northmen, and Magyars

The achievements of Britain and Francia (as modern France was then known) in the eighth century might have become more general and more permanent if it had not been for new waves of attacks from the outside. They were threefold. From the north came the Northmen, or Vikings; from the east, the Magyars, or Hungarians as they were called in Europe; from the south, the Muslims. Europe had not yet achieved sufficient internal coherence to withstand these attacks without disruption and loss of cultural momentum.

Muslim attacks were a continuation of the conflict with the Christian world that had begun in the seventh century. The

great period of Muslim expansion had been the century after
the death of Muhammad (632–732), during which the Muslims
had erupted out of Arabia, conquered Syria and Iraq, Egypt,
the coastal region of northern Africa, and Visigothic Spain in
the West, central Asia and northern India in the East.
Charlemagne's grandfather had set a northern limit to their
raids into Francia from Spain in a great battle near Poitiers
in 732. But this was the beginning rather than the end of the
battle for definition of frontiers between them and the Frankish kings. Furthermore, irreconcilable Christians had taken
refuge in northern Spain in the mountains of the Pyrenees
and of Asturias, waiting their time for a counterattack.
Charlemagne fought the Muslims and established the Spanish
March south of the Pyrenees. But they continued to attack the
south coast of Francia and established bases there from which
they could prey on the Rhone river traffic and that coming
through the western passes of the Alps. In the ninth century
Muslims from northern Africa crossed to Sicily and set up a
strong base at Palermo. With Palermo as the seat of their operations they conquered the island from the eastern Romans and
launched attacks on the mainland, even sacking the basilica of
St. Peter in 846.

In the north during the eighth century the Northmen, or
Vikings, began raids on Britain and Francia for plunder and
trade. As the years passed, they stepped up their forays and
fanned out to Russia in the east, to Ireland, Iceland, and
eventually America in the west and ranged as far south as
Rome and Constantinople. In their first major attack on Britain
in 793, the Vikings plundered and burned the rich Celtic-
Christian monastery at Lindisfarne. In the Frankish empire
their first attacks came about 800 on the coast of the Netherlands. In Russia, at about the same time, they built a stronghold on the shores of Lake Ladoga. The raids were hard to
meet because no one knew where or when they would strike.
Their ships were better built and faster than any west European ships of the day, and they commandeered horses for
mobility on land. In the second half of the ninth century they

began to settle down where they could find a landhold. In Russia they made themselves masters of the trade route from Novgorod, through Kiev, to Constantinople. In Francia, in 911, they got Normandy, one of the richest parts of the country, as the price of peace for the rest of the Frankish kings' domains. Their leader, Rollo, was asked to do homage to the Frankish king for this land. Everything seemed to go smoothly until the bishops said to Rollo:

> "Whoever receives such a gift should salute the king's foot with a kiss."
> Rollo replied, "I will never bend my knee to anyone's knee, and I will never kiss anyone's foot."
> But moved by the entreaties of the Franks, he ordered one of his warriors to kiss the king's foot. The warrior immediately lifted up the king's foot, threw the king on his back, and kissed the foot, while he was standing up and the king was flat on his back. At this there was a great roar of laughter and great excitement among those present.[18]

The Vikings brought to Europe chiefly this bold independence of spirit and sense of equality among fighting companions, their techniques of shipbuilding, and, perhaps, some innovations in agriculture. Their culture was not markedly different from that of the Germanic nations to whom they were closely related. In Britain, they founded harbor towns in Ireland, the Orkneys, and western Scotland, and they settled in northwest England. They won from Alfred the Great (862–899), who united the English against them, a peace (886–890) that guaranteed them legal equality with Englishmen. Eventually, though briefly, under Canute and his sons (1016–1042), they ruled the whole of England. In England they left the mark of their culture in place-names, vocabulary, and greater freedom among the peasantry of the "Danelaw," the area of their settlement.

In the east the Magyars were just one in the long series of nomadic peoples who attacked Europe from the steppes of southern Russia. They moved over the Carpathian Mountains at the end of the ninth century, conquering and enslaving the local Slavs and appropriating the land. They established a kind of headquarters in the area of modern Hungary, but this did not mean that they settled down and abandoned their marauding and plundering habits. In 899 they devastated northern Italy; they conquered and captured a local king, exacting heavy ransom. In 947 they penetrated as far south as Apulia in southern Italy. They carried out annual and devastating raids against the people of Germany. More spectacular raids carried them west into Francia as far as Aquitaine. Such armies as could be gathered by local bishops and secular rulers to meet them were no match for them in speed of movement and ruthlessness. It was not until the German king, Otto the Great (936–973), succeeded in arraying a large army against them at Lechfeld in 955 that they settled down to become rulers of Hungary. Perhaps the most important effect of their attacks was that they cut the northern Slavs off from Constantinople, the source of their conversion to Christianity, and opened the way for a reconversion from the West by bishops deriving their authority from Rome.

The effect of these diffuse yet violent attacks of the Muslims, Vikings, and Magyars differed in the various parts of Europe. England achieved unity in the ninth and tenth centuries, after a long period in which there had been seven or more kingdoms yielding only hegemony to a dominant king. Alfred's sons and grandsons were rulers of a united England, and England has never since suffered division. The burhs (the fortresses built by Alfred for defense against the Danes) became administrative centers and, some of them, commercial centers. But the wars with the Northmen had had their destructive effect. The great monastic schools suffered. Alfred, a man of considerable education himself, deplored the decline of learning in England. He recalled the days when scholars came from continental Europe to England's schools and when churchmen in England were masters of Latin and other ancient languages. To supply knowledge of the substance of the Christian classics, he himself translated or caused to be translated into English some of these great works, Augustine's *Soliloquies* and Pope Gregory the Great's *Pastoral Care,* for example. And, like Charlemagne, he tried to encourage the better education of nobility and clergy. Yet the ninth and tenth centuries were a period of relative dearth in English literature and scholarship.

On the continent the effect of the threefold attacks was not only to destroy learning, but also to destroy Charlemagne's extended and precarious empire. It had already been divided by treaty in 843 among Charlemagne's three surviving grandsons. The invaders completed the work of disintegration. Kings could not be everywhere at once with large armies. Charles the Bald, who inherited the western part of his grandfather's empire, tried Alfred's tactics of building fortresses in the basins of the Seine and Loire rivers, where the Vikings made their most persistent attacks. But the effectiveness of fortresses was nil without soldiers to man them. It was increasingly hard for Charles and his successors to call together the general assembly of the free fighting men. Raids were annual and unpredictable as to locality. Crops had to be sowed and harvested. Fighting had become a more specialized occupation of professional soldiers on constant alert in the season for raids. One result was that people turned more and more to local leaders for protection. Counts and dukes assumed hereditary power, ignored their allegiance to kings, and treated the lands granted to them conditionally as payment for their services, as personal and heritable possessions. In Francia this led to a pattern of government and personal relationships that came to be designated "feudal" (see Chapter III). In Germany, the eastern part of Charlemagne's former empire, dukes set themselves up as rulers of provinces bearing the names of ancient German nations: Frisia, Saxony, Thuringia, Swabia, and Bavaria. The kings and the counts and bishops as their representatives lost power. In Lorraine and Franconia, which had been more thoroughly integrated into Charlemagne's empire, something like the feudal conditions in France developed.

Technological Change in the Early Middle Ages

Early medieval society was predominantly military and agrarian. Mediterranean commerce had begun to decline before the collapse of Roman power in the West. It never disappeared altogether; Jews and Syrian merchants continued to bring Eastern luxury wares into the Frankish kingdom, but trade was difficult because Francia had no products to exchange for these goods. The result was a drainage of coin, particularly gold, from the West and a continued decline in trade. Early Frankish kings neglected coinage and shipping, two essentials for anything but local exchange. Nevertheless, commerce continued in locally unavailable products such as salt and metals, and there was a temporary recovery of trade under Charlemagne. Trade in slaves with the Mediterranean world continued throughout the period in spite of injunctions of the Church and kings against selling Christians to non-Christians. The chief source of slaves were the Slav peoples of the Baltic region and Anglo-Saxon England, and the chief market was the Muslim world. In northern Europe commerce fared better than in the south. The Frisians were traders as were the Vikings. Anglo-Saxon England was hospitable to merchants, selling cheese, silver metalwork, precious embroideries and woolen cloth, as well as slaves in return for such luxury goods as silks, jewels, gold, glass, wine, and oil.

However, the predominant occupations of most people in western European society were fighting and raising crops and domestic animals. Therefore, for students of history improvements in technology in these occupations become important. The facts concerning such improvements are hard to obtain. Documents describing weapons, tools, and methods of fighting or farming are nonexistent after Roman times. Pictorial representations are scant. Archeological remains have not been fully explored and are hard to date.

Certain changes did occur in fighting tactics, but it is not possible to attribute dates or other details to them. Cavalry replaced infantry as the principal element in medieval armies. Roman legions had fought on foot, and Germanic armies, though moving about on horses, had also fought mainly on foot. Sometime, probably in the eighth century, owing to the introduction of the stirrup, men began to fight more successfully on horseback. The stirrup gave the horseman a firm footing and enabled him to use not just the force of his arm, but also the weight of his entire body and the horse in thrusting at his enemy with a spear. But fighting from the back of a horse required more skill than fighting on foot. Professional training was needed. To do this, the trainee, the *gwassus* (boy) or vassal, had to be recruited at an early age and educated to his calling. In the eighth and ninth centuries, when attacks from Muslims and Northmen were most severe, many vassals were drawn from the ranks of the household servants or slaves to form trained armies. But in the following years they increasingly were freemen drawn from those possessing a specified amount of landed wealth. They were rewarded with *feoda* ("fiefs," holdings of office or of land) for past and future military service. The result was the creation of a new class of men—a fief-holding or "feudal" class, who neither worked in the fields nor supervised those who did. Their function in society was to fight and to rule those who produced the food and other necessities of existence (see Chapter III).

In this same early period, but even more difficult to date than the advances in fighting techniques, came some changes in agricultural techniques. Possibly borrowed from the Slavs and brought in by the Germans were the heavier and more efficient plows that came into use. These proved more suitable to the culture of the heavier soils of northern Europe. Their greater efficiency derived from metal-toothed colters that cut deeply into the earth, from mold boards that turned the soil in ridges making for better aeration and drainage, and, in some, from wheels that helped the ploughman to drive his furrow straight. These plows were pulled by yokes of from two to eight oxen. Many historians believe that the open-field system of cultivation (see Chapter II) derived from the need for cooperation in the use of animals necessary to draw these heavy plows. Poor peasant families were unlikely to own the necessary ox power.

Other technological improvements that are thought to have contributed to improvement in agricultural production are the increasing use of horses in cultivation and the introduction of the three-field system of crop rotation to replace the two-field system more common in Mediterranean lands, or the more haphazard system used by people who could find virgin land to plow when they had exhausted fields that had been long in use. A three-field system entailed the planting of a winter crop sown in November, a spring crop sown in March, and a portion of the land left to lie fallow. It produced more crops for less man-hours, and it made possible a greater variety of crops. The horse was not of much use in agricultural work in Europe until the introduction from Asia of the horse collar to replace the yoke. A collar around the horse's shoulders attached to lateral traces increases a horse's pulling power at least fourfold. And because a horse works faster and pulls harder than an ox he offered definite advantages to a medieval farmer. The main drawbacks are that he eats more, needs oats for food as well as grass or hay, doesn't live as long as an ox, and is not very good eating himself when he can no longer pull plows and carts. For these reasons, medieval farmers were slow to accept the horse as a substitute for an ox.

The use of water and wind power in the milling of grain is another improvement expanded in the early medieval period. The Romans had used water mills, but there seem to have been very few in use in Francia in the time of Charlemagne. They were expensive to build and, therefore, could be built only by wealthy landowners. Thus, as long as there was sufficient manpower or womanpower on an estate, they were not worth the expenditure. Small farmers or poor peasant villagers could not be expected to abandon hand-milling methods. Windmills, an obvious need in areas like the Netherlands where there are no swift-running streams, were either a local invention in the north of Europe or a borrowing from the East, and were not much in use until the twelfth century.

Conclusion

This chapter has attempted to give some account of the 600-year period in which the Europe of cathedrals and crusading knights was formed, the Europe that is recognizable to most people as characteristically "medieval." The essential ingredients were the Greco-Roman tradition as transformed by Christianity and by the pagan Germanic tradition with which it came to conflict because of the incursion of Germanic nations into the Western Empire. The next six chapters will attempt to describe European society of the so-called High Middle Ages in sufficient depth at least to persuade the reader that he should go beyond a textbook to find out more for himself about this early European world that influences his own world in ways that he hardly suspects.

II

Agrarian Economy
and Peasant Life

It is a commonplace of medieval history that society was borne on the backs of the peasantry. Their toil in the fields produced the food that kept the whole society alive and created the surpluses of food and other goods that supported the clergy and knights in nonproductive functions and provided them with luxuries. It is a somewhat less well-known commonplace that a striking increase in productivity made possible the cultural surge forward that marks the centuries 1000–1300. In these centuries the population of western Europe doubled in an "explosion" that, though not comparable in extent or volume to that which accompanied the industrial revolution of the nineteenth century, was at least a preview of western Europe's expanding future. What caused this population increase cannot be reduced to a single factor. However, in relation to an economy like that of the Middle Ages in which most people lived on the bare margin of subsistence, one can perhaps assert with certainty that there must have been an increase in the food supply.

Agrarian Expansion, 1000–1250

The increase in the food supply in the period under consideration came from the technological improvements discussed in the preceding chapter and from an expansion of western Europe's frontiers, both external and internal. Wasteland within Europe (most dramatically the polders reclaimed from the sea in the Netherlands) and new lands on all the fringes of European settlement were cultivated. Arable lands crept up the slopes of the river valleys or up the downs in the south of England. New orders of monks pushed into moorland and mountain valleys, converted wilderness to arable acres and pasture for cattle and sheep. Lost villages were reclaimed from the forest, and new villages were built where none had existed before. For example, the duke of Brittany and two lesser lords converted the forest of Rennes to rich farmland. During the same centuries the Teutonic Knights extended the frontier against the Slavs and opened up new lands in the Baltic region for settlement by west Europeans. In order to attract settlers to new lands, landholders sent agents through settled lands to promise more favorable conditions for peasants. The resurgence of commerce and the growth of towns helped greatly in drawing people to agriculture, for merchants, weavers, metalworkers, and other specialized craftsmen in newly founded towns provided markets for agricultural surpluses. Regional fairs drew trade from wider areas and attracted both luxury goods and specialized agricultural produce such as wine and wool.

Regional and local diversity, seasonal fluctuations, the pace of change, and the familiar medievalist's problem of dearth of sources make generalizations difficult. Yet some general statements are possible. Landlords, ecclesiastical and secular, led in the agrarian expansion. Despite improvements in peasant status and periodic peasant economic gains, they managed to deprive agricultural workers of most of the surplus they created. Karl Marx in the *Communist Manifesto* describes landlord-peasant relations as "patriarchal and idyllic" and charges the bourgeoisie of later times with putting an end to such relations of men with their "natural superiors" in favor of "callous cash payment." Study of medieval documents suggest that payment, whether in cash or in kind, was the main interest of the landlord; preservation of his subsistence and, if possible, his surplus was the main interest of the peasant. Estate management improved in the twelfth and early thirteenth centuries. Good landlords tried to maintain their peasant labor force, their most valuable asset. Peasants endured harsh conditions and exercised their ingenuity to resist the landlord's collecting agents. Periodic bad harvests were disastrous for those who had no surplus. Yet some peasants became rich and even joined the landlord class by lending to impoverished neighbors, buying up lands from the destitute, and marrying sons and daughters to their "natural superiors."

Increased exchanges in fairs and markets and the increasing use of money in all transactions meant an increasing emphasis on payments in kind or in money rather than on labor services of peasants to landlords. The substitution of payments, along with other social forces such as intermarriage, led to a blurring of legal distinctions among rural social classes. In A.D. 1000, there were domestic slaves, semifree peasants owing labor services of various sorts to their lords, and free cultivators recognizing and paying only for the protection and jurisdiction of lords. By 1300 there were wealthy peasants, a large class of peasants of middling income, and a vast multitude of peasants living on the margin of subsistence, supplementing their living from their small parcels of land by working for hire on the lands of the more wealthy. Freedom was important. If it had not been so, the serfs of Rosny-sous-Bois would not have fought for sixty-seven years of the twelfth and early thirteenth centuries an action in the royal courts (finally appealed to the papal curia itself) in order to affirm their freedom against their lord, the abbey of St. Genevieve in Paris. Nor would individual peasants and peasant communities have paid large sums for their manumission. Lawyers influenced by the revived study of Roman law tried to make clear the distinction between the free and the unfree but found it hard to establish precise distinctions. The most distressing fact by 1300 was that the countryside was overpopulated. A bad growing year meant death by starvation to an increasing number of the poorest peasants.

Agrarian Organization

Peasants lived in villages or hamlets. There were few isolated farmsteads of the sort typical in the United States except in some remote and newly reclaimed frontier regions. Villages with the fields surrounding the nucleus of church, manor house, and peasant dwellings patterned the river valleys and plains. In mountainous or wilderness areas, hamlets, that is, smaller and less orderly aggregations of huts surrounded by small patches of arable land, were more characteristic. In particularly well-adapted regions, some specialized farming, like the growing of wine grapes and the raising of sheep, comprised the prime use of the land. Fishing villages ringed the seacoasts. In spite of the increase in trade that accompanied the expansion of the three centuries from 1000 to 1300, the tendency to local self-sufficiency noticeable in late Roman times and continuing through the early Middle Ages persisted. No village could, of course, live in complete independence of the larger world. Salt, a necessity for all animal life, was not available everywhere. Metals used for horseshoes, nails, and increasingly in the making of plows and other farm tools could not be dug out of every hillside. Thus there had to be commerce between communities.

The great diversity of village organization from one region to another makes it difficult to describe a typical village of the twelfth or thirteenth century. However, some common features may be listed. There had to be water, preferably a running stream that could be dammed to provide a fish pond and a mill. There had to be arable land and meadow and pasture for the sustenance of beasts. There had to be woodland or heath to provide fuel, building materials, acorns for the pigs and game. Ideally, there was some wasteland into which the village might expand. (See Map 3.)

Arable fields lay "open"; that is, one peasant household's holdings lay beside those of another without internal fencing. Only "balks," or unplowed ridges, separated them. The land was plowed in long strips comprising an "acre" of land, that being the extent that a plow team (Latin: *acer*) could turn over in one day. The strips were distributed in "cultures," or plots in which the furrows lay parallel, following in some fashion the contours of the land. Whether or not contour plowing resulted from intelligent foresight based on experience or from chance, it must have helped to avoid erosion. Holdings were distributed among cultures and fields, probably according to some principle of fairness in sharing the land among peasant households when the particular site had first been settled, then expanded as the arable land was extended. An average peasant holding in England was about thirty acres, but it might be much more or much less.

The open-field system came, in modern times, to be considered inefficient. In the twelfth century it was an adaptation to the fact that cultivation was cooperative. The average peasant household could not support all the animal power necessary to pull the new heavy plow in the clay-filled soils of northern Europe. Thus, the head of the family joined his yoke, or yokes, of oxen to those of his neighbor. The principle, however, was cooperative, not the collective principle of modern Russian collective farms or Israeli *kibbutzim*. Each peasant household held its own strips and took the produce from them from generation to generation. Workers did not share the produce according to the work hours they had put in to produce the crops, nor was the land redistributed periodically as in nineteenth-century Russia. More fortunate peasant families became richer than their neighbors and bought up their holdings in the fields.

By the eleventh century the three-field system predominated in northern Europe. Its greater productivity as against the older two-field systems is self-evident. If villagers planted 200 out of 300 acres of arable land each year instead of 150 out of 300, they obviously gained the produce of 50 acres. In the three-field system new crops were added, and the rotation was, perhaps, as follows: Field I—winter-sown crops, mainly rye and wheat; Field II—spring-sown crops, such as quicker-growing grains (barley, oats) and pulse vegetables (peas, beans, vetch, lentils); Field III—fallow land. Fallow land was not planted. It was fenced off, and animals were turned into it to crop the stubble and drop manure. Stubble, weeds, and manure were plowed under twice in summer to form a compost for the enrichment of the soil. Manure was precious. It was the only

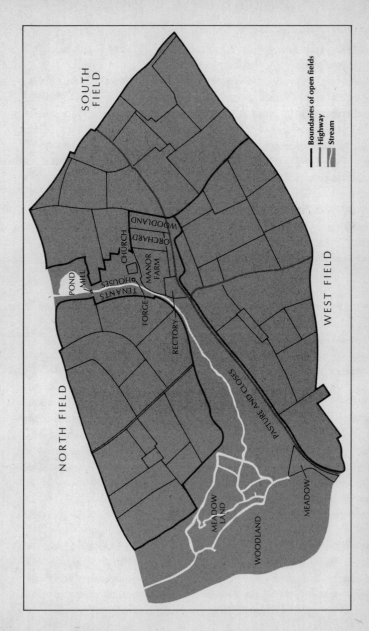

Map 3. Plan of Seignorial Village

fertilizer other than marl, a kind of soil rich in calcium carbonates found only in fortunate areas. Where possible, the soil was marled every twenty years or so.

Though rights in the arable acreage were private, many peasant rights were communal. Villagers joined with others in "commoning" their beasts in the pasture. Village ox herds, shepherds, swine herds, and cattle herds were chosen in village courts. Villagers cut the grass in the meadow and shared it out according to customary procedures. Turves or peat used for fires, marsh grass and reeds, marl from the village marl pits (if any), and other complements to "farmland" were shared. Woodland, once limitless in extent, by the thirteenth century seems for the most part to have come under the protection of lords who appointed foresters and other officers to guard it and demand payment for its resources.

Landlord and Peasant: Exploitation of Land and Labor

In seignorial villages, subject to economic exploitation as well as rule by lords, many peasants did some forced labor on the lord's demesne. The demesne was the land reserved by the lord for his own use to supply his own household and such surpluses as he could command from the market. It was sometimes compact, sometimes distributed in strips in the open fields like the peasants' lands. Serf laborers owed a customary amount of labor to the lord on the demesne ranging in amount from a few days a year at plowing and harvest time to "week-work" of three or four days and additional "boon-work" at the critical times in the agricultural year. The serf received his food in the lord's household when he worked on the demesne, and for the intensive "boon-work" the lord rewarded him in the spirit of the boon with feasts and games. Free peasants owed more specifically defined amounts and kinds of services. Some villagers, perhaps because they had been manumitted from slavery or because their ancestors had lost their landholdings through adversity, had very little or no land in the arable areas. These "cottagers" were sometimes specialized workers who hired themselves out for wages to work on the demesne or on the lands of wealthier peasants. All serfs were part of the *familia,* or household, of the lord. Their *sequela,* or offspring (the same word was used for people or pigs), were part of the lord's assets. He looked them over for prime workers on the demesne, especially skilled workers, like plowmen, vine dressers, spinners and weavers. Serfs could be bought and sold and deeded to others by their lords, although they could not themselves leave their lord without his permission:

> To all whom these presents may concern, Brother John, Abbot of Bruerne and the monks of that [Cistercian] Abbey, greetings in the Lord. Know that we have sold to William, Squire to the lord Nicholas de Noers, Hugh the Shepherd our serf of the manor of Certelle, with all his chattels and livestock, and we have quit-claimed him of us and our successors for ever, so that we henceforth may exact or vindicate no right or claim in him. For which sale and quit-claim the aforesaid William hath given us four shillings sterling; in testimony whereof we have set our seal to this present deed.[1]

The *sequela,* though not mentioned with the chattels in this transaction, probably went, if there were any, with the serf in the transfer. Medieval serfdom, in contrast to modern American slavery, respected family ties. Diversities in status and tenure of serfs, not only from region to region but from manor to manor, are manifold, and status and tenure did not necessarily correspond. A free peasant might hold serf lands through marriage, inheritance, or purchase. This was risky. For these lands he was held to servile obligations and might easily forfeit his free status.

Not only free individual peasants but also free peasant communities existed in various parts of Europe. In England in the Danelaw, for example, and in Frisia and Saxony in Germany these were survivals from earlier times. In France, in this period of intensification of landlord and peasant enterprise, communities bought their freedom at high cost. For example, we have this charter dated 1248:

> To all those who shall see these present letters, William, abbot of St. Denis in France and the convent of the said place, greetings in the Lord. We make known that which follows. Having regard to the danger which the souls of certain of our bondsmen run, as much by marriages contracted by them as by excommunications which bind and could in the future bind many of them (for it is not only the annual rent due by reason of their servitude towards us, it is also their own persons, which are seen and may in the future be seen furtively removed from our church). Moreover having taken counsel of good men we have liberated and liberate by piety our bondsmen of the warren villages, that is, of Villeneuve . . . [six villages], laborers in these villages at the time of the grant of this liberty, with their wives and their heirs issued or to issue in the future from their bodies. We have delivered them in perpetuity from all the burdens of servitude by which they were formerly held to us, that is, from *formariage, chevage,* mortmain and all other kind of servitude by whatever name it shall be called, and we give them their liberty.[2]

They were not to be free of dues on wine sales and other dues, river tolls, and customs in the town of St. Denis, nor were they freed from the abbey's judicial power; and they were warned that they would forfeit their liberty if they married servile women belonging to the abbey. The sum to be paid was 1700 Parisian livres, far more ready cash than any peasant community could be expected to possess. The solution was long-term credit and annual payments until the sum was paid off.

The payments from which these peasants were freed were just some among the many to which peasants, both free and servile, were subject. The landlord's largest income in this period evidently came from monopolies of one type or another and from tithes. The lord generally maintained the mill, hired the miller, and exacted a part of the grain in payment for the peasant's use of the mill. The village bake oven was his oven, and he exacted a payment for the baking of bread. The wine press was his, and the peasants were required to pay him for its use. The stud bull and boar were his, and he exacted stud fees for their services. Sometimes he held a monopoly on the sale of wine and beer. The forest was his forest, and he charged the peasants for the pasturing of pigs and other animals. Less understandably, perhaps, he collected parish tithes. The church in the village was, often enough, founded by himself or his ancestors. He appropriated the share of tithes due to the parish priest and gave the priest land in the fields for his support.

The lord had a number of choices as to how to exploit a seignorial village. He could live there, periodically or permanently, and use the produce directly. He could have the produce carted by the peasants to his favorite seat of residence. He could have the produce sold and take the money. He could rent the demesne to peasants and take in return a money rent or a share of the produce. Devices for increasing profit differed from one estate to another. The twelfth and thirteenth centuries seem to have been a time of increasing emphasis on money payments. Many landlords began to use hired labor on their demesne lands and to take from the peasants money in commutation of their labor services. Hired labor was more efficient, and in a time of improved techniques of cultivation, customary labor services often produced a surplus of inefficient labor that the efficient landlord could do without. In times of rising prices and wages, however, substitution of money rents for payments in kind and commutation had drawbacks for the landlord. In solution of the problem of fixed income from these sources, short-term leases and temporary sales of labor services were in many instances substituted for long-term leases and permanent commutations. Some reactionary landlords even attempted to restore forced labor services toward the end of the period. In general, the leasing out of the demesne was a more common phenomenon on the continent than in England.

In addition to land rents and labor-service payments, a battery of demands for other payments assailed the rural population. Peasants were subject to arbitrary tallage, that is, the lord could exact from them whatever he could get to meet his own emergency needs. To reduce the arbitrary character of this payment, it was usually put on an annual basis at a fixed rate, and in practice only serfs had to pay it. The lord was owed hospitality for a night's visit. He had the option of taking money or goods in its stead. A head tax, or *chevage,* was levied in recognition of the former slavery of members of the lord's *familia* and in payment for his protection. At the death of the head of a serf household, the lord's bailiff exacted as *mainmorte*—or, in English, *heriot*—the best beast that the family possessed in token of the lord's ultimate right in their land, their persons, and their possessions. The lord received a marriage payment (*formariage*) for every peasant who married off the estate. This payment became more profitable as village communities became more inbred since the Church had strict prohibitions against the marriage of cousins too close in blood to one another. In many places, the lord got a payment called *leyrwrite* for girls caught in adultery. Free peasants were less burdened by these dues than the unfree, but distinctions were not always kept clear and custom varied from manor to manor.

Landlord and Peasant: Governmental Power

The village, free or seignorial, was a governmental and social unit as well as an economic one. Where the village was free, it held its own court under its own officers. Where a lord ruled a village, the lord's bailiff or his steward presided over the court. The villagers elected a "reeve" to speak for them. All of them, free or serf, owed attendance at the court. The court made agricultural decisions, settled disputes, punished offenders against the lord's rights, and, if the lord had powers delegated by or usurped from the king, enforced royal administrative orders and other legislation, and administered justice against criminals. In England it was uncommon for the manor court to administer any criminal justice except for small offenses; in France great lords more normally had full royal powers. Lurid examples can be found of arbitrary and brutal use of powers of justice. It is harder to collect statistical evidence as to the extent of hangings or other cruel punishments. Lords and their agents must always have had to balance loss of income from the work of the peasant against the maintenance of discipline.

For England numerous manor court records exist. Typical entries are the following for the years 1246–1249:

Hugh Free in mercy for his beast caught in the lord's garden. Pledges, Walter Hill and William Slipper. Fine 6d.

The twelve jurors say that Hugh Cross has right in the bank and hedge about which there was a dispute between him and William White. Therefore let him hold in peace and let William be distrained for his many trespasses. Afterwards he made fine for 12d.

Roger Pleader is at law against Nicholas Croke to prove that neither he nor his killed Nicholas's peacock. Pledges Riner and Jordan. Afterwards he made his law and therefore is quit.

From the whole township of Little Ogbourne, except seven, for not coming to wash the lord's sheep, 6s. 8d.

Gilbert Richard's son gives 5s. for license to marry a wife. Pledge, Seaman. Term for payment the Purification.

William Jordan in mercy for bad ploughing on the lord's land. Pledge, Arthur. Fine, 6d.

The parson of the church is in mercy for his cow caught in the lord's meadow. Pledges, Thomas Ymer and William Coke.

From Martin Shepherd 6d. for the wound that he gave Pekin.

Ragenhilda of Bec gives 2s. for having married without licence. Pledge, William of Primer.

The Court presented that William Noah's son is the born bondman of the lord and a fugitive and dwells at Dodford. Therefore he must be sought. They say also that William Askil, John Parsons and Godfrey Green have furtively carried off four geese from the vill of Horepoll.

It was presented that Robert Carter's son by night invaded the house of Peter Burgess and in felony threw stones at his door so that the said Peter raised the hue. Therefore let the said Robert be committed to prison. Afterwards he made fine with 2s.[3]

The record tells only the bare facts relevant for the lord's officers who are to collect the fines. The reader will have noticed some survivals from earlier Germanic custom. Martin Shepherd paid sixpence for the wound to Pekin. Roger Pleader "made his law" against Nicholas Croke. That means that he produced oath-helpers who vouched for his honesty. The manor lord's officers have borrowed the king's device of trial by jury in the case of Hugh Cross in default of the ordeals prohibited since 1215. The court itself accuses Carter's son and the men who have stolen the geese. It advertises the escape of William Noah's son.

Various treatises and "how-to-do-it books" for budding lawyers and estate managers produced in the thirteenth century suggest that the tone in dealing with peasants in the manor court was not unduly harsh. From a manual for would-be bailiffs or stewards, for example, is the following:

Bailiff, says the Steward, cause those to come to us who should make their law on this day. . . .
William de C. you are attached to answer in this Court wherefore your son who is of your household entered the lord's garden beyond the walls which are built around it and was found therein . . . and carried away at his will apples and pears and all manner of fruit to his house and there they were found by the sworn bailiff. . . . How will you make amends for this trespass?
Sir, I am ready to do as you will for by my advice he never entered nor carried away any manner of fruit.
Fair friend William you cannot deny that he was found therein and carried away divers fruit to your house.
It is indeed true, Sir, wherefore I put myself on your mercy. . . .

Walter de la More you are attached to answer in this Court wherefore the other night against the lord's peace you entered his fish pond and carried away at your will divers kinds of fish. . . . How will you defend yourself or how will you make amends?
Now be advised, Sir, and for God's sake do not take it amiss, if it please you. My wife has been in bed all these months continually and has neither eaten nor drunk anything that has pleased her. And for the great wish and the great desire which she had to eat of a tench I drew near to the bank of this fish pond to have a tench only and I neither took nor carried away any other fish of this pond. . . .

Walter you have at least made acknowledgement in this Court of having taken and carried away a tench otherwise than you ought to do; . . . wherefore we say that you are in the lord's mercy and moreover at law sixhanded that you have taken and carried away at this time no other manner of fish.[4]

Instructions are also given for the dialogue with a baker who has sold bread not baked according to the king's laws and a fishmonger who has sold "stinking and putrid" fish contrary to local ordinance. In almost every case the penalties were fines. Justice was a not inconsiderable source of income; secure places for confinement of prisoners were few, and it was better to get money if possible and then to release the peasant to do his work.

Peasant Life

The life of the peasant centered on the local parish church. The steeple with its bell or bells identified the village on the horizon. The bells announced the hours of the day, tolled the passing of the dead, or summoned the villagers to meet an emergency. The priest was frequently a more important figure than an absentee lord. He was often also scarcely distinguishable in his appearance or occupation from his parishioners. It has already been noted that lords who founded churches in the years of Christianity's expansion often took the priest's share of the tithes and gave him in return a parcel of strips in the open fields. The priest was lucky if he had the necessary laborers in his household to work his lands for him. The villagers were lucky if he was a man of education and spirituality who could educate selected children and give to his adult parishioners counsel and comfort in time of need and if he could intercede for them with the lord, his agent, or the king's officers.

The peasant family was the strongest unit in village society. Family patterns differed from one part of Europe to another, but the typical family was a "stem family," that is, one in which inheritance went from father to son. Normally, the son who inherited (the oldest or the youngest) the family holdings would not marry until he took over the rule of the household and the family holdings in the fields. If his father was still alive at this time, the son was expected to provide for him in his old age. Other sons worked for the head of the household and did not marry as long as they remained at home. Opportunity for them consisted in marrying a rich widow or a daughter of a peasant household that had no sons. Freemen could become clergy (serfs, too, by dispensation). Serfs could learn a trade and/or escape to a town. There was more mobility than is sometimes thought. Widows and orphans were protected and provided for by local custom. Numerous manor court cases and tales of peasant life were generated by the frictions arising from the close family life.

The peasants' year was punctuated by the great holidays taken over and regulated by the Church but incorporating many survivals of pagan festivals. Michaelmas (September 29) —the feast of St. Michael and the Archangels—marked the beginning and end of the agricultural year. The crops had been gathered in; the animals were turned loose in the stubble. Plowing and planting of the fallow with the winter crop of wheat and rye began. The animals that could not be fed through the winter were killed; the meat salted or smoked to preserve it. In good years this was the fat season when both men and beasts fed well. The twelve days of Christmas were a time of rest, revelry, and rejoicing. Lent was celebrated as now with fasting. The spring plowing was supposed to be done by Lady's Day (March 25) or at the latest by Easter Sunday. May Day was a largely pagan festival for the young people of the village. Boys and girls spent the night in the fields to bring May in, and wedding and bedding were likely to follow soon after.

> Between the acres of the rye,
>   With a hey, and a ho, and a hey nonino,
> These pretty country folks would lie
>   In the spring time . . .[5]

Midsummer marked the beginning of the heaviest work season of the year. On the eve of the Nativity of St. John the Baptist (June 24), just after the summer solstice and before the hard work of the summer began, the boys built great bonfires in the fields, and the lords supplied extra meat for the feasting.

The life of the peasant was hard. He lived in a hovel equipped with little more than a hearth, straw pallets for sleeping, a few sticks of furniture, and a few utensils. His diet was scant and monotonous at best, consisting of bread, cheese, ale, stew, some fruit, and fresh vegetables in season. In winter it might drop to starvation level or below; fortunately there was also less work to do. Bad harvest years were disastrous. The man who works the land for his living works hard in any age. Nature is exacting, unpredictable, often harsh. And nothing can change the fact that cows have to be milked at inconvenient intervals, chickens have to be fed, and eggs gathered. Hay has to be taken in between rain storms, and harvesting of grains and vegetables does not conform itself readily to rigid patterns about hours of work and overtime pay. The medieval peasant often had to take care of his lord's needs at the expense of his own, and he was more helpless in relation to natural forces than the modern farmer. He did not know or understand the science of what he was doing. Experience summed up in rhymes dictated the timing of the work:

> The rye in the ground, while September doth last:
> October for wheate sowing, calleth as fast
> What ever it cost thee, what ever thou geve,
> have done sowing wheate before halowmas eve.[6]

Pagan superstitions persisted in the countryside although the clergy attempted to curb them. Fairy trees and fairy rings were identified and visited in the woodland. Every village doubtless had its witch credited with magical powers. Spells and incantations became prayers to persuade the bees to swarm in the beehive, to insure a good harvest or pregnancy of cattle and wives. Would you call the following invocation a charm or a prayer?

Christ, there is a swarm of bees outside,
Fly hither, my little cattle,
In blest peace, in God's protection
Come home safe and sound.
Sit down, sit down, bee,
St. Mary commanded thee.
Thou shalt not have leave
Thou shalt not fly to the wood.
Thou shalt not escape me,
Nor go away from me.
Sit very still,
Wait God's will![7]

Waiting God's will played a large part in peasant life. Whether he was reasonably comfortable or not depended on whether the weather was good, whether his lord was a "good lord," whether the bailiff was a kind man or a cruel and grasping one. Yet the peasant was not necessarily submissive and passive. Villagers fought in the courts for their customary rights, and they had both peaceful and violent ways of dealing with an abusive bailiff. They were many, and he was one. And if food was simple and often scarce, and houses were dark, unsanitary, and unsubstantial, the comforts of a corner at the hearth fire and a full stomach were the more valued.

III

Feudal Society

What we call "feudalism" was a method of maintaining some sort of security and order in a society in which centralized government had become weak. The term is modern, an invention of seventeenth-century lawyers to describe a system based on the *feodum* (fief or fee in English), land or an office granted by a lord to his vassal. It was never a "system." It emerged haphazardly from Carolingian practices and from the chaotic conditions of the ninth and tenth centuries when western Europe was under attack from Muslims, Northmen, and Magyars, and it operated effectively only until kings had rebuilt centralized territorial government in states that were the predecessors of the nation-states of modern Europe. It originated in France and achieved its fullest development there, spreading later to other parts of Europe with peculiarities adapted to local conditions. Change and diversity, as in all medieval phenomena, make generalization difficult. Feudalism affected, to a greater or lesser degree, most of western Europe in the High Middle Ages and left a heritage of social and political attitudes, some of which are still important.

Vassals and Fiefs

The landlords referred to in the previous chapter constituted the feudal class. They were the nobles, knights, and monastic and secular clergy, who ruled the peasants and exploited their labor. Among them the central relationship was the personal one of vassalage of a man to his lord. This relationship was a development of the lord-follower relationship that the Germans brought with them into Europe. It was expressed in the sym-

59

bolic acts of doing homage and taking the oath of fealty. To do homage, the vassal knelt before his lord, placed his hands in the lord's hands, and promised to be his man against all other men. This was conceived of as a real surrender of freedom and could, therefore, only be made by a freeman. The vassal then took an oath of fealty similar to the following model given in a thirteenth-century lawbook:

> Hear this, lord N., that I will bear you fealty in life and limb, in body, goods, and earthly honour, so help me God and these sacred relics.[1]

This oath of fealty may also have been a survival of older Germanic custom. It evidently had taken on a religious character and often included explicit definition of the services to be rendered as a kind of limitation on homage. Because the relationship between lord and vassal was personal, it had to be renewed with the new incumbent in case either lord or vassal died.

The lord "invested" the vassal with a "fief" after homage and fealty by placing in his hand a piece of sod or a symbol of office. He then raised the vassal up and gave him a ceremonial kiss in token of the bond between them. A fief consisted of lands or office from which he derived economic resources that freed him to fight and to rule. Landed fiefs were populated by peasants who raised the crops and animals that supported the fief holder. The vassal, in other words, was not an estate administrator on his lord's behalf. He ruled the peasants on his lands and used the peasants' labor for his own support. The income from administration of justice on his peasants or the income from an office fief went to him, not to his lord. Fiefs were, by the eleventh century, generally inheritable but, in recognition of the fact that in Carolingian times they had been *precaria,* that is temporary grants, the heir owed to the lord a "relief" before he could claim the inheritance. Fiefs ranged in size from whole provinces like Normandy given to Count Rollo to a few acres of land given to a single knight or other freemen. Reliefs correspondingly varied from vast sums to a few shillings. The rate in England in the twelfth century was five pounds for a knight's fief, the amount of land considered to be essential to maintain one mounted and armed knight.

Service for land fiefs was typically military, the service of one or more armed knights or some equivalent. The vassal who owed more than his own service had a choice of alternatives of finding the other knights for service to his lord. He could maintain knights in his own household, providing them with bed and board, mounts, and armor. Or he could grant these knights fiefs that would enable them to find their own bed and board and to provide themselves with their own arms and mounts. The household knight was ordinarily a young landless man who aspired to get a fief for his services.

Obligations of Lord–Vassal Relationship

The vassal owed to his lord, in addition to service, other obligations and courtesies. One of these, expected in northern France and England but not necessarily in the Mediterranean lands, was "suit of court." The vassal was required, when summoned, to come to his lord's court. The lord's court of vassals was a body of multiple functions. It was ceremonial. That is, it might be summoned to witness the knighting or marriage of a son or merely to celebrate Christmas. The court was also a judicial body that sat in judgment in cases of breach of feudal agreements or breach of the peace. The court had advisory functions too. The vassals advised the lord on problems such as whether he should go to war against a neighboring lord or whether he should go on a Crusade to the Holy Land. Any great lord—a king, duke, or bishop—had administrative officers who formed the hard core of his feudal court. Stewards, chamberlains, and the like, might incidentally be fief-holding vassals as well as administrative officers, but their presence in the court was demanded as a consequence of their administrative duties.

Courtesy demanded that the vassal entertain his lord if the lord came into his part of the country. By custom, the vassal helped the lord with the expense for knighting his eldest son, for the marriage of his eldest daughter, or for the ransom of the lord from captivity. He was also expected to give special financial aids on the lord's request—such as funds to finance the lord's going on Crusade or to help the lord meet the king's demand for money. If the vassal, for any reason, could not or chose not to perform his military service, he owed "scutage" (a monetary payment) in commutation of it. The classic statement of the duties of the vassal is in rather negative terms, perhaps because of the difficulties involved in defining a relationship in which both men were free and often equal in general social status but in which one was subordinated to the other with respect to his fief:

> He who swears fealty to his lord ought always to have these six things in mind: what is harmless, safe, honorable, useful, easy, possible. Harmless, in that he should not do his lord bodily harm; safe in that he should not betray his secrets or defenses; honorable, in that he should not weaken his rights of justice or other matters that pertain to his honor; useful, in that he should not attack his possessions; easy or possible in that he should not hinder his lord in doing good . . . or make difficulties in what is possible for his lord to do.[2]

The writer goes on to say that it is not enough to avoid evil, that the vassal must also do good, "give aid and counsel to his lord in the six things mentioned above."

The lord owed reciprocal good faith toward his vassal. In return for homage and service, he owed the vassal protection against enemies and respect for the integrity of his possessions, including his wife and children. Often the lord took into his own household the young sons of his vassals for their training to knighthood. From some of his responsibilities he derived considerable profit. When a vassal died leaving as heir a son or daughter under age, the lord became the legal guardian, administered the land himself through his agents, or sold the administration to someone else. He was entitled to appropriate the proceeds of the land provided only that he took care of the elemental needs of the heir for food, clothing, shelter, and education becoming his rank. The heir's marriage, whether boy or girl, was for the lord to arrange. Because other lords might be willing to pay handsome sums for marriage to an heir or heiress of great estates, this became an important source of revenue for lords. If the vassal died without heirs, the fief escheated, or reverted, to the lord. The legal relationship between a lord and a landholding vassal was often (but not always) made explicit in a written deed or charter such as this one from twelfth-century England:

> Gilbert de Gaunt to all his men French and English, greeting. Know that I have given and conceded to Seyer de Arceles his inheritance, that is, Lucebyam, with all the holdings which belong to it. Wherefore I wish and command that he, Seyer, well and peacefully and freely and quietly and honorably hold [it] to himself and his heirs after him from me and my heirs with all the liberties and the holdings which belong to the land in wood and field and meadow and in pastures and ways and paths, in waters and mills and ponds, with soc and sac and toll and team, infangenethef, by the service of one knight. Witnesses . . . etc.[3]

"Soc and sac," "toll and team," and "infangenethef" are the words used in England for powers of administering justice and of levying tallage on the peasantry living on the land. This kind of deed was characteristic of England in the high medieval centuries. In France, especially in the south of France, written charters often included a statement about homage and fealty, sometimes even incorporating the terms of the oath.

Enforcement of the obligations of lord and vassal toward one another was difficult until kings began to build up their power in relation to such matters. Legal theory had it that the vassal could renounce his allegiance if his lord failed in his obligations or if he wished to surrender his fief. The lord could summon the vassal to his feudal court for failure to fulfill responsibilities, and, if the vassal was found guilty of treachery to his lord, he forfeited the fief as well as his life. It was obviously difficult for the lord, in the case of a powerful vassal, to enforce the decision of his court by peaceful means. The ultimate recourse was war, as it is between nations in our times.

Many complexities were inevitable in the loose organization of feudal society. A man might, for example, be vassal to many different lords. For example, the counts of Champagne in 923 held lands from ten different lords, including the king of France, the duke of Burgundy, the archbishop of Reims, and seven other bishops. To take care of the conflict of loyalties deriving from this state of things, a principle of "liege homage" was devised. This meant that a vassal must choose among his lords the one to whom he owed his prime loyalty. This did not solve all the problems. Vassals often, as the result of marriage or inheritance, owed liege homage to more than one lord. The complexities in which such multiple homage involved him are well illustrated by the problems of John of Toul, a vassal of the counts of Champagne in the thirteenth century:

> I, John of Toul, make it known that I am the liege man of Lady Beatrice, countess of Troyes and of her son, my dearest lord count Thibaud of Champagne, against all persons, living or dead, except for the liege homage I have done to lord Enguerran of Couçy, lord John of Arcis, and the count of Grandpré. If it should happen that the count of Grandpré should be at war with the countess and count of Champagne for his own personal grievances, I will personally go to the assistance of the count of Grandpré and will send to the countess and the count of Champagne, if they summon me, the knights I owe for the fief which I hold of them. But if the count of Grandpré shall make war on the countess and count of Champagne on behalf of his friends and not for his own personal grievances, I shall serve in person with the countess and count of Champagne and I will send one knight to the count of Grandpré to give the service owed from the fief which I hold of him . . . .[4]

Women and Ecclesiastical Vassals

Two sorts of lords and vassals did not fit into the general pattern of feudal relations. They were women and ecclesiastics. Women could not perform the service of vassals, not, that is, the basic military ones on which the system rested. Neither could they perform homage or take oaths of fealty. On the other hand, they could, in the height of the feudal age, inherit land held in military tenure, could hold movable property, and could dispose of it by will. Single women, unmarried or widowed, could enter into contracts and sue and be sued in court. They were often formidable adversaries in the English courts. They did not preside over courts, nor did married women *officially* advise their lords or, indeed, their husbands. As married women, they were under the protection of their husbands and could not act independently in law. As heiresses under age, they were under the protection of the lord of the fief and subject to his disposition with respect to marriage. Essentially, they were pawns in the game of men trying to build up holdings of land and followings of vassals. As such, they could be beaten, knocked about, and treated as adjuncts of estates. However, they also held great responsibilities. They often had to command household knights and men-at-arms defending a castle in the absence of a husband. They managed a complex household consisting of servants, knights, squires, men-at-arms, pages, poets, young girls in training for marriage, and old men and women living out their last days. They were responsible for the welfare of the peasants who were the main labor resource of the landed fief. Under the spirited leadership of Eleanor of Aquitaine (1122–1204) and her entourage they began to demand more respectful treatment for themselves from the men of the society.

Ecclesiastical vassals, who acquired by gift or by pioneer enterprise great tracts of land in the early medieval centuries, were from an overlord's point of view economically not profitable, whether they were bishops, priests, or abbots. The theory that the Church, not the individual member of the clergy, held the fief from the lord meant that the lord could never expect escheat, nor wardship, nor the profit from the marriage of heirs. The only effective way in which the lord could make something of his relationship with ecclesiastical vassals was through postponing the election of a new bishop or abbot, or the appointment of a new priest for a considerable period. Doing this, he could take the proceeds of the fief. King John of England (1199–1216) did this fruitfully with English bishoprics for a number of years in resistance to Pope Innocent III (1198–1216). Theoretically, ecclesiastical vassals could not render military service because the tenets of Christianity forbade their shedding of blood except in just war. Yet Odo, Bishop of Bayeux, was in the thick of the fight at Hastings when William, Duke of Normandy, invaded England, and in the twelfth century *chanson de geste, The Song of Roland*

> Archbishop Turpin led the Franks
> Against the Paynim host, riding the steed
> Of a great king whom he aforetime slew
> In Denmark . . .[5]

Turpin killed a Muslim champion, and the Franks cried: "Here is true knightlihood! In the Archbishop's hand the Cross is safe." Even bishops and abbots who were not as lusty in battle as Odo or Turpin often owned a contingent of knights. Grave question was raised as early as the ninth century whether ecclesiastical vassals should do homage or take the oath of fealty, evidently in protest against a widespread custom:

> The churches entrusted to us by God are not royal property, nor benefices of such a sort that the king can give them or take them away as he sees fit, because everything which belongs to the churches is dedicated to God. . . . And we bishops, consecrated to the Lord, are not men of such a sort that, like laymen, we should commend ourselves in vassalage to anyone . . . nor should we in any fashion take a solemn oath [of homage] which scriptural and apostolical and canonical authority forbid. It is abominable that hands anointed with holy oil, hands which through prayer and the sign of the cross can make the body and blood of Christ out of bread and water . . . that such hands would be touched in a secular ceremony of oath-taking. And it is sinful that the tongue of a bishop, which by the grace of God is a key to heaven, should pronounce an oath over holy relics like any common layman. . . .[6]

The climax in the conflict over this problem did not come until the eleventh century (see Chapter VI). By that time, the Church was thoroughly enmeshed in the feudal world.

War and Chivalry

War was the profession of the noble. When the Muslim, Viking, and Magyar attacks had subsided, and there were no longer outside enemies to fight, the feudal noble turned his fighting propensities on his neighbors and rivals. When kings, princes, and ecclesiastics began to try to check this private warfare, tournaments or war games were devised to take its place, to keep the knights in fighting trim, and to supply the noble with the spoils in horses, armor, and ransom needed to supplement his income from the peasants' labor. The typical tournament of the High Middle Ages was not the individual combat of two knights made so famous in later romantic tales. It was the *melée*, a simulated general battle, in which knights were often killed though there were more rules of courtesy than applied in real warfare. It was in these general battles that heraldic devices began to be used to distinguish one knight from another. Individual combat following intricate rules was a further elaboration in the later Middle Ages dictated by the desire for renown that motivated every knight worthy of his calling.

The code of the knight, called "chivalry," was in itself an elaboration of the code of the primitive Germans. The prime requisites of this code from the knight were prowess, loyalty, generosity, and courtesy toward his fellow knights. A boy of the feudal class underwent a long period of training in these virtues. He was taken from his parents at the age of seven and placed in the household of a patron for training. Here he learned the difficult art of fighting from the back of a horse, he learned swordplay, and he built up his physical stamina. But he also learned, as a page or servant in the lord's household, the modesty and obedience that would make him a good vassal. He was trained in courtesy toward his equals and superiors and in proper behavior toward women and the lower orders. The physical training was basic. If he failed in that, the best he could hope for was to become a monk or cleric. Although book learning was no part of the course, there were some learned knights of the twelfth century—Robert, Earl of Leicester, justiciar to Henry II, for example, or King Henry himself. Knighthood was conceived of as a degree awarded for the successful completion of training to arms. The dubbing of a knight, in early centuries, had no religious overtones. It was not until the ecclesiastical hierarchy began to try to moderate the brutalities of feudal society that the ceremony became a religious one.

From the time of St. Augustine, the clergy had had the concept of the "just war," the war fought for God and sanctioned by the hierarchy. Interpretations were crude, however, and were hard to enforce in relation to the knight's code of honor. The latter required a knight to avenge insult and to defend his estates and his household. Ideally, it demanded kind and courteous treatment of a fellow knight. The hero of one twelfth-century epic refused to kill his treacherous enemy, although he made him step naked into a fountain where he stood helpless in the hero's power.

The knight's code did not require that he treat peasants kindly nor even the women of his own class. Other men's peasants and even one's own, where self-interest did not intervene, could be and were killed with impunity from censure. The pillage of fields and the burning of peasant villages were a normal part of feudal warfare. Noble women were expected to bear with husbands who boxed their ears, slapped them or beat them "for their correction," and divorced them if they did not bear male heirs. The romantic literature of the age is full of instances of callous cruelty.

Yet the clergy and women did attempt and perhaps succeed during the twelfth and thirteenth centuries in moderating somewhat the brutality of the life of the castle. John of Salisbury, a twelfth-century ecclesiastic and scholar, states the ideal of knighthood as follows:

> But what is the office of the duly ordained soldiery? To defend the Church, to assail infidelity, to venerate the priesthood, to protect

the poor from injuries, to pacify the province, to pour out their blood for their brothers (as the formula of their oath instructs them), and, if need be, to lay down their lives.[7]

Faced with the knights' resistance to Christian teaching, the best that the clergy could hope to do was to harness knightly aggressiveness by encouraging moderating rules and by turning warfare against non-Christians. They tried to persuade the knights of Europe to accept the "Truce of God" and the "Peace of God." According to the former, fighting was prohibited on weekends and religious holidays. The "Peace" attempted to protect clergy, women, merchants, and peasants from attacks by knights and men-at-arms. Churches provided sanctuary for even the red-handed murderer. But chronicles and court records suggest that none of these prohibitions was overwhelmingly effective. Warfare was the profession of the knight. He could hardly be expected to give it up. The Crusades were the culminating expression of the attempt to Christianize warfare. If the warlike proclivities of the knight could not be extirpated, they could at least be turned against non-Christians (see Chapter VIII).

The conflict between reality and the ideal is best illustrated in the deathbed words of William Marshal, by reputation one of the greatest knights of Christendom:

> Henry, listen to me a while. The clerks are too hard on us. They shave us too closely. I have captured five hundred knights and have appropriated their arms, horses, and their entire equipment. If for this reason the kingdom of God is closed to me, I can do nothing about it, for I cannot return my booty. I can do no more for God than to give myself to him, repenting all my sins. Unless the clergy desire my damnation, they must ask no more. But their teaching is false—else no one could be saved.[8]

William had started as a landless knight, had risen to great fame and fortune, dying a great earl and chief ruler of England on behalf of the boy-king Henry III. In his will he left his rich garments to his household knights, with a proviso that the residue be distributed to the poor.

Courtly Love

Women tried to tame feudal manhood through the game of courtly love. The "game" per se originated in Provence, France, in the twelfth century. It received its first great impetus from the court of Eleanor of Aquitaine (1122–1204), a redoubtable woman who was successively wife to Louis VII of France and Henry II of England. Eleanor suffered adversities as a wife in feudal society, but, on the whole, she received what she deserved. She was unfaithful to her first rather monkish husband and treacherous to her second, encouraging her sons to twice rebel against him. Henry II finally shut her up in polite imprisonment as a precaution against her brilliant rebelliousness. She had been a great heiress, to the duchy of Aquitaine, which included a large part of southern France. Before her imprisonment, Eleanor spent a great deal of time at her palace in Poitiers, the capital of the duchy. Here she ruled over a splendid court frequented by poets from her domain and from other parts of Europe. And here was played the elaborate game of courtly love.

The game was not only a protest of women against their treatment in feudal society, but also a rebellion of both sexes against the strictures of the Church on the enjoyment of sexual love. The Fathers of the Church and contemporary theologians considered sexual desire to be a punishment for the original sin of Adam and Eve, and they tended to frown upon intercourse except between spouses for procreation of children. In courtly love, the pain as well as the pleasure of sexual love was recognized. It was thought to have an ennobling effect on lovers, especially the men, for whom frustration was often the reward of their devotion. Andrew the Chaplain, who wrote a textbook on courtly love, says that

> Love is a certain inborn suffering derived from the sight of and excessive meditation upon the beauty of the opposite sex, and which causes each one to wish above all things the embraces of

the other and by common desire to carry out all of love's precepts in the other's embrace.[9]

The rules of courtly love, if carried out with serious intent, would have turned the feudal world upside down. The lady of the castle rather than the lord became the object of the knight's service, his homage, and his fealty. As his *midon* (a French word for lord), she required his whole devotion even when it led to insult and disgrace in terms of the fighting man's code. *The Knight of the Cart* carried the theme of devotion to an absurd extreme. The hero Lancelot subjected himself to ridicule at a tournament by command of his lady and, finally, in a culminating episode, rode in the hangman's cart in order to rescue her. She, by the way, was the wife of his lord, the king. His adultery with her was treason, not just sin.

What more delightful game could there be for women languishing of boredom in the company of a medieval household from which the master and his knight vassal were absent in war or on Crusade? Noble women set up "courts of love" in which the delicacies of the knight's duties were defined and refined. Poets and the minstrels who sang their songs cooperated. Churchmen fulminated against adultery, yet priests notoriously indulged in it. Andrew the Chaplain, himself probably a priest, said that priesthood was no bar to the role of true lover. It is doubtful whether the game resulted in a total increase in adultery. The conditions of feudal society encouraged that sin since men rarely chose their wives for love, and women rarely had any voice in choosing their husbands. Boys and girls married at puberty and were often pledged to each other in the cradle. In any human society monogamous fidelity is a difficult rule to enforce.

The most important effect of courtly love was probably an improvement in the treatment and social status of women of the noble class and the emergence of the concept of romantic love, in which tenderness, courtesy, and respect were added to lust as the basis of relations between the sexes. This development reached its culmination much later in nineteenth-century England when women were placed on a pedestal on which they suffered unbearable strain.

The Life of the Castle

Feudal relationships in their prime provided a loose form of government within the ranks of the professional soldiery as well as a system of education and a code of social behavior. They provided also a means of governing the men and women who produced the food, clothing, and shelter for medieval society. They worked reasonably well in terms of the standard of values for the times. The lord got as much as he could from the peasants' labor and treated peasants with a mixture of contempt, compassion, and *noblesse oblige*. The lord himself lived a life of hardship in modern terms. Even though he might be able to afford luxuries denied to the peasant, he had few physical comforts. Castles, whether they were modest and primitive wooden fortifications built on top of natural hills or man-made mounds, or were more elaborate stone fortifications, were not very comfortable in the centuries from 1000 to 1300. They were cold, drafty, overcrowded, and, inevitably, dirty, having been built for defense in war, not domestic comfort. They offered little privacy for any of the residents. The noble lord and lady of a twelfth-century castle usually slept together in the same room with their children and upper maid servants and men servants. Food supplies often fell low even for the members of the aristocracy. Military campaigns were difficult and often dangerous—not so much because men died in combat, but because they fell ill of eating overripe fruit or diseased meat foraged from the countryside, or because they succumbed to epidemics of typhus or other devastating plagues not understood by medieval doctors. The worst of these plagues, the bubonic plague, invaded Europe in the middle of the fourteenth century and catalysed significant changes in the social and economic order. The Crusades, undertaken with exaltation and hope, in the end provided no solution to west European problems. There were men, then as now, who thought that the problems of society could be solved by realizing more fully the traditional ideals. And there were some who thought that the whole social order must change.

Changing Feudalism of the Later Middle Ages

Feudal society did, in fact, change in the later Middle Ages. Feudal military techniques became outmoded. Before the end of the twelfth century paid knights, men-at-arms, and archers began to replace the feudal host, and technically trained engineers for siege work became an essential part of any army. By the fourteenth century foot soldiers equipped with pikes or bows had demonstrated that in certain conditions and under good leadership they could defeat mounted knights, however valiant. By the fifteenth century gunpowder and artillery had come into use, and the armed, mounted knight began his long demise as the chief strength of an army. This does not mean that nobles and knights ceased to be important elements in armies, in government, and in society. However, they had to adapt their abilities to new conditions. They became leaders of paid armies. Lord-vassal relationships became lord–paid retainer relationships, and the personal loyalties within the feudal class became a threat to attempts of kings to set up states in which law and order prevailed (see Chapter V), instead of a means of maintaining order and security in a time of weakness of kings and princes. Chivalry, a product of the prime centuries of feudal society, became a matter of ritual, of romantic fantasy, and of wistful nostalgia.

IV

Medieval Commerce:

Towns

Trade had never wholly died out even during the chaotic ninth and tenth centuries. Jews and Syrians continued to carry on commerce with western Europe. Muslim conquests caused some disruption and redirection of routes in the eighth century, but the Muslims were themselves traders and soon were exchanging goods with their Christian neighbors. The Vikings were also traders as well as pirates and plunderers. They followed the rivers of Russia to Byzantium to establish trade relations there in the ninth century, and their explorations to the west took them as far as "Vinland" by 1000.[1] Regional trade in western Europe did continue for such articles as wine, wool, fish, dairy products, and grain. Throughout the early medieval period Venice had maintained her sea route through the Adriatic Sea to the industrial centers of the eastern Empire, including great Byzantium itself.

The enterprise of the Jews, in particular, is illustrated in this passage from a Muslim commentator of the ninth century:

These merchants speak Arabic, Persian, Roman, Frankish, Spanish and Slavonic. They travel from the East to the West and from the West to the East by land as well as by sea. They bring from the West eunuchs, slave girls, boys, brocade, beaver skins, marten furs and other varieties of fur and swords. . . . Sometimes the Jewish merchants, embarking in the country of the Franks on the Western Sea, sail toward Antioch. From there they proceed by land to al-Jabiya, where they arrive after three days' journey. There they take a boat on the Euphrates and they reach Bagdad, from where they go down the Tigris to al-Ubullah. From al-Ubullah they sail for, successively, Oman, Sind, Hind, and China. . . .[2]

Yet during the centuries of inroads from the outer regions into "civilized" Europe there undoubtedly had been a serious decline in the volume of trade and a breakup of the single trading area that had centered on the Mediterranean in Roman times and included in its farthest outposts China and the British Isles. The problem of the flight of gold from the West because of an unfavorable balance of trade with the East and the conquest of gold-bearing areas by the Muslims had been solved by substituting silver. Charlemagne and other eighth- and ninth-century kings had adopted better minting policies, reserving the privilege of minting to themselves or persons they had licensed.

Revival of Long-Distance Trade

By the year 1000 commercial recovery was well under way, and by 1100 Venice, Genoa, and other Italian mercantile cities may have rivaled in wealth the greatest commercial centers of the ancient world. In the north, recovery was slower. Yet, even there, when society had become more peaceful after the subsidence of attacks from Northmen and Magyars, small urban centers began to emerge under the protection of kings, nobles, and bishops. Part of the stimulus came from the production of agricultural surpluses and the population increase of the period. The main factor, however, was the revival of long-distance trade and the restoration of contacts between north and south, east and west. Muslim importation of slaves, metal goods, timber, furs, and other northern commodities by the tenth century had reversed the drainage of gold and begun to restore a more normal balance of trade. In the eleventh century Venice won new trade concessions from the eastern Empire as the price of her help against attacks of Norman adventurers in southern Italy. Genoa and Pisa began attacks on Muslim strongholds in Corsica, Sardinia, Sicily, and northern Africa. By 1052 they had captured the Muslim base at Palermo. The Crusades stimulated the commercial enterprise of north Italian cities by creating a pilgrim passenger trade to the East and by enabling them to establish ports on the coast of Syria and Palestine. Venice dominated the eastern Mediterranean routes, but Genoa and Pisa put up strong competition. The ancient Mediterranean ports of Marseilles and Narbonne, on what is now the French coast, began to recover, and in the thirteenth century Louis IX (1226–1270) built a fortified port in the salt marshes west of Marseilles to provide a base for the departure of his crusading fleets. In the same century, the commercial movement spread westward to Catalonia in northern Spain.

Trade routes followed old Roman roads and convenient waterways. But the traveling merchants of this period sought more than passes through mountains, fords across streams, and navigable channels. They also wanted comfortable inns, busy markets, safe and well-kept roads and bridges, low tolls, speedy justice in disputes, and strong protection from thieves and robbers. From northern Italy the earliest land routes went up through the Brenner Pass into Germany or through the western passes of the Alps into the Rhone valley, then up the Rhone and Saône rivers into the upper Seine valley and from there north and west through the Rhine, Scheldt, and Seine valleys to the English Channel and North Sea coast. The medieval county of Champagne experienced a century and a half of wealth and glory in the twelfth and early thirteenth centuries. Her counts had built up a strong state around well-fortified centers in which commerce was safe. Swift justice for merchants could be had in their courts. Fairs and markets at Troyes and other centers drew merchants from all over the Western world. Yet Champagne's preeminence proved ephemeral because the land had insufficient produce of its own to exchange for goods of other areas and because the French kings built up competing routes and centers and eventually absorbed Champagne into their demesne.

Access to the north by sea was limited. Merchants sailed from northern Italy to Marseilles and Narbonne and then traveled overland to Atlantic coast ports because they were unable to use the sea route through the Strait of Gibraltar.

Impenetrable Gibraltar was held by the Muslims, who allowed no one else through. Not until 1277 did the Genoese break through the Muslim guard on Gibraltar and open up an all-sea route to the north.

In the high medieval period the Low Countries were the northern pole of an axis of trade of which northern Italy was the southern pole. The counts of Flanders and the dukes of Brabant offered order, peace, and protection for commerce in their domains. Towns like Bruges, near the North Sea coast, Ghent, and later, Antwerp, on the Scheldt River began to complement the Italian cities as centers of trade and industry. They distributed woolen textiles, and they drew trade from the Baltic Sea, from Scandinavia, and from Britain, as well as from southern Europe. From the Baltic region came furs, hemp, flax, honey and beeswax, timber, and pitch. From Britain the main products were wool, wool fells (sheepskins with the wool still on them), and hides. From Italy came fine textiles, steel, glassware, spices, dyes, and other luxury products of the eastern Mediterranean and beyond. In Germany the thirteenth century was a time of commercial growth. Merchants from Bremen, Hamburg, Lubeck, and Stettin established trading posts further to the east at Riga, Reval, and distant Novgorod in Russia and plied their commerce between them and posts in Britain and Flanders.

Growth and Spread of Towns and Cities

Neither towns nor merchants fitted readily into the pattern of feudal society. Merchants were more mobile than peasants. They probably traveled no more than did the top and bottom levels of the feudal class, that is, the kings and great nobles, the mercenary soldiers and the knights in pursuit of their livelihood. But unlike the feudal nobles they needed "outside" protection for their goods and security for their residences and warehouses. In the law courts they needed swifter and more flexible procedures for collecting debts and getting compensation for breaches of contract. These peculiarities led to the recognition that townspeople were a new and different category of people from peasants, although in the early stages of town development town dwellers were often referred to as "villeins" and owed labor services to lords and were subject to tallage.

The history of the growth of towns is so different from one part of Europe to another and from one town to another that it is difficult to generalize. In southern Europe (northern Italy and southern France) towns emerged out of the surrounding countryside as reconstructions of the city-states of the ancient world. Urban centers drew the feudal nobility from the environs and absorbed them into the town population. Nobles joined the ranks of the merchants and built their town palaces with gains from trade. Peasants, too, were drawn to the cities until city governments restricted their immigration by denying rights of citizenship except to those who had lived in the town for periods as long as twenty-five years. A city-state needed a rural agricultural population to cultivate the fields and supply the urban nucleus with food. Italian city-states gained autonomy with relative ease because there was no consistently strong centralizing monarchy at work to oppose their increasing influence as in France or England. The kings of Germany, claiming and asserting, whenever they were able to, the title to be emperors of the Holy Roman Empire, descended through the Alpine passes to exploit the wealth of the north Italian towns, by upholding their rights to tolls, mints, and judicial powers. In the end they were driven to exact large sums of money in return for concessions of autonomy. They needed north Italian wealth and military support in their quarrels with the papacy. Frederick Barbarossa, second and perhaps greatest in the Hohenstaufen line (1152–1190), in 1183 conceded city-state autonomy, free elections of the consuls of these states, and the right to form alliances among themselves. Italian cities hired armies, engaged in war with one another and with kings, popes, and emperors and, indeed, behaved like very princes themselves. A contemporary historian, writing of Frederick Barbarossa's attempt to subdue the Lombard cities, says that they raised to knighthood

. . . young men of low condition, even workmen of contemptible mechanical arts, such as other people drive away like the plague from the more honorable and liberal pursuits. From which it happens that they are preeminent among the other countries of the world for riches and power. And to this they are helped also, as has been said, by their own industrial habits, and by the absence of their princes, accustomed to reside north of the Alps. In this, however, they retain a trace of their barbarous dregs, forgetful of ancient nobility, that while they boast of living by law they do not obey the laws. For they seldom or never receive the prince reverently, to whom it would be their duty to show a willing reverence of submission . . . .[3]

In northwestern Europe towns grew up under the protection of kings, great nobles, bishops, and monasteries. Here there were two general types—*organic* towns, which grew out of older settlements, villages, or merchant colonies outside castle walls, and *planted* towns, newly founded by kings and lords for military and commercial purposes. Merchant constituencies offered many advantages to lords in need of money in a time of rising prices and expanding horizons. Tolls could be collected for sales in markets or fairs and for passage along the roads and bridges leading to the commercial centers. Tallages or other taxes could be levied on the residents, and fees for justice brought in needed revenue. Enlightened self-interest or desperate emergency suggested the advantage of conveying to the townspeople the right to manage their own affairs in return for a compounding of the money exactions. Town "freedoms" were conferred by charter. Townsmen paid large sums for these documents. In the case of planted towns, freedoms were offered to attract settlers either from the countryside or from other towns. Richard the Lion-hearted (1189–1199) and his brother John (1199–1216) of England made extensive grants of charters to meet the cost of their wars. John's son and grandson built fortress towns in frontier regions to maintain their power against the Welsh or the French kings.

On the continent the French kings also made extensive grants of town charters and founded new towns. The great period of "planting" towns both in England and France was the thirteenth century. Most towns in England by 1200 held royal charters. However, on the continent developments were more complex and stormier. The earlier towns, many of them founded by bishops and monasteries, had to fight for the rights so readily granted to new communities. "Communes," or associations of townsmen, were formed, and members took oaths to support each other in the struggle for emancipation from the lords. A twelfth-century abbot tells of the violence at Laon where a revolt broke out against the bishop and nobles in 1115. During the absence of the bishop, the inhabitants were offered the opportunity to form a commune by paying a sum to cover the customary services and dues. The bishop, on his return, was displeased with the arrangement, and friction developed between him and the townsmen.

> He determined to urge the annulment of the Commune, to which he had sworn, and had by bribes induced the King to swear. . . . The compact of the Commune being broken, such rage, such amazement seized the citizens that all the officials abandoned their duties and the stalls of the craftsmen and cobblers were closed and nothing was exposed for sale by the innkeepers and hucksters, who expected to have nothing left when the lords began plundering. For at once the property of all was calculated by the Bishop and nobles, and whatever any man was known to have given to arrange the Commune, so much was demanded of him to procure its annulment.[4]

On the Thursday or Friday of Easter week the citizens entered the bishop's palace "with swords, battle-axes, bows and hatchets, and carrying clubs and spears." The nobles rallied to the bishop's side; many were killed in the fight against the invaders. Others fled in disguise. The bishop himself took refuge in a wine cask but was ultimately discovered and brutally killed. He was dismembered and thrown into a corner in front of his chaplain's house. One man, seeing his ring, cut off his ring finger to get it. And so, the abbot states "because he had wrongly and in vain taken up another sword, by the sword he perished."

In Germany merchant enterprise was more important than in the west in the planting of new towns. Groups of merchant entrepreneurs, rich from their participation in long-distance trade, entered into contracts with the territorial lords to establish bases on the shores of the Baltic Sea and in the Danube region. For the Baltic–North Sea trade, a league of cities was formed to protect and encourage the expansion. Originally called the Gotland Association, it adopted the more familiar name Hanseatic League in the fourteenth century. Both the king-emperor of Germany and the towns recognized the mutual advantages of alliances with one another. The emperor needed money; the townsmen needed freedoms, which were hard to win from the lords. By requesting these from the emperor, who granted them for financial reimbursement, the towns won for themselves by the thirteenth century a position in relation to imperial authority more or less equivalent to that of the princes.

By negotiation or by violence town dwellers all over Europe ultimately won recognition of their special needs. They achieved this by acting in community with one another as citizens, not by individual negotiation or action. In town charters five privileges were basic: (1) the right to farm the taxes and tolls, that is, to collect them through town officers and to pay the lord or lords an annual sum; (2) the right to personal freedom—residence in a town for a year and a day conferred freedom on runaway serfs (the saying was, "Town air makes free."); (3) the right to hold their own courts for trial of cases arising within the town; (4) burgage tenure, a tenure more flexible than feudal tenure, allowing freer conveyance of real estate by will or deed of sale; (5) the right to organize their own defenses, including patrol of the walls and the maintenance of a militia.

Fairs and Markets: Protection of Trade

Fairs and markets, that is, periodical gatherings for the exchange of goods, were held under the auspices of lords or of the towns themselves. Fairs were held at special seasons and attracted buyers and sellers from all over Europe. The Champagne fairs at Troyes, Provins, and Lagny-sur-Marne were famous in the twelfth century. There Genoese and Venetian merchants met Flemings and Germans and exchanged spices and fine textiles for raw wool, furs, and other northern products. Great lords bought horses and armor; their ladies fine cloth for dresses. Markets were held more often and drew a local clientele. To market went peasants with their eggs and cheese to buy metal for tools and other products not available in the village. The right to hold fairs and markets entailed also the power to administer justice. There grew up a special body of law called the "law merchant," and special courts called "piepowder" courts (courts for the dusty-footed merchants—*pieds poudrés* in French). A man could start an action in such a court at sunrise and hope to get his remedy by sunset. For seamen, as always a class of mixed cultural origins, there evolved a special law and custom of the sea that applied to all countries. The Code of Oléron, an island off the French coast near Bordeaux, became standard for northwest Europe. It regulated sailors' pay, freight charges, and the like.

Kings and other rulers of great feudal states recognized the advantage of promoting and protecting the interests of merchants traveling in their realms. In the Magna Carta, for example, King John granted to merchants safety and security in moving about and selling or buying goods and freedom from unjust tolls except in time of war between England and their own country.

> But if they come from a country at war against us; and if such [merchants] are found in our country at the beginning of a war, let them be seized without harm to their persons or goods until it is known by us or our chief justiciar in what fashion the merchants of our realm, who are to be found at that time in the land at war against us, are being treated. And if our [merchants] are safe there, let the other [merchants] be safe in our realm.[5]

King John's grandson granted a general charter to merchants in return for which they agreed to pay import and export duties. These custom duties became an important source of income to

English kings of the later Middle Ages. French kings granted similar protection. In Germany, where the king's power was weaker in the high medieval period, the cities themselves banded together to defend and further their interests. The Hanseatic League cities, under the leadership of Lubeck, maintained a fleet, fought wars (particularly with the king of Denmark), and negotiated with princes and other cities to establish and maintain their overland and sea routes. They set up trading posts all over Europe where merchants from the alliance could be safe in their goods and persons. In London they maintained an enclave called the Steelyard, where their ships docked and where their merchants could reside in safety.

Town Government and Social Classes

Internally, the towns developed great complexity in social structure and government. As in all medieval phenomena, there is great diversity from one town or city to another, and there was change from one period to another in each town's history. Venice, for example, in the twelfth and thirteenth centuries came under the control of a small hereditary commercial oligarchy. This oligarchy constituted its Great Council and elected the doge (the chief magistrate). Florence was briefly a "gild democracy," in which the power rested in the leaders of the gilds. London and Lincoln in England had a mayor and council type of government. In the north the town's constitution depended on the terms of its corporation charter. Certain town charters were used as models so that all the liberties need not be written out in full. The oldest and most famous of these models was the charter of the Norman town of Breteuil. A new town could simply be granted the liberties of Breteuil without spelling out all the details. Lynn, founded by the bishop of Norwich in 1204, obtained from King John the right to choose its own model charter:

> . . . the lord king granted that we should choose a borough in England, whichever we willed; and then that our town of Lynn

should have the same liberties as that town has: and we have chosen Oxford.[6]

In general, the wealthier merchants dominated town government. In twelfth-century England merchant gilds were the prevailing organization. Their membership coincided with the participating citizenry, and their officers often held the main offices in the government. Their main objective was to protect their monopoly of the town's market. By the fourteenth century craft gilds had replaced them in control of the town's life and government. But it was still the wealthier members of the wealthier gilds who held the power. Florence had seventy-three gilds of craftsmen in 1316: cloth manufacturers, furriers, butchers, tanners, money changers, proprietors of bath rooms, sewer cleaners and garbage removers, teachers of grammar, arithmetic, reading, and writing, and the like. A craft gild not only regulated prices, wages, quality of produce, conditions of work, and other economic aspects of the craft, it also performed social and religious functions. Craft gilds maintained alms houses and cared for widows and orphans and other victims of misfortune. They founded schools for poor scholars and performed the cycles of "mystery" plays familiar to every student of English literature. Craft gilds were ruled by the "master-craftsmen," men who, having qualified by producing a "masterpiece," had their own shops. Journeymen worked in the masters' shops by the day (or *journee* in French). To learn the craft, apprentices were contracted to masters as children. They received bed and board and training but were not paid until they became journeymen.

The power of the wealthier merchants and gildsmen was not accepted without protest by those of lesser wealth. In some Italian city-states a three-way struggle between *grandi*, or nobles, the *populo grasso*, or merchant oligarchy, and the *populo minuto* gave the poorer people some temporary bargaining power. (See Chapter VIII.) They allied themselves with the *grandi*. Until the fierce conflicts were resolved by calling in outsiders as elective princes to maintain peace, the poor did achieve some recognition of their interests. Conflict between the poor and the rich occurred in the north too, particularly in Flanders where weavers rose against the merchant oligarchies. Even England, where the power of the king was strong in the towns, was not free from civic conflict. Roger of Wendover, a twelfth-century chronicler, gives for 1194 a vivid account of

> . . . a dispute in the city of London between the poor and the rich on account of the tallage, which was exacted by the king's agents for the benefit of the exchequer; for the principal men of the city, whom we call mayors and aldermen, having held a deliberation at their hustings, wished to preserve themselves free from the burden, and to oppress the poorer classes.

William Fitz-Robert (called William with the Beard because he carried on a family tradition of refusing to shave in token of resistance to tyranny) led the opposition to the mayor and council of aldermen. The rebels were defeated, but the king's officers had to be called in to subdue William. He was smoked out of his sanctuary, dragged tied to a horse's tail through London, and hanged. Thus, says the chronicler:

> William of the Beard was shamefully put to death by his fellow citizens for asserting the truth and defending the cause of the poor; and if the justice of one's cause constitutes a martyr, we may surely set him down as one. With him also were hanged nine of his neighbors or of his family who espoused his cause.[7]

Life in the Towns

Medieval towns were laid out in relation to three essentials: the walls, the markets, and the cathedrals and churches. The walls were the most important of the three. They offered protection. However, they obviously confined the available space and made growth difficult. As towns grew, their walls had to be extended to take in the new settlements. Depressions or shifts in trade routes led to depopulation of some communities. Houses and shops were deserted, and this added to the burden of taxes for the surviving population. Market places were sometimes near the gates, sometimes in the center of the town. The cathedral, if there was one, tended to be central and to dominate the town landscape. Churches were centers of the parishes into which any sizable town was divided. New towns were laid out on a grid pattern; older ones grew somewhat more haphazardly in relation to land contours and human settlement.

Medieval towns and cities were not large by modern standards. Florence reputedly had 100,000 inhabitants in 1340. London, in the same period, had only 30,000–40,000. Köln (Cologne), the largest city in Germany, had 30,000. Most towns and cities were considerably smaller. They were noisy and dirty (although perhaps not as much so as their eighteenth-century counterparts or modern industrial centers). Street vendors called their wares, cart wheels ground over cobblestones, horses' hooves clopped or rang on stone. Church bells marked the passage of the hours or the passing of a man. Filth, bad smells, and fires were constant hazards. Fires were, of course, less easy to control than in modern cities. Houses were built of combustible materials, open lamps and candles were used, and water was harder to command in the right spot. Rapid growth meant overcrowding, and overcrowding aggravated problems and dangers.

Florence did have public baths, sewers, and garbage collectors. However, in many towns garbage was thrown in the gutter along with human excrement and urine. Plumbing was primitive or nonexistent. Butchers slaughtered animals within the city limits. Without the means of refrigeration, fish and meat became stinking and putrid. Houses, to save space, were sometimes built out over the streets. Thus they cut off light and air for passers-by and even endangered horsemen's heads. Municipal authorities were not indifferent to these conditions. Avignon, in 1243, decreed:

> That no one shall throw water into the street, nor any steaming liquid, nor chaff, nor refuse of grapes, nor human filth, nor bath water, nor indeed any dirt. Nor shall he throw anything into the

street under his house nor allow his family to do so. . . . And he who commits this offense, be he head of the family or not, shall pay a fine of two shillings for every offense; and his accuser shall receive a third of the fine.[8]

London's government similarly forbade dumping, ordered that streets and lanes be kept clear of pigs and pigsties and that stalls for the sale of foods should stand midway between gutters. It also forced householders to cover their roofs with tiles to reduce the fire hazard from thatch. It established specifications for the construction of privies and forbade butchers to slaughter animals within the city. Curfews were common. When the curfew bell rang, the city gates were closed, taverns and wine shops were shut. The inhabitants were expected to retire to their houses, to cover their fires and put out their candles. In London six men were appointed to each ward to enforce the regulations and to protect the sleeping citizens. Boatmen were forbidden to take anyone on the river at night.

Despite noise, dirt, and other hazards, medieval townsmen took pride in their cities. A thirteenth-century Italian writer has described the wide streets of Milan, the beautiful palaces, the "houses packed in, not scattered but continuous, stately, adorned in a stately manner." Milan had 12,500 dwellings, "many in which many families live together with crowds of dependents." Its public buildings and the Chapel of St. Ambrose surrounded a central square or piazza in which stood a tower hung with the four bells of the commune. Porticoes covered other squares open to all residents and protected them from the rain and brilliant Mediterranean sun. Northern houses tended to be smaller and porticoes were more unusual. William Fitz-Stephen's description of London in the time of Henry II illustrates how close the inhabitants of that city still were to the countryside:

Among the noble and celebrated cities of the world that of London, the capital of the kingdom of the English, is one which extends its glory farther than all the others and sends its wealth and merchandise more widely into distant lands. . . . It is happy in the healthiness of its air; in its observance of Christian practice; in the strength of its fortifications; in its natural situation; in the honour of its citizens; and the modesty of its matrons. It is cheerful in its sports, and the fruitful mother of noble men. . . . Everywhere outside the houses of those living in the suburbs, and adjacent to them, are the spacious and beautiful gardens of the citizens, and these are planted with trees. Also there are on the north side pastures and pleasant meadow lands through which flow streams wherein the turning of mill-wheels makes a cheerful sound. Very near lies a great forest with woodland pastures in which there are the lairs of wild animals: stags, fallow deer, wild boars and bulls. The tilled lands of the city are not barren gravel but fat Asian plains that yield luxuriant crops and fill the tillers' barns with the sheaves of Ceres. There are also outside London on the north side excellent suburban wells with sweet, wholesome and clear water that flows rippling over the bright stones. Among these are Holywell, Clerkenwell and St. Clement's Well, which are all famous. These are frequented by great numbers and much visited by the students from the schools and by young men of the city, when they go out for fresh air on summer evenings. Good indeed is this city when it has a good lord.

After describing the Tower of London to the east he continues:

London was once also walled and turreted on the south, but the mighty Thames, so full of fish, has with the sea's ebb and flow washed against, loosened and thrown down those walls in the course of time.[9]

It is worth noting that there were still salmon in the Thames at London in 1320. Today Englishmen go to distant Scotland or Norway to catch salmon.

Medieval Businessmen

The medieval businessman did not succeed without really trying. Apart from the risks to body and goods as he traveled the roads or waterways, the just and unjust tolls he had to pay at every turn, the struggle for recognition of his special needs and interests, he endangered by his very occupation his immortal soul. The love of gain was avarice, one of the seven deadly sins. As St. Thomas Aquinas put it, a man may without sin profit only if profit is not an end in itself:

> . . . as when a man uses moderate gains acquired in trade for the support of his household, or even to help the needy; or even when a man devotes himself to trade for the public welfare, lest there be a lack of the things necessary for life of the country . . .[10]

As for receiving a price for the use of money lent, this was usury and was prohibited to Christians. A Christian might safely take a just price for goods sold, that is, a price based on the intrinsic value to buyer and seller of the thing sold. He could not safely make a profit by buying goods where or when they were cheap and selling them where or when they were dear. And yet a widely popular story was the Dick Whittington story of the boy who sold his cat to the king of a distant country infested with mice and so founded a great fortune. This story was associated with a lord mayor of London. It was told also of Francesco di Marco Datini, a fourteenth-century merchant of Prato, near Florence in Italy. But perhaps the more important moral of Datini's life story lies in the anxiety that he suffered all his life concerning his salvation. A few years before his death he joined a band of 30,000 pilgrims who, dressed in white linen and barefoot, walked through the villages of Tuscany praying in the churches and scourging themselves for their sins. Their pilgrimage ended at Fiesole, where they heard the bishop preach. "And then each man returned to his own house and the journey and pilgrimage were ended. God make it profitable to our souls, if it be his will."[11] At his death Datini bequeathed his whole fortune of 70,000 gold florins, his house, and (fortunately for history) his papers to the poor people of Prato.

Jews were the moneylenders of the early Middle Ages, but Christians soon found ways to get around the prohibitions to their engaging in money lending. Legitimate interest was defined as payment for the inconvenience to the lender for not getting his money back on time. For example, a cloth merchant of

Dijon agreed to pay back 312.5 gold francs to three Italian merchants.

> [The debt] is to be paid within the next six months. . . . And in addition to this, once the said six months have passed, for each of the said francs not paid 2 [deniers] Tournois [will be due] as increment each week, for so long as, etc., together with all expenses. . . .[12]

The weekly payment of 2 pennies is hidden interest. Another example: an Italian merchant lent money to the king of England, the debt to be repaid in sacks of wool. Since the market value of the wool was greater than the amount of the loan, the Italian got his interest. That is, he got it if he ever got the wool. Three great Italian banking houses failed through overgenerosity in lending money to Edward III of England. A third example: a partnership was formed in which one of the partners put in money, the other his labor and enterprise. The "sleeping" partner shared the profit on his investment.

Medieval businessmen were ingenious in inventing or borrowing from the Arabs new tools for their trade. Letters of credit were useful not only to them but also to the Crusaders traveling to and from the Holy Land. Checks were also used. The introduction of Arabic numerals and a decimal system facilitated accounting and made possible double-entry bookkeeping. Coin, especially gold, was not readily accessible in northern Europe, hard to carry about in any quantity, and its value hard to regulate or control, especially in international transactions. Kings, bishops, and townsmen often kept their reserves in the form of jewels or gold and silver plate. The Polos—father, son, and uncle—on their travels to distant China carried their funds in jewels sewed into the lining of their clothes.

The life of the medieval merchant was beset with difficulties and risks; but, for born adventurers, it offered compensating challenge and excitement. Anyone who doubts this should read Marco Polo's tale of his journeys to the court of Kublai Khan in faraway China, or even Pegolotti's The Practice of Commerce, a "how to do it" book written by an Italian merchant of the early fourteenth century.

The most important contribution of the medieval townsman or bourgeois to civilization was to reintroduce the civic spirit. In the communes that won liberties from kings, bishops, and nobles, in the gilds that exercised privileges and protected their members, and in the town corporations through which they governed themselves, they learned the effectiveness of dealing with problems by acting together.

V

Feudal Monarchy: The Formation of Territorial States

Medieval kings were absolute neither in theory nor in fact. They had to dominate a not notably submissive aristocracy and resist papal efforts to establish supremacy over themselves. Theory about monarchy helped them only a little because it was neither monolithic nor clearly applicable to their problems. The prevailing concepts of kingship derived from Germanic tradition, Christian ideals, and the principles of Roman law, and there was no one accepted synthesis. By Germanic tradition, kings were chosen from a royal family thought to be descended from a god. They were leaders of the folk in war and custodians of its law and custom in peacetime. In Christian teaching, all power being derived from God, kings held power by God's grace. Consecration to their office made them God's vicars on earth. Law was divine law interpreted by duly constituted monarchs and their advisers. Where Germanic "kin-right" (the right of a royal family to the kingship) failed, as when the Carolingians usurped the power of the last Merovingians, consecration helped to strengthen the weak title of the usurper. The trouble was that it also seemed to give color to the claim that ecclesiastical power was superior to temporal power even though the king was conceived in Christian thought to be priest as well as king. From Roman law came two important concepts. One was that the ruler's power derived from the Senate and people; the other was that the prince's will had the force of law. The first of these survived long after the Senate and people as sources of public power had ceased to exist in the West. The second conflicted both with Germanic tradition and Christian thought.

Theory and Actuality

The reader will note that there were many contradictions between and within these concepts and will also recognize that, when medieval thinkers tried to reconcile theory with the facts of monarchy in feudal society, they encountered many thorny difficulties. Christian ideas of monarchy might be expected to have swept the field. As a matter of fact, they did not; Roman law was as strong as Christian theory. John of Salisbury, a twelfth-century bishop, writing a handbook for rulers, described the king's office as follows:

> Between a tyrant and a prince there is this single or chief difference, that the latter obeys the law and rules the people by its dictates, accounting himself as but their servant. It is by virtue of the law that he makes good his claim to the foremost and chief place in the management of the affairs of the commonwealth and in the bearing of its burdens; and his elevation over others consists in this, that whereas private men are responsible only for their private affairs, on the prince fall the burden of the whole community. . . . Therefore, according to the usual definition, the prince is the public power, and a kind of likeness on earth of the divine majesty. . . . However, it is said that the prince is absolved from the obligations of the law; but this is not true in the sense that it is lawful for him to do unjust acts, but only in the sense that his character should be such as to cause him to practice equity not through penalty of the law but through love of justice; and should also be such as to cause him from the same motive to promote the advantage of the commonwealth, and in all things to prefer the good of others before his private will. . . . For in these matters his will is to have the form of a judgment, and most properly that which pleases him therein has the force of law, because his decision may not be at variance with the intention of equity.[1]

John had been studying Roman law. He had difficulty reconciling it with conditions in a society in which public power was dispersed and exercised by private persons who ruled vassals, peasants and others by reason of holding fiefs with grants of powers of justice. He also knew Christian theory and was trying to find an answer to the question how the king can be both subject to the law, God's law, and the law and custom of his realm, yet the chief administrator of it.

As for the actualities of feudal monarchy, they varied from state to state and from time to time within the same states. They nowhere agreed wholly either with feudal or with traditional monarchical theories. Feudal theory grew up after the fact as a kind of rationalization of chaotic actuality. According to it, the members of the ruling class formed a hierarchy, a pyramid of power from the king to the lowest knight who held of him directly or mediately. In actuality, even in England after its conquest in 1066 or in the Latin kingdom of Jerusalem, where there were opportunities to apply strict feudal principle in building the state, west European rulers never formed the perfect pyramidal hierarchy that conscious feudalism would have required. The kings of Jerusalem were never more than first among equals, and their precarious hold on this position scarcely survived the fall of Jerusalem in 1187. In England, William, the Norman conqueror, saw fit in 1066 to take over without change what he recognized as useful strengths of the old English monarchy. England, France, and Germany, between 1000 and 1300, had monarchies that can be called feudal, although they differed markedly from one another. Not one of them was strictly feudal. In all three the vicissitudes of dynasties, the tendency toward fragmentation by inheritance, the complexities arising from multiple lordship, multiple vassalship, and intermarriage within the ruling class created an ever changing balance of power. Italy and Christian Spain were ruled by many different princes or magistrates and did not fit the pattern of the more feudal north. To draw a wholly satisfactory map of feudal Europe at any given date is impossible. The lines are really lines of personal allegiance rather than the territorial boundaries appropriate to maps. Individual people knew who their lord was and perhaps who the dominant lord of the region was. They did not know a "country" to which they belonged. The only rulers who could claim power that extended to the whole of western Europe were the popes, and their claim to supremacy over kings led to protracted conflict that, in the end, aroused rebellion against their authority in the West.

Three Western Monarchies in the Early Eleventh Century

Anyone looking at the three western monarchies in the first quarter of the eleventh century might have said that Germany was the strongest and most likely to dominate Europe for the next several hundred years. England was engulfed in bloody conflict, of which the outcome was the crowning of Canute, King of Denmark and Norway, as King of England (1016). England briefly became part of a large maritime empire which depended for its lines of communication on the stormy Baltic and North seas. The French monarchy under Robert II (996–1031), second of the Capetian line, was very weak. Robert controlled directly only the Ile de France, a small island of territory reaching from Laon to Orleans and centered on Paris. The great vassals of the crown, like the counts of Champagne and of Flanders and the dukes of Normandy and Aquitaine, recognized Robert as suzerain but refused to do homage or to render service. The trusted military vassals of the crown of Carolingian times had been decimated by the wars with the Vikings. Robert depended for support on ecclesiastical vassals, the archbishop of Reims by whom French kings were crowned, the bishops of Sens, Tours, Bourges, and others. No one would have projected for the Capetian kings a great future as rulers of a united France and the dominant secular rulers of Europe. The German monarchy, however, under Henry II (1002–1024), seemed secure in its power as a result of the sound work of the Saxon line of kings (919–1002) that

Map 4.   Europe in 1250

had preceded him. Building on the resources of the royal estates, on the personal loyalty and obligations of the counts to them, and on their alliance with German bishops and monasteries, they had prevented the rulers of the great duchies from gaining the kind of independent power that the great royal vassals had in France. But there were inherent weaknesses. Germany was a country not yet of lords and vassals but mainly of free landowners, and these men gave their primary loyalty to the dukes of Franconia, Saxony, Thuringia, Swabia, and Bavaria, states built up by the Carolingian rulers of these regions. The monarchy was elective among the dynasties of these dukedoms, and whenever a line failed or a claimant was weak, the line changed. A resource and, at the same time, a problem to the German kings was their possession of a part of Lotharingia (the inheritance of Lothar, eldest grandson of Charlemagne) and of Burgundy and their lordship over the increasingly wealthy city-states of northern Italy. These had been won by the Saxon kings under claims arising from the treaties dividing Charlemagne's empire among his grandsons. (See page 36.) Along with the rule of these lands they also held claim to Charlemagne's title of Emperor and Augustus in the West, later called Holy Roman Emperor. They had asserted this claim successfully and had been crowned in Rome. This title gave them enormous prestige and involved them fatefully with the popes as rival claimants to ascendancy in western Christendom. The weaknesses in the power of German king-emperors in the early eleventh century were concealed behind the veil of the future.

Aims and Methods of Feudal Kings

Medieval kings aimed at building territorial states with boundaries that could be defined and defended. This was easier for the kings of England and France than for the king-emperor of Germany, Burgundy, and northern Italy. For English kings in England the chief problems were the Welsh, Scots, and the

Irish. The Welsh were conquered and brought under English rule at the end of the thirteenth century. Scotland successfully resisted union with England until the eighteenth century. The Irish were never wholly conquered. The most distracting problem for the English in the high medieval period was their continental possessions. As dukes of Normandy, Brittany, and Aquitaine and counts of Anjou and Maine, the English kings were vassals to the king of France. These possessions involved them in almost continual warfare against their royal overlord throughout the period from 1066 to 1328. After that date other factors led to a long war dubbed the Hundred Years War, though it lasted from 1337 to 1453. The English kings lost, but that is a story for a later chapter. The French kings, in the High Middle Ages, were generally successful against English kings but were handicapped in the drive toward territorial unity by the *appanage* principle. Whereas in England, after 1154, the eldest son inherited the kingdom as a whole, in France younger sons of the royal line had to be given large fiefs to govern. This was a survival of the ancient Frankish principle of division of the royal domains among the sons. Appanages held by royal princes could in time become great feudal states rivaling the king's. For Germany the existence of the great dukedoms bearing the names of the old "nations" among the Germans, the barriers of the Jura mountains and Alps, and the great diversity in development between different parts of Germany, Burgundy, and Italy enormously complicated the problem of achieving territorial unity.

Medieval kings hoped for robust sons to perpetuate their dynasty and enable them to insure the succession. They tried to abolish private warfare between feudal rulers and to engage the loyalty of vassals toward themselves. They built up a bureaucracy of royal administrators and tried to reclaim the powers of justice dissipated by their predecessors. As their financial needs expanded, they extended their powers of taxation. In general, whether they observed feudal law and custom or not, they tried to make subjects rather than vassals of the feudal class and to extend their power over the lower orders in society. In their objectives they found the increasing wealth and professional ability of townsmen and middle-class men from the rural areas useful to their purposes. The close alliance between kings and the middle class was not fully consummated until the later Middle Ages; but it began in the twelfth and thirteenth centuries, and it was important in the formation of feudal monarchies. One of the signs that it was important was the incorporation into the assemblies of "estates" of the realm, the descendants of the old assemblies of fighting men, of the representatives of the new middle class in town and country. In England "knights of the shire" and "burgesses of the boroughs" were invited to a body more and more often called a "parliament." In France the Capetian kings began to summon the Estates General as well as regional estate assemblies and to call to them representatives of all free classes. In Germany the Diet met, including not only the great dukes but also the lesser princes and the representatives of the free cities holding imperial charters. In northern Italy the German king-emperors called councils of representatives of the city-states. In Spain the kings of Leon, Castile, Aragon, and Barcelona called assemblies of nobles, clergy, and representatives of the wealthier members of the lower orders to ask them for advice and for money.

The feudal kings of the High Middle Ages laid the foundations for the later national monarchies. Specific aims and methods differed from state to state, varying according to specific conditions and possibilities. England, France, and Germany only will be used in illustration. Spain, divided under a number of Christian princes and many Muslim rulers, presents too intricate a pattern to follow in this context. Italy, too, had a woefully complex history. The city-states of northern Italy were under the general overlordship of the German king-emperor. The central part of Italy including Rome was under the temporal power of the popes. Sicily and southern Italy, conquered by adventurers from Normandy in the eleventh century, were brought under German rule at the end of the twelfth, then transferred first to French, then to Spanish rule at the end of the thirteenth. The details, though important and full of interest for the historian, are not essential for a general understanding of feudal monarchy.

The English Feudal Monarchy

In England the Norman and Angevin kings contributed, by deliberate policy and also by some mismanagement, two major strengths of the English state. One was the "common law," that is, a law and custom common to the whole realm. The other was a sense of the "community of the realm," which became the basis of the English parliamentary system. William, Duke of Normandy, who became the King of England by conquest in 1066, took over from his predecessors the concept of "the king's peace" and the instruments for its local enforcement. The king's peace had covered not only royal palaces and estates, royal dependents, but also highways, merchants traveling on them, and the *burhs* (fortified centers) set up to resist the Danes, some of which had become commercial centers. By the reign of William's son, Henry I (1100–1135), the king's peace extended to the whole realm, and the king's writ or written command extended everywhere except where he had granted immunity from it. William also adopted from his Anglo-Saxon predecessors the old Germanic popular courts of shires (or counties) and hundreds (subdivisions of the shires) and their officers—the sheriffs and bailiffs respectively. He took over the lands of the English aristocracy and gave them to his great vassals as fiefs in return for the service of a specified number of knights. His vassals, in turn, subinfeudated, that is, granted land to their own vassals in return for the service to the king as well as feudal duties toward themselves. For a brief moment in history, before multiple allegiances developed and knights' fees got subdivided, the feudal structure in England may have borne some resemblance to the ideal feudal pyramid. The old assembly of the "wise men" of England, which the Anglo-Saxon kings had called to advise them, became a court of feudal vassals. From this *curia regis* (king's court) emissaries went down into the shires to settle disputes about land. In 1086 William's officers made a comprehensive inventory of all the lands of England, who had held them before the conquest, who held them at the time of the conquest, and who was in possession by 1086. This remarkable survey, still preserved in the English Public Record Office, has come down in history as Domesday Book and has provided an incredible amount of contemporary information from a time for which records are scarce.

Under William's successors the same kind of technique was applied to other judicial matters. Itinerant justices went down into the counties and asked questions of local juries, then made decisions based on their findings. A special committee of the *curia regis* was set up to deal with the king's revenues. This committee was called the Exchequer (so-named because it did its accounting on a chequered table). Records of its accounts from 1130 do survive today. Henry II (1154–1189), first of the Angevin kings, greatly furthered the cause of royal justice. In his time justices were sent out on regular circuit to hear indictments for crime and to try the accused, as well as to determine rights of possession of land. The principle was established that no man need answer for his landholdings except by writ of the lord king. A writ was the king's command engrossed on parchment and sealed with his seal. The normal way of beginning an action in the king's courts, that is, the *curia regis,* and the courts held before his itinerant justices, was to get a royal writ from the Chancery, the chief writing office in the king's entourage. Each case considered provided precedents for other cases, and so a body of "common law" for the whole country was built up. The *curia regis,* in order to take care of the increasing flow of business, set up subdivisions called the King's Bench and the Court of Common Pleas. The Exchequer also exercised some judicial functions, and these three constituted the central courts of common law.

Henry II and his sons, Richard I (1189–1199) and John (1199–1216) also experimented with new forms of taxation.

The old income from the royal estates, from fees and fines for justice, from feudal dues, and from a land tax inherited from the Anglo-Saxon kings proved inadequate in a time of rising prices and constant war in France and Wales and on the Scottish border. The most successful experiment was a tax on movable property. In 1207 this brought in £60,000 as against the £9,000 to £11,000 that could be levied from a scutage. Tallages were levied from the peasants on royal domain and from towns, and townsmen were persuaded to pay substantial sums for the renewal and the extension of their freedoms. All freemen began to be subject to direct royal taxation.

Under John, youngest of Henry II's sons, resistance to new taxes, to arbitrary and excessive feudal exactions and seizures of land, and to John's sadistic cruelties created a crisis. John levied taxes for war in Normandy but lost the war. He became involved in a quarrel with Pope Innocent III (1198–1216) and was excommunicated. England was put under an interdict. A large faction among the baronage then joined together in corporate action, announced their repudiation of homage and fealty, appealed to the French king for help, and levied war against John. John hastily made peace with the pope at the price of surrendering England to him as a fief to be held for the service of an annual payment of 1,000 marks. Despite the pope's support, however, John was forced to agree to the grant of Magna Carta (June 15, 1215), a charter of liberties mainly concerned with the feudal rights of the barons but also showing some concern for the Church in England, for merchants, and for townsmen, if not for serfs, excepting insofar as they were possessions of their lords. The barons professed to speak for "the community of the whole land," and they attempted to set up a mode of enforcement of the charter, which, though clumsy, nonetheless expressed the principle that if the king did not rule by law, he could be held to that responsibility by his subjects. In the course of fifty confirmations before 1422 and some fruitful distortion of its most important clauses, Magna Carta came to be considered a symbol of the liberties of all free Englishmen. As more men became free, more came under its protection. Moreover, the idea basic to the charter that the king could be held to his responsibility under the "law and custom of the realm" foreshadowed the "social contract" theory of the seventeenth and eighteenth centuries.

John died soon after the charter had been sealed. His nine-year-old son, Henry III (1216–1272), was allowed to succeed without protest, and the first confirmation of the charter was issued in 1217 to win baronial support. Henry inherited his father's political "unwisdom" and little of his ability. He, too, became involved in war with a group of the baronage who claimed, as in John's time, to represent the community of the realm. Both the dissident group and the king's party attempted to enlist the direct support of the wider community of the realm by calling to meetings of the feudal vassalage representative townsmen or "burgesses" and knights from the shires. Edward I (1272–1307), Henry's son, saw the wisdom and usefulness of this procedure as a means of getting grievances presented to the "king in his council in his parliament" for adjudication and as a means of obtaining consent to taxation for his wars. And so he continued the practice. In the midst of a crisis over taxation toward the end of his reign, he granted that:

> No tallage or aid shall be laid or levied by us or our heirs in our realm without the good will and assent of the archbishops, bishops, earls, barons, knights, burgesses, and other freemen of our realm.[2]

He also confirmed Magna Carta. His son and successor, Edward II (1307–1327), in his coronation oath, added to the ancient oath guaranteeing the rights of the Church and promising justice in his judgments the following dialogue with the archbishop:

> "Sire, do you grant to be held and observed the just laws and customs that the community of your realm shall determine, and will you, so far as in you lies, defend and strengthen them to the honour of God?"
>
> "I grant and promise them."[3]

The terms of this oath still leave open the question who constitutes the "community of the realm." Bracton, who wrote a book on the *Laws and Customs of England* during the period of Henry III's war with his barons, had said:

> For the king, since he is the minister and vicar of God on earth, can do nothing save what he can do de jure [by right] . . . nor is that anything rashly put forward of his own will, but what has been rightly decided with the counsel of his magnates, deliberation and consultation having been had thereon, the king giving it auctoritas [authority].[4]

But, in the reign of Edward II's son, it became regular practice to summon to the meetings called parliaments the representative knights and burgesses, and by the end of the fourteenth century their participation was essential to the making of statutes or the grant of taxes. The community of the realm meant the king, the magnates, and the freemen in town and country. England's great achievement in the medieval period was this sense of community and a lasting means of implementing it.

Feudal Monarchy in France

The reign of the Capetian kings of France started, as has been said above, with much fewer of the circumstances present for the establishment of a strong, centralized kingdom than the Norman kings of England. France was already feudalized. That meant that the king of France was recognized only as nominal overlord by the great dukes and counts. Descendants of the royal appointees of the Carolingian period, they claimed their power by hereditary right, enforced it in relation to their own vassals and refused to do homage to the king for it. The king they tolerated and helped against his enemies when it suited them. He was not a serious threat to their power. He had the support of the great ecclesiastical vassals because of their antagonism toward the powerful secular vassals. Royal officers, the *prévôts*, exercised no power outside the royal domain. They were financial officers whose main job was to collect the revenues from the royal estates. And because they bought their offices at auction, they paid only the income agreed on in the contract of sale. They often succeeded in making their offices hereditary. Thus the king's power was not very great even in his own domain. The kings lived by moving about from estate to estate and by exercising the guest rights due from royal vassals in their own narrow lands. The old Germanic popular courts had ceased to function in Merovingian times and the Carolingian *missi dominici,* who had exercised royal jurisdiction throughout the empire, had long since disappeared.

By the beginning of the fourteenth century, the Capetian kings ruled a reasonably unified state, one capable of surviving a sporadically strong and persistent attack from the kings of England during more than a hundred years. The story of how they achieved this position is hard to dig out from the surviving sources. Narrative sources, mainly monastic chronicles, were compiled with the interest of the monastery mainly at heart. In comparison with England, the surviving documentary sources are few and fragmentary. Medieval kings carried their current archives around in carts as they moved from place to place. In fact, Philip II "Augustus" (1180–1223) lost all his records to Richard I of England in a battle at Fréteval on the banks of the Loire:

> The plunderer neither spared the chests bursting with coin, nor the sacks in which jewels and plate were hidden, the evidences of dues and the contracts for taxes, nor did he fail to steal the sacred relics and the royal seal.[5]

The Capetians, however, had some important assets, not all of them immediately apparent to medieval men. France has a basis for unity greater than has either England or Germany. The Massif Central in southern France does not seriously interrupt the geographic unity enclosed by the Alps, the Pyrenees, and the Rhine basin rivers. Furthermore, the Capetians were fortunate in the vitality of the line. There was at least one surviving son in every generation until 1328. This was not altogether a matter of luck. Many of the kings of the line married several times in order to get a male heir. Working somewhat counter to this was the appanage principle under which younger sons of the royal line had to be given large estates to govern. Appanages held by royal princes could in time become great feudal states rivaling the crown. But when the Capetian line failed in 1328, there was a collateral line to turn to for a successor.

The Capetians were shrewd in their policies. They made the most of escheats and forfeitures, rights of wardships and heirs, and other feudal prerogatives for increasing their power. They got land to add to the royal domain through marriage and inheritance wherever possible, and they acquired new vassals by offering protection or partnership to lay and ecclesiastical lords who were involved in private warfare. Like English and German kings, they granted town charters as a means of extending royal power and increasing royal revenues. The decisive acquisitions in their aggrandizement came from their recovery of Normandy, Brittany, Maine, Anjou, and the major part of Aquitaine by war against the kings of England in the twelfth and thirteenth centuries. In the same period they recovered overlordship in Provence through the Albigensian Crusade (see Chapter VI). By the end of the first quarter of the thirteenth century only the counts of Champagne and the dukes of Burgundy were still independent. Champagne was won in the course of the thirteenth century by a policy of undermining the country's economic wealth, by diverting trade from her fairs and markets, and by dynastic luck. The male line of the counts of Champagne failed in 1274. Philip IV (1285–1314) married Joan, heiress to Champagne and the kingdom of Navarre, and in due time the hold of the kings of France over Champagne was secured. In spite of shrewd marriages by the last Capetian kings, Burgundy eluded their grasp and was added to France only in early modern times.

The most permanently constructive work of the Capetian kings was probably that of building a viable bureaucracy. No governmental system can function adequately without a corps of officials loyal and devoted to its aims. In England the Norman kings had been able to take over the royal household and the sheriffs and bailiffs in the counties and hundreds. In France there were no royal local officers except within the royal domain, and the household offices, particularly that of the chancellor and the seneschal, or steward, had tended to become hereditary in the families of the Ile de France. Philip Augustus was probably the first to appoint new royal officers to exercise power outside the old royal domain. He sent out *baillis* to supersede the hereditary *prévôts* and to establish their judicial and financial power outside as well as inside the domain. They offered royal justice throughout France on the theory that the king was the fountain of justice for the whole kingdom and that such powers as existed in the hands of feudal vassals were exercised only by delegation from the king, the king being (as had been said) the vicar of God in this respect. The *baillis* were based in new towns chartered by the king, and they were able to extend their power in direct relation to the extension of the prestige of the monarchy. Before he left on Crusade in 1190, Philip Augustus issued the following ordinance to guide the work of the *baillis* and his deputies during his absence:

> First, we order our *baillis* to establish in each of our towns four prudent, law-abiding and respectable men; no business of the town shall be transacted without the advice of at least two of them. . . .
>
> And we establish *baillis* in each of our lands, who shall fix a day called an assize each month in their *bailliages*. On this day all those who have complaints shall receive justice without delay and we shall have our rights and justice. . . .
>
> Moreover, we order that our dearest mother, the queen, and our beloved and faithful uncle, William, archbishop of Reims, shall hold a court at Paris every four months to hear the complaints of the men of our realm and to decide them for the glory of God and the welfare of the realm.
>
> We also order that at these meetings . . . our *baillis* shall come before them and tell them of the affairs of our land.
>
> If any of our *baillis* shall do wrong . . . we order the archbishop and the queen . . . to send us letters, telling which *bailli* has done

wrong and what he did. . . . Then we, with the aid of God, shall punish them in such a way . . . that others may have good reason to be deterred.[6]

These new royal officials were appointed and paid by the king in order to prevent them from developing local attachments or becoming hereditary as had the older *prévôts*. Local seneschals were added to supervise the work of administering justice and collecting royal revenues. By the end of the Capetian period two subdivisions of the *curia regis*, each equipped with a permanent staff of officers, met in periodic sessions to deal with financial and judicial matters. They were respectively the *Chambre des Comptes* and the *Parlement*, the counterparts to the Exchequer and the central courts of common law developed in Norman and Angevin England.

All these officers of the crown had to be paid in order to keep them faithful, and wars cost increasingly more as the pay of soldiers and the price of supplies rose. Money was a great problem for the French kings, as for the English. The Capetians tried to solve the problem by positing a basic responsibility for military service due from all freemen, then commuting this for a money payment, which they negotiated on a local basis. They still called out the "host" of feudal vassals and townsmen who owed military service for forty days and three months respectively, but they paid them in order to insure their not leaving the army in the middle of a campaign. And the last of the Capetians resorted heavily to debasement of the coinage. This was a device that, for obvious reasons, could be only an opportunist measure. The Capetian monarchy died out in an atmosphere of emergency arising from the failure of the direct line of succession and monetary problems.

In spite of emergencies, the French king in the early 1300s was strong within France and dominant in the affairs of Europe. He won a long battle with Pope Boniface VIII (see Chapter VI) with support of his clergy, nobles, and representative commoners called together in an Estates General. This body did not enlist quite the sense of community on which the English Parliament rested, but it was useful to the French king in meeting

general national emergencies in the medieval period. The Capetians had won their dominant position by patient persistence in
the task of building a strong monarchy. Making the most of
their rights and powers under feudal law and custom and of
central lines of communication and a well-situated capital city,
they had bided their time and seized opportunity as it offered.
Moreover, they had allowed themselves to be relatively little
distracted by foreign adventure, although three kings, Louis
VII, Philip Augustus, and Louis IX, had gone on Crusade.

The German Feudal Monarchy

The German monarchy had a very different history in the
eleventh, twelfth, and thirteenth centuries. From a position of
great strength and prestige, it fell into insignificance and weakness. If one has to choose any one factor that, more than others,
made this outcome inevitable, it was the effect of the fifty-year
long investiture controversy with the papacy (see Chapter VI).
This so undermined the foundations of royal power that the
monarchy never recovered even in the prestigious days of the
Hohenstaufens (1138–1254). The strength of the monarchy in
the early eleventh century rested mainly on the concept of the
king as both king and priest and, therefore, head of the national
church. Monastic and other ecclesiastical reforms were fostered
by the monarchy, and extension of the frontier to the eastward
had been carried out through the founding of new bishoprics
to bring into the Christian fold the Slavs and the Magyars. Governmental powers exercised by monasteries were in the hands
of advocates who could only be chosen with royal assent.
Servile *ministeriales* were the bearers of royal power throughout the land. The power of the great dukes rested only on their
leadership of free people, and the Saxon kings had successfully
prevented their efforts to achieve provincial autonomy.

During the eleventh century all this began to change. New
monasteries (from 108 in 973 to 700 in 1075) were founded
under the patronage of the nobility within the duchies. These

provincial nobles succeeded, owing to the principles of the Cluniac reform movement—under which the new monasteries should be subject to the pope alone—in getting control of the advocacy and in using the monastic expansion for their own improved economic welfare. Forest and waste areas were reclaimed and brought into cultivation. These now contributed to the wealth of the local aristocracy rather than to that of the crown. Feudal rights and powers of the monarchy could not be used and extended in the manner of the Capetians because Germany was not feudalized in this period. Independence was the mark of the German nobility. Vassalage was not, as in France, the sign of membership in a free and noble class. On the contrary, it was associated with the ministerial vassals who, like the early Carolingian *vassi dominici,* were drawn from the upper ranks of the unfree. New members from the internal and external frontier were constantly joining the ranks of the independent aristocracy. The minority of the king at the beginning of the reign of Henry IV (1056–1106) and the consequent regency opened up opportunity for this free spirit of the German aristocracy and countered royal efforts to keep the situation under control by rewarding the *ministeriales* with silver from newly discovered resources in the Hartz Mountains, not with royal estates. The Saxon rebellion (1070–1073) was put down but was followed so soon by Pope Gregory VII's attack on the priestly powers of the monarchy in the investiture struggle (see Chapter VI) that Henry IV could gain no real strength from this early victory.

The kings did not immediately lose all their power over the bishops and monasteries in this critical period. Indeed it was the very success of the German kings, especially Henry II (1002–1024) and Henry III (1039–1056), in carrying forward the work of ecclesiastical reform in Germany that invited the papal lightning. Compromise was easier with the English and French rulers because their power in relation to the Church was always more ambiguous. William I had conquered England with papal sanction and had separated church and lay courts, thus allowing the opportunity for independent development of ecclesiastical jurisdiction. The French clergy needed royal support in their resistance to the feudalizing tendencies of the French nobility. The German kings' pretensions to full headship of the Church in Germany and their constant interference in episcopal and even papal elections under imperial powers made the German monarchy the major target of Pope Gregory VII's effort to establish papal supremacy.

Combined with pretensions were weaknesses that helped to destroy the German monarchy. None of the German dynasties had as good luck as did the Capetians in having sons to succeed them. This helped Gregory in advocating a theory of monarchy as an office to which, as to the papal office, the king-emperor must be elected. The princes of Germany, not God under a principle of inheritance, chose the German king. This fitted with the older Germanic theory still effective in Germany under which regality, or royal power, was based on a pact with the nobility. It did Henry IV no good to hold out for the Christian theory of hereditary monarchy by God's grace. The German nobility with papal encouragement turned against him in 1077 and chose Rudolf of Swabia. The intransigent pope eventually confirmed Rudolf although he would have preferred to bring a repentant Henry to his terms.

A compromise was ultimately won under Henry's son and successor in 1122 at Worms. Elections of bishops were to take place in the presence of the king-emperor or his representatives. He was permitted to invest with the royal powers, or *regalia,* and to take homage before investiture with the symbols of the spiritual authority. These ecclesiastical symbols, the ring and staff, were to be conferred by the properly constituted ecclesiastical authority. In contrast to England and France, where the outcome of the investiture conflict hardly changed church-state relationships at all, in Germany it proved to be a papal victory that dislodged the king-emperor from his place at the head of the German ecclesiastical hierarchy. Henceforward, he was a secular ruler only, and his authority was comparable only to that of archbishops and bishops. He had to be elected and to be subsequently consecrated as king, and he had to have papal consecration in order to become emperor. Civil war in Germany, in which peasants and townsmen fought for the monarchy and the clergy and the independent nobility against it, had contributed to these disastrous effects.

Feudalism, which in France and England had been exploited to contribute to the elevation of the monarchy to the apex of a hierarchy of church and state, in Germany contributed mainly to the growth in power of members of the nobility. The princes got control of the judicial authority that had belonged to the king or to the local courts. Italy was peripheral to the problem in Germany. It contributed wealth and prestige to the monarchy, and the kings were bound by their inheritance to maintain their power south of the Alps. Yet fifty years of relative inaction in Italy during the investiture crisis gave the Italian city-states a chance to assert their independence. Both in Germany and in northern Italy the trend after the investiture conflict was toward local particularism rather than toward the kind of unity that the Saxon king-emperors had established and their successors had tried to maintain.

The Hohenstaufen dukes of Swabia (Frederick I Barbarossa, Henry VI, and Frederick II, 1152–1250), when they became kings, tried to reverse this tendency by concentrating attention on wealthy Italy. By marriage alliance and by war they established their power in Sicily and southern Italy and threatened the papal power in central and northern Italy from two sides. Frederick I tried, and succeeded temporarily in his attempt, to maintain power both north and south of the Alps and to recover the old unity of Germany, Burgundy, and Italy. In Germany he based his power on Franconia, the central and most manageable of his domains there. In Italy he centered it in Tuscany for similar reasons. He married the heiress of Burgundy and, on the first of his five trips to Italy, helped the pope against revolutionary forces in Rome. At the same time he refused offers of the Roman aristocracy to give him the imperial throne, using the following terms:

> We have turned over in our minds the deeds of modern emperors, considered how our sacred predecessors, Charles and Otto, wrested your City with the lands of Italy from the Greeks and Lombards and brought it within the frontiers of the Frankish realm,

not as a gift from alien hands but as a conquest won by their own valor. . . . I am the lawful possessor.[7]

In other words he claimed the throne by inheritance from Charlemagne and from Otto, the first of the Saxon kings, and repudiated both the old Roman theory of imperial power and Gregory VII's papal pretensions.

He reasserted the old power over the Church in Germany, nominating bishops and archbishops and insisting that all *regalia* derived from him. By his ecclesiastical nominations he gained several loyal royal servants. Against the nobility he tried to enforce an end to private warfare. He conciliated the great dukes, especially Henry the Lion, Duke of Bavaria and Saxony, to whom he gave a free hand on the frontier, thus diverting his fighting abilities against the Slavs.

In Italy he tried to reclaim the *regalia* from the city-states at the Diet of Roncaglia (1159), where his officers asserted the derivative nature of all governmental power. Rulers of the city-states were in the future to obtain his confirmation. He interfered, in the manner of Saxon and Franconian kings, in the papal election of 1159 and supported an antipope against Pope Alexander III, who took refuge in France. The turning point against him was the battle of Legnano in 1176, where his feudal cavalry was defeated by the infantry of the city-states. Frederick was forced to make peace with Alexander III and to agree that popes in future should be properly elected by a two-thirds vote of the cardinals. In a general reconciliation in 1183 the Lombard city-states were put on a loose rein under the administration of imperial legates and vicars. (See Chapter IV.) The pope recognized imperial suzerainty in northern Italy. After this, in 1186, a triple coronation took place in Milan. Frederick himself was crowned King of Burgundy. Henry, his son, was crowned "King of the Romans and Caesar," successor to the imperial title. And Constance of Sicily, young Henry's wife, was crowned Queen of Germany.

It would seem that this should have consolidated the position of the German monarchy throughout its dominions. It did not because Frederick himself went off on Crusade and was drowned. It did not because his son, Henry, lived only seven years after his father and died leaving a two-year-old infant son. Henry strengthened the imperial position in Sicily and in central Italy at the pope's expense and had his son recognized as elective heir in Germany. But his premature death left the infant Frederick subject to the whims of papal guardianship under Innocent III, successor to Gregory VII, in his aims for extending papal power. Germany, having no ruler of an age or incontestable legitimacy to control it, suffered a long interregnum from 1197 to 1215, when Frederick, recognized by Innocent III as the legitimate successor, asserted his power in Germany.

Frederick II, called *Stupor Mundi* by his contemporaries, and "the first modern monarch" by his leading modern biographer, never took Germany seriously. He founded a university in Naples (1224), established a modern law code for his Mediterranean realms, and adopted economic policies for these southern realms that were a preview of the acts of seventeenth-century monarchs in northern Europe. But he made constant concessions in Germany for the sake of support in his Italian campaigns against the pope. In 1220 he surrendered the right to erect castles and charter towns in ecclesiastical territories, an important part of the *regalia*. And in May 1231 he granted to the princes of the Princely Estate, recognized as such by his grandfather as early as 1180, the absolute right to their own domains to the exclusion of the rights and powers of the crown. As a result, the princes could legislate with the consent of their subjects in local diets or assemblies and could ignore legislation enacted by the assemblies or diets of princes and representatives of imperial cities called by the king-emperor. In the Diet of Mainz (1235) the power of the princes was somewhat modified by a repetition of Frederick I's ordinance against private warfare and by insistence on the king-emperor's power of judgment over princes. But meanwhile Frederick had deserted his son Henry in the latter's efforts to maintain power in Germany. (Henry was arrested and imprisoned and committed suicide in prison in 1244.)

Frederick, at this time, was more interested in his struggle with the most formidable of his papal adversaries, Innocent IV (1243–1254), a Genoese jurist, who, under protection of Louis IX of France, excommunicated Frederick (his third excommunication), declared him deposed, and initiated a crusade against him as guilty of sacrilege, suspected of heresy and other infamies. The outcome, after Frederick's death (1250) was the fall of the house of Hohenstaufen and the splitting up of its lands. After a brief exposure to a ruler of the French royal house (1268–1282) Sicily revolted. At the end of a civil war, it was turned over to Peter of the Spanish house of Aragon. Rudolf of Habsburg, the first of a new line, was elected as king of Germany (1273), after a long interregnum, and recognized though not crowned by the pope. He renounced imperial claims to the papal states and to Sicily (1279) and left Italy to the mercy of its own local rulers and foreign contestants. Henry VII (1308–1313), of the house of Luxembourg, briefly tried to restore effective imperial control in Italy but failed. The papacy, after Philip of France's victory over Pope Boniface VIII (see page 108 and page 125), fell under French domination. Germany and Italy both remained divided until modern times.

And so ended the period of feudal monarchies. England and France locked each other in a protracted war that exhausted their financial resources and brought misery and starvation to the French peasantry. The war did, however, contribute to a growing sense of English and French nationality. Feudal monarchy became in these states national and territorial monarchy. Germany and Italy, because of their distraught medieval history, remained backward in this national and territorial development and did not finally achieve national unity until the nineteenth century. Spain achieved her unity in the fourteenth and fifteenth centuries and became the dominant power in western Europe in the early modern period. But that triumph is beyond the scope of this book.

VI

Christianity
and the Church

Christianity was the one nearly universal influence in
European life. Missionary and military enterprise had
carried the faith out to and far beyond the outermost
limits of the old Roman Empire into Ireland, Scotland, Scandinavia, and Russia. Within the area of modern Europe by A.D.
1000 all men except the widely-scattered Jews, the Muslims
concentrated in the Spanish peninsula and southern Italy, the
Finns, the Lithuanians, and some other Baltic peoples and the
steppe people on the north shores of the Black Sea were
Christians. The East Roman or Byzantine Empire was Christian.
Moreover, Christendom extended beyond the frontiers of
Europe into Asia and Africa.

Disunity Within Christendom

Near universality of the faith, however, did not mean complete uniformity of belief, nor did it mean complete unity under
the rulership of the pope. Although the Byzantine Empire was
Christian, differences between East and West in church organization, in ritual, and in theological definition had led to a series
of disputes and misunderstandings that culminated in mutual
condemnation and schism by 1054. Byzantine missionaries had
converted the Slavs in the ninth and tenth centuries, including
the medieval Russian state based on Kiev. Even within western
Europe universality meant neither monolithic unity nor complete papal control. Christianity's expansion had been the work
of ten centuries and many individuals. Not unnaturally, bishops
and missionaries had concentrated on the saving power of

baptism and communion and on the importance of receiving these through properly constituted authority. The appreciation of the fine points of theology and the enforcement of Christian ethics against conflicting codes had to wait for a long process of education. The price of the drive for conversion had been the incorporation into Christianity of many extraneous or even anti-Christian elements. The Saxons converted by Charlemagne at the point of the sword may not have gotten the full message of peace and brotherly love. Pope Gregory the Great (590–604) understood the problem and accepted the consequences. In a letter of advice to the missionary monk he had sent to convert the Anglo-Saxons of Britain, he enjoined Augustine not to destroy indiscriminately all pagan temples nor to try to cure converts of all their old religious practices immediately, "For there is no doubt that it is impossible to cut off everything at once from their obdurate hearts, for he who strives to ascend to the highest place, rises by degrees or steps, not by leaps."[1]

The work of propagation of the faith had been carried out largely by cooperation of kings, bishops, and monks. Only strong popes like Gregory the Great had been able to direct and control the movement. King Oswiu called the council that settled the conflict between Celtic and Roman Christianity in the north of England (663). Charlemagne summoned church councils in Francia to strengthen discipline and to further the work of converting the heathen. The Saxon kings of Germany (see Chapter V) took the initiative in establishing the archbishopric of Magdeburg and the bishopric of Prague for the reconversion of the north Slavs and the conversion of the pagan Magyars. Their aim was to extend their own power as well as the frontiers of Christendom after the disorders of the eighth and early ninth centuries.

The Church as an Institution

The Church in its most inclusive sense had meant to St. Augustine the whole body of the faithful, living and dead, who truly seek God:

And so the Church now on earth is both the kingdom of Christ, and the kingdom of heaven. The saints reign with Him now, but not as they shall do hereafter: yet the tares reign not with them though they grow in the Church amongst the good seed. . . . Lastly, they reign with Christ who are withal His kingdom where He reigns. But how do they reign with Him at all, who continuing below, until the world's end, until His kingdom be purged of all the tares, do nevertheless seek their own pleasures, and not their Redeemer's?[2]

It included both laity and clergy, and of the latter both the seculars living in the world and responsible for the care of souls and the regulars living in monasteries according to a *regula*, or rule.

The power of the secular clergy was organized territorially in dioceses, a term borrowed from the later days of Roman imperial administrations. Each diocese was governed by a bishop. Groups of dioceses were administered as provinces and governed by archbishops. Within the dioceses parishes were presided over by priests. They had often been somewhat haphazardly organized by lay initiative. Parish churches had been founded by lay lords and were attached to their estates or to monasteries. Lay lords or monasteries often had the right to appoint priests and take their cut from the tithes. Tithes, or tenths of their income, contributed by parishioners for the support of religion, consequently, had to be divided among the needs of the parish for the maintenance of the local church and the poor, the priest, the diocesan bishop, and the local landholder.

The main responsibility of this secular hierarchy from the parish priest to the pope was to maintain the worship of God in the churches and, through administering the saving power of Christ and the saints, to save the souls of themselves and the rest of mankind. Parish clergy were expected to say mass daily, to educate the children in the faith, to hear confession, to give absolution and penance, to join parishioners in matrimony, to administer the last rites. Often they had neither the education nor the spiritual leadership to perform these duties satisfactorily; often, also, they were distracted by personal economic necessities. The sacraments, defined in the middle twelfth century as baptism, penance, Holy Communion, confirmation, marriage, ordination, and the last rites,[3] were, by canon law, to be freely administered, but gifts in money or in kind had come to be expected. Confirmation of boys and girls in the faith into which they had been baptized as infants and ordination of priests were sacraments reserved for the bishop to perform. In administering the sacraments, the priest was considered to be a vessel of God's power, able after ordination to administer His power even though he might as a man be weak and sinful. In Holy Communion he was enabled to perform the miracle of transforming bread and wine into the body and blood of Christ. As a matter of custom (determined perhaps by economy and sanitation), the consecrated bread only was administered to the laity.

The secular hierarchy had always had disciplinary authority in relation to its own membership and over the laity with respect to sin. Sin and crime overlap, and in the chaotic early centuries no very clear distinction had been made between the spheres of ecclesiastical and lay government. Lay government being weak, there was no serious clash of power. Men who had grievances or disputes to settle took them to popular courts, to lords' courts, or to bishops' courts without much concern for fine points of distinction between jurisdiction. In England, before its conquest by William, the bishop and earl had jointly presided over the county courts. By the second half of the eleventh century kings had built up monarchies strong enough to threaten the jurisdiction of bishops and to challenge even the universal authority of the bishop of Rome.

Ecclesiastical Reform: The Secular Hierarchy

Problems of discipline within the secular clergy were many. It is worth noting, however, that some of them arose not so much out of decadence or corruption as out of a new perception of responsibilities. Secular clergy had been permitted to marry, although high value had been placed on celibacy and chastity. The lower ranks in the Eastern Church continued to marry, and their caste had become hereditary. In the West a rule of the fourth century prohibiting marriage was reaffirmed in 1059, but it took two centuries or more to enforce it strictly. The common human problems of clerical discipline are well-illustrated in the thirteenth-century report of an archbishop's visitation of rural churches in Normandy:

> We found that the priest of Ruiville was ill-famed with the wife of a certain stonecarver, and by her is said to have a child; also he is said to have many other children; he does not stay in his church, he plays ball, and he rides around in a short coat. . . .
> Also, the priest of Ribeuf frequents taverns and drinks to excess. . . .
> Also, the priest of Oville keeps his daughter with him against synodal prohibition.
> Also, the priest of Poierville is drunken, quarrelsome and a fighter.[4]

Less personal, more public, were the problems of simony and lay investiture. Simony was the buying and selling of church offices, an evil likely to crop up in any large-scale bureaucracy in which offices provide valuable income and power. The problem of lay investiture arose in the context of the feudal world. Archbishops, bishops, and monasteries were vassals of kings and other lay lords and held lay fiefs of them, their so-called "temporalities." Kings and other lords naturally wished to participate in the election of their vassals. Characteristically, they did not stop at interfering in elections. They also invested their chosen candidates with the symbols of spiritual office, the bishop's ring and staff, and they took homage from them before ecclesiastical confirmation had been received. The upper clergy were drawn for the most part from the lay nobility. They did not disassociate themselves from the lay world. Of the four sons of the count of Cerdana who died in 990, two became counts, one an abbot, the fourth a bishop. Of his eight recorded grandsons, three were counts, five were bishops or archbishops. The family, having contributed heavily to the founding of bishoprics and monasteries in Barcelona, insisted on being rewarded for this.

The papal office itself was subject to these involvements. Rival families in Rome vied for the office, and the method of election by clergy and people encouraged factionalism. Benedict IX, a young profligate elected to the office in 1032, sold it in 1044 to Gregory VI, alleged by some to be a Jew by descent. There followed a confused conflict in which three popes, or ex-popes, were involved. Resolution came only when Henry III, King of Germany, descended into Italy in 1046 and enforced the selection of his own candidate, a German bishop.

The reaction against these disorders was a reform movement led by a group of able young men in the papal curia. The central tenet of this group of reformers was that the corruption of the Church was due to the power in it of lay members of the ruling class. In an eleventh-century charter to a bishopric, for example, is the following statement:

> The whole body of Holy Church was endowed, through the mercy of God and the Blood of His only Son, our Saviour, with His own eternal freedom; but through the cunning of evil men and the neglect of the pastors, many churches have fallen into the hands of earthly rulers.[5]

The solution, therefore, was to put the chief power in the Church back where it had always belonged—in the hands of ecclesiastical rulers.

One of the first necessities was to reform papal elections and to assert papal supremacy over secular rulers. An election decree in 1059 provided that, henceforth, the Roman bishop was to be chosen by the cardinal[6] bishops of the city and its environs. Cardinal priests and deacons of the diocese, authorized at this time only to approve the choice, were, a century later, given the power of participating in elections. Hildebrand, a fiery leader among the reformers, became Pope Gregory VII in 1073 and launched an ambitious program to enforce papal supremacy within the Church and in relation to secular rulers. In the *Dictatus Papae*, a rather unsystematic compendium of statements culled from early medieval canon law collections, Gregory announced, among other precepts:

2. That the Roman Pontiff alone can by right be called universal.
3. That he alone can depose and reinstate bishops.
12. That he ought to be allowed to depose emperors.
17. That no chapter and no book shall be considered canonical without his authority.
19. That he ought to be judged by no man.
22. That the Roman Church has never erred, nor, as Scripture proclaims, will it ever err, through all eternity.[7]

This was an ambitious manifesto. It would, if it had been successfully implemented, have placed the pope's power above that of any other ruler. The immediate issue in the first phase of the dispute was a matter of detail. A Roman synod, or council, denounced lay investiture. King Henry IV of Germany responded by summoning the German bishops to a council that charged Gregory with unlawful seizure of the papal office and renounced allegiance to him. To Hildebrand, "not pope but false monk," Henry wrote "you have mistaken our humility for fear, and have dared to make an attack upon the royal and imperial authority which we received from God."[8] Despite these bold words, Gregory won this first round beteween ecclesiastical and royal authority (in medieval terminology, *sacerdotium* and *regnum*). By excommunicating Henry and releasing his nobles and clergy from their allegiance to him, Gregory forced Henry into submission. The young king crossed the Alps in the bitter cold of winter, descended to the castle of Canossa in Tuscany, to seek the aging pope's pardon.

> There, dressed in coarse woolen garments, with bare feet and freezing, he stayed outside the castle, even to the third day, with his friends, and thus, most strictly tested by many trials and temptations and found obedient as far as human judgment extends, he demanded with tears, as is the custom of penitents, the favor of Christian communion and the apostolic reconciliation.[9]

This dramatic confrontation had its effect on men's minds, no doubt, but it did not end the struggle over investitures. That went on until long after both original participants were dead, and it involved England and France as well as Germany. In France the struggle was relatively undramatic. For England, a compromise was reached between Archbishop Anselm, King Henry I (1100–1135), and Pope Paschal II in 1107 whereby the king agreed to relinquish investiture with the ring and staff but was permitted to continue to receive homage from ecclesiastical vassals. Substantially the same compromise was reached in Germany in the Concordat of Worms (1122). The papacy won on principle, but kings continued to interfere in ecclesiastical elections.

Debate concerning the boundaries of judicial power between kings and ecclesiastical rulers also continued. A particularly acute crisis developed in England between Henry II (1154–1189) and Thomas Becket, the king's personally chosen archbishop of Canterbury. The most important issue was whether clerics who committed crimes should be tried by secular judges and subjected to the same penalties as laymen. In the Constitutions of Clarendon (1164) a compromise provided that clerics accused in lay courts and found guilty by trial in bishops' courts should be turned over to lay authorities after Church authorities had first deprived them of clerical standing. Becket agreed to this, then repudiated his agreement. The controversy dragged on for six years. Becket won in the end, but only through martyrdom. An angry, hasty explosion of temper on Henry's part led to Becket's murder in Canterbury Cathedral by four of Henry's knights. Henry was forced by public criticism to do penance and to yield to the Church on the main matter of jurisdiction over the clergy. Thomas Becket was canonized, first by popular opinion, then by papal authority.

The pope who most nearly succeeded in achieving Gregory VII's objective of papal supremacy was Innocent III (1198–1216). He forced Philip II, "Augustus" (1180–1223), of France into taking back a wife whom he hated and refused to live with. He induced John of England (1199–1216) to accept his appointee as archbishop and to do homage to him for the realm of England, promising a service of 1,000 marks. Innocent was the guardian during his minority of Frederick II, King of Germany and Emperor of the Holy Roman Empire. A long contest over the succession in Germany was finally settled by

Innocent's decision to accept Frederick as king and emperor. He called and presided over the Fourth Lateran Council in 1215. The 412 bishops and 800 abbots, priors, and lay delegates who gathered in Rome tightened the definition and discipline of the Church under Innocent's statesmanlike leadership.

This prolonged strife between popes and emperors, continuing, as it did, to the end of the thirteenth century, exhausted the prestige and resources of both papacy and empire. The French kings of the period made the most of opportunities to strengthen and consolidate their own power. Boniface VIII (1294–1303), the last strongly assertive pope of the medieval period, issued the bull *Clericis laicos* in 1297 forbidding clergy to pay taxes to lay rulers. In the next year he had to follow it with *Romana mater,* in which he conceded that clergy might in separate convocation make gifts to lay rulers. Yet, in 1302, he attempted the boldest assertion of papal power made thus far. The bull *Unam Sanctam* stated it as follows:

> And we learn from the words of the Gospel that in this Church and in her power are two swords, the spiritual and the temporal. . . . Both are in the power of the Church, the spiritual power and the material. But the latter is to be used for the Church, the former by her; the former by the priest, the latter by kings and captains but at the will and by the permission of the priest. The one sword, then, should be under the other, and temporal authority subject to spiritual.[10]

This statement expressed the concept that led to the most important outcome of Gregory VII's program of reform. By attempting to raise the ecclesiastical hierarchy above the world in power and discipline, the reformers separated it from the laity. "The Church" came to mean only the secular and regular clergy, no longer the whole body of those professing Christianity. In his conflict with Philip IV of France Boniface was defeated and driven into exile from Rome by Philip's soldiers. After the pope's death in 1303 the French cardinals were dominant in the college and were able to elect a French pope, who removed the papal headquarters from the political chaos of Italy to papal estates at Avignon in the south of France.

Monastic Reform

Parallel with the long struggle for reform of the secular hierarchy ran a less centralized movement for monastic reform. Serious problems in the practice of monasticism had been recognized as early as the beginning of the tenth century. One source of corruption in the monasteries was, as Pope Gregory and his party thought, that kings and other lay lords gave lands for monastic foundations. They tended to retain some measure of control, often appointing abbots and in other ways interfering with the operation of the Benedictine Rule. Kings' employment of monks as royal administrators took them out of the cloister. Peasant workers attached to the land grants did the work that, by St. Benedict's prescriptions, should have been done by the monks themselves. Some monasteries were lax about food and drink. A weak or corrupt abbot meant progressive deterioration, for corruption and lack of discipline begat more of the same. Moreover, postulants were no longer, as in early days, individuals who had chosen the monastic life for themselves. Often they were dedicated as children by their parents because they were misfits in feudal society or because their fathers were unable to make other adequate provision for them. The latter reason for entering monastic communities applied probably the most to women. Girls who had no landed endowments and no personal charm were not easy to provide for in the feudal world.

Early in the tenth century a widespread reform movement began. Spearheaded by the founders and early rulers of Cluny, it brought a sharpening of discipline throughout western Europe. William the Pious, Duke of Aquitaine, founded Cluny in 910. He gave land in "free alms" to the monks, meaning that they should owe no feudal service to him or to his descendants. Statesmanlike abbots of Cluny and reform popes ruled that the monastery should be subject to no local lords, kings, or bishops but only to the bishop of Rome himself. By 1100 there existed 1,450 Cluniac communities in which probably 10,000 monks lived. Many of these were new foundations; some were old communities that had placed themselves under Cluny's rule. They all retained ties with the original community at Cluny and were subject to visitations by its abbot. Cluny emphasized service to the poor and elaboration of the offices—that is, the prayers that the monks chanted together. Kings chose Cluniac monks as administrators to reform monastic and general ecclesiastical discipline within their domains. Yet by the middle of the eleventh century even Cluny was criticized for wealth and luxury.

In the latter half of the eleventh century another reform movement started. The two most important new orders of that century were the Carthusians and the Cistercians. The Carthusians, founded in 1084 by St. Bruno of Cologne, practiced a rigorous rule of withdrawal from the world, ascetic self-denial, and complete silence within the community. They were never as popular as the Cistercians and did not expand as rapidly. The Cistercian order was founded in a remote valley at Cîteaux in 1098. Its members pioneered the opening up for agriculture or sheep-raising of unoccupied wastes and wildernesses like the Yorkshire moors. They practiced rigorous austerities, and in their early years did all their own work in fields, pastures, and forests in compliance with the original rule of St. Benedict. Their enormous success was mainly due to St. Bernard, founder of the Cistercian monastery of Clairvaux (1115). He was so persuasive in enlisting recruits for the order that parents are reported to have concealed their sons and wives their husbands when he came into a neighborhood. He was more than a great abbot. He dominated his age until his death in 1153. Through the power of his dedication and his eloquence he guided popes and kings, settled theological and other controversies, and roused Europe to undertake the Second Crusade.

In contrast to these eleventh-century orders, the friars went out into the world instead of withdrawing from it. They frequented the towns to preach, to teach, and to care for the poor and the sick. The two major orders—the Franciscans and the

Dominicans—were founded in the early thirteenth century. St. Francis of Assisi (1181–1226) renounced the gay life of an Italian merchant's son to live a life of labor, poverty, and mendicancy and to help the sick and the poor. His personal qualities and the purity and simplicity of his rule attracted many followers, and his movement spread rapidly. But, even before his death, controversy arose within the Franciscans between those who thought absolute poverty impractical (if not impossible) and the "spirituals," who wished to follow strictly the example of the founder. The very popularity of the order helped to undermine its purity of aim. Benefactors gave houses and money to the order, and the order grew rich. By the time that Pope John XXII, a century after St. Francis' death, burned "spirituals" for heresy, corruption had set in.

St. Dominic (1170–1221) founded his order to teach, preach, and combat heresy. Admirably organized under a systematically conceived rule setting up a tight chain of command from pope to individual friar, the Dominicans became the chief instruments in the fight against heresy. The Franciscans soon joined them in this work, but the typical inquisitors were the *Domini-canes*, "God's hounds."

Meanwhile, many of the clergy who served cathedrals and larger parish churches had been organized under rules like those that applied to monastic communities. The Premonstratensians and the Augustinians were the most important orders. They adopted austere rules enjoining fasting and silence like those of the Carthusians and Cistercians and in the twelfth century founded seminaries to train priests.

Heresy and the Inquisition

Heresy was a profoundly troublesome problem in twelfth- and thirteenth-century Europe. Heretics were those who deliberately dissented from accepted Christian belief and repudiated ecclesiastical authority in matters of faith. Differences in belief had disturbed Christian unity from the beginning and had contributed to the split between East and West. But Western Christendom had never confronted a large-scale attack on its unity before the twelfth century. The main attack came into Europe through the Balkans from the East. Essentially, it was a revival in a new form of Manicheism, an old heresy condemned by St. Augustine of Hippo and other Church Fathers in early medieval centuries. There had always been Christians who, from an orthodox point of view, had put too great emphasis on the problem of evil. The Catharists, as these medieval Manicheans were called, deified the principle of evil as a god of darkness. For them God was spirit and Satan, matter, and the two were engaged in a cosmic struggle in which man must take his part. He must deny his body, particularly his sexual functions. The *perfecti,* or leaders among them, were expected to live entirely without sin. For the mass of believers the chief duty was reverence toward the *perfecti.* Catharists rejected the Christian doctrine of the incarnation, believing that Christ could not have appeared in a corrupt human body. They also rejected the sacraments. In their religion, there was one sacrament only, the *consolamentum,* a last absolution for sin usually administered just before death.

This dualistic faith arose in a new movement that achieved great strength in the Netherlands, in the Rhineland, and in southern France in an area centered on Albi, a town in Provence, from which was derived the name "Albigensians" as an alternative to Catharists. Efforts to check the spread of the heresy by prosecuting its adherents in the bishops' courts and by teaching and preaching had little effect. The heresy spread most strongly among townspeople, but it was supported by powerful nobles like Count Raymond VI of Toulouse. After a papal emissary had been assassinated in 1208, Innocent III authorized a "crusade" against the heretics. Landless nobles from northern France went into Provence and perpetrated bloody massacre in the name of orthodoxy. They were rewarded with the lands of their victims, but they did not succeed in wiping out the heresy. Ultimate victory came through the organization of a papal inquisition in the second quarter of the thirteenth century. A special "apparatus" was set up directly under the pope's supervision. Inquisitors were freed from supervision by local bishops and were to be assisted in the arrest and punishment of heretics by lay rulers. Methods of trial followed established procedures based ultimately on Roman law, but they were interpreted and operated with ruthless determination to save Christian unity and wipe out the contagion. Strong rumor was enough to bring a person under suspicion. Informers flourished. Suspects were investigated by taking secret depositions from witnesses. Those arrested on suspicion were examined under oath in secret trial on the basis of evidence they had not seen beforehand. The only available counterweapon for the defendant was a charge of malice in the witnesses. However, since he usually did not know who had accused or denounced him, success in this defense must have been infrequent. Persistent heretics (particularly those who recanted, then repudiated their recantation) were burned at the stake publicly to deter others who might be tempted into heresy. Lesser penalties, such as branding, the wearing of special identifying badges, pilgrimages, and imprisonment, were more commonly imposed. As in the secular courts of the times, torture was used to extract confessions. The accused's property was confiscated, and inquisitorial zeal was stimulated by a share in the proceeds. Many heretics died miserably in the filth and neglect of medieval prisons.

This chapter in medieval Christianity's history is not one to be proud of. But before passing absolute judgments on the events, one should consider the problem from the point of view of medieval men. The medieval Manicheans threatened the unity of Christendom in a time of war against the Muslim infidel. The medieval inquisition, however, never reached the level of sophisticated cruelty practiced in the later Spanish inquisition. And we cannot in all honesty feel self-righteous in an age in which we have inflicted barbarous suffering on people guilty of no more than belonging to a despised culture or race.

As a result of the conflicts of two centuries, Western Christianity became more rigidly authoritarian in its dogma and more insistent on conformity. Decisions and definitions, once made, closed paths that might fruitfully have been explored further. The tightening of internal discipline of the Church achieved by the Fourth Lateran Council did not last into the fourteenth and fifteenth centuries and the spirit of self-renewal in monasticism flagged. But that is a story for a later chapter.

Contributions of Christianity

The contributions of medieval Christianity to Western society are monumental. Christianity introduced, and in spite of the hierarchical order of society fostered, the idea of human equality and universal brotherhood. If the ploughman labored hard to serve knight and priest, his labor was, at least in the ideal, considered worthy, entitling him to respect in the world and reward in the hereafter. Slavery was both condoned and condemned by Christian leaders. It had largely ceased to exist in northern Europe by the twelfth century. If it later reappeared, modern, not medieval, man was responsible for the relapse. Christianity encouraged gentler and more humane treatment of women and children. Marriage became a sacrament, and men and women were taught to look upon it as a divine instrument for the procreation and protection of new life. Concern for the poor, the handicapped, the aged, and the helpless was channeled through Christianity into constructive uses. Hospitals, alms houses, and homes for the aged were founded in the name of Christian charity. The clergy attempted to moderate the violence of feudal society by introducing the Truce and Peace of God. Monks and secular clergy preserved, attempted to interpret, and spread the learning of the classical world. They created libraries, established monastic and cathedral schools, and eventually created universities. They aided kings in furthering law and justice. There is perhaps no need to emphasize the importance of Christianity for art. Drama, poetry, architecture, and all the visual arts derived dynamic inspiration from religion.

What Christianity meant to the individual medieval man is as hard to generalize about as what democracy means to modern man. The articulate minority, even in the two greatest centuries, differed greatly in thought and expression. Thomas Aquinas' coldly logical objectivity in proving the existence of God is poles apart from St. Bernard of Clairvaux's mystical exaltation:

> For when the Lord has been sought in watching and prayers, with strenuous effort, with showers of tears, He will at length present Himself to the soul; but suddenly when it supposes that it has gained His Presence, He will glide away. Again He comes to the soul that follows after Him with tears; He allows Himself to be regained, but not to be retained, and anon He passes away out of its very hands. Yet if the devout soul shall persist in prayers and tears. He will at length return to it. . . .[11]

As for the peasant, how can we know what he thought about his soul's salvation? Writers of the times present us with an upper-class view of what he felt or what they thought he ought to feel. The evidence of the acts of the Fourth Lateran Council would suggest that he did not go regularly to confession. Yet Church holidays and feast days did serve to punctuate his life, to alleviate some of its rigors, and to fill his stomach. At best the village priest was his counselor and his comforter in adversity. He at least had the opportunity to feel his oneness with a larger society joined in rejoicing at Christmas and Easter time. One suspects that he may often have tried, on Sunday, particularly in planting and harvest time, to catch up on his own work neglected in favor of labor for his lord or interrupted by weather. A twelfth-century sermon on the Lord's day tells the story of how God sent St. Paul, the apostle, and St. Michael, the archangel, down into Hell "to see how the folk fared there." St. Paul returned weeping at the horrors of the damned and petitioned God to give them rest "at least on Sunday ever until doomsday come." God granted Paul's petition, and the sermon ends:

We ought to honour Sunday very much and to observe it in all purity, for it hath in it three worthy virtues, which ye may hear. The first virtue is that it on earth gives rest to all serfs, men and women, from their servitude. The second virtue is in heaven, because the angels rest themselves more than on any other day. The third virtue is that the wretched souls in hell have rest from their great torments. Let each one then always observe the Sunday, and the other holy days which in church we are commanded to keep . . . and let him be a participator of heaven's bliss with the Father and the Son and the Holy Ghost without end. Amen.[12]

VII
Learning
and the Arts

The intellectual and artistic influences that went into the
making of the thought and the art of the High Middle
Ages are many and diverse and hard to weigh. Medieval
men, when they began to express their feelings about themselves and their relations to the past, were so naive, so spon-
taneous, and so unself-conscious that one is impressed chiefly
with the zest and freshness with which they tackled the problems of origins:

> By the books which we have the deeds of the ancients are known
> to us and the world as it formerly was. This our books have taught
> us, that Greece had the first fame of chivalry and learning. Then
> chivalry came to Rome and the totality of learning now domiciled
> in France. God grant that it be kept there and that the place may
> please it to the end that never may the honor which is established
> there leave France.[1]

The twelfth-century poet who wrote these lines was chiefly
impressed with the continuity of the medieval European world
with the Mediterranean classical world. Hindsighted perspective may lead us to say that medieval men did not fully
understand the ancient world, not in the historical, anthropo-
logical, sociological, and psychological sense in which we
understand it—or profess to do so. They did recognize their
common humanity with the men of the classical past, and they
tried to understand and to assimilate their inheritance. If
David, King of the ancient Hebrews, making adulterous love to
Bathsheba (in a twelfth-century manuscript illustration) lies

134

in a medieval bed and wears a crown modeled on that of Henry II of England, who is to say that the artist did not all the better understand King David's sin? Or, if Abelard, the great twelfth-century teacher in the Paris schools, in discussing Aristotle's *Categories,* drives a syllogism to the point of absurdity (and his students presumably to hysterical laughter), has he not caught the play spirit of Greek dialectics?

From their Muslim neighbors medieval scholars obtained scientific knowledge and techniques, translations of the classics, and stimulation for the solution of common philosophical problems. The first full texts of Aristotle came to them through Muslim Spain. From the Muslims also they began to increase their knowledge and improve their tools in astronomy, chemistry, mathematics, and medicine. From their Celtic background they had preserved some skills in metalworking and of design in illuminating manuscripts. From their German-Scandinavian inheritance they retained a sense of the sound and rhythm of the spoken word and a heroic concept of man engaged in an eternal struggle with the overpowering forces of nature—the sea, death, the cold of winter. Throughout the medieval period, but especially in the early centuries, Byzantine art and architecture overawed them.

From all these elements they created a new amalgam of great originality, especially in architecture, sculpture, and poetry. Many historians, from the fifteenth-century Italians to twentieth-century Americans, have disparaged medieval achievement. It is hard to understand how anyone can ever have stood in Chartres or Durham cathedrals and not felt himself in the presence of awe-inspiring creativity. Greek temples have greater serenity and Roman public buildings more sturdy self-assurance. However, in medieval cathedrals we recognize our own restless forbears reaching higher and higher into the sky with their towers and spires, and cutting ever more intricate patterns into it with Gothic arches and flying buttresses. Serenity, too, is present in a medieval cloister, particularly on a day of spring sunshine.

Gothic Architecture

Medieval cathedrals are a product of mathematics and mysticism. Their dimensions and proportions were based on ancient mathematical principles and formulas, but, combined with these, went a mystical faith that gave to the designers the courage to experiment with new shapes in stone and with new stresses and thus to produce the awe-inspiring Gothic arches and vaulting. Suger, the twelfth-century abbot of St. Denis near Paris, a pioneer of Gothic building, reveals his feelings thus:

> *For who am I, or what is my father's house,* that I should have presumed to begin so noble and pleasing an edifice, or should have hoped to finish it, had I not, relying upon the help of Divine mercy and the Holy Martyrs, devoted my whole self, both mind and body, to this very task? But He Who gave the will also gave the power; because the good work was in the will therefore it stood in perfection by the help of God. How much the Hand Divine which operates in such matters has protected this glorious work is also surely proven by the fact that it allowed that whole magnificent building [to be completed] in three years and three months, from the crypt below to the summit of the vaults above, elaborated with the variety of so many arches and columns, including even the consummation of the roof.[2]

Earlier medieval churches (*ca.* 1000 to *ca.* 1200) had been constructed on the plan (and sometimes in and from the remains) of old Roman basilicas. The style of architecture that evolved is usually called Romanesque in token of its use of Roman forms. It is characterized by round Roman arches, barrel vaulting or a flat wooden roof, and massive columns supporting ceiling and roof. Light entered only through a clerestory, that is, a tier of windows cut through the walls on a level above the main part of the nave. The interior of Romanesque churches was very dark on a rainy day. In southern Europe, where the Byzantine influence was strong, the darkness was relieved by wall paintings or by variations in the color of the stone. In the earlier churches of Ravenna and Verona mosaics constructed of small squares of glass or gilded paintings over the apse had reflected what light there was. Northern Romanesque churches, particularly those built in the Norman Romanesque style introduced into England by William the Conqueror, were more massive and less decorated than the Italian edifices and thus quite dark at any time. But dark or not, the rugged strength of a structure like Durham Cathedral in the north of England is overwhelming—even, or perhaps especially, on a stormy, gloomy day.

In Gothic architecture a new principle is introduced—that of light entering through windows. Roman and Romanesque buildings consist of walls and roofs enclosing space. A Gothic cathedral is essentially a skeleton of stone on which windows are hung to introduce light. Light was associated in the mysticism of cathedral builders with the power, love and glory of God. In Gothic building it was fragmented and bejeweled by stained glass windows. Stained glass was not unknown in northern France when the Gothic style was first developed. It was there to be used by the Gothic builders. Abbot Suger, inspired both by the writings of the supposed titular saint of his abbey —St. Denis the Areopagite—and by the beauty of light reflected from jewels, used stained glass to finish his new choir. St. Denis had written of God as the "superessential Light" or the "Father of the lights" and Christ as the "first radiance which has revealed the Father to the world." Suger expressed his joy in the jeweled light of his church in these words:

The church shines with its middle part brightened.
For bright is that which is brightly coupled with the bright,
And bright is the noble edifice which is pervaded by the new light;
Which stands enlarged in our time,
I, who was Suger, being the leader while it was being accomplished.[3]

and again:

Thus, when—out of my delight in the beauty of the house of God— the loveliness of the many-colored gems has called me away from external cares, and worthy meditation has induced me to reflect, transferring that which is material to that which is immaterial, on the diversity of the sacred virtues; then it seems to me that I see myself dwelling, as it were, in some strange region of the universe which neither exists entirely in the slime of the earth nor entirely in the purity of Heaven; and that, by the grace of God, I can be transported from this inferior to that higher world in an anagogical manner.[4]

Suger surely hoped that the worshippers in his church would share his anagogical experience, that is, his sense of increasing nearness to God through contemplating the light in his church.

The characteristic forms of Gothic architecture—the pointed arch, ribbed vaulting, the buttressing devised to support the outward thrust of the vaulting over nave and side aisles—had all been used by Romanesque builders. Gothic architects achieved a new harmony or order based on more daring uses of these forms. Whereas Romanesque builders had used ribbed vaulting to roof only square spaces in quadripartite patterns, Gothic builders covered oblong or rectangular spaces with multiple-ribbed vaulting. They also split up the solid columns supporting the vaulting into multiple supports and built them on up through the clerestory. This increased the strength and emphasized the height of the nave. To counteract the intensified outward thrust from the more elaborate vaulting and heavy stone roof made possible by it, they devised increasingly elaborate "flying buttresses." Architecturally speaking, they created a vigorous yet balanced tension, a feeling of life and movement rather than of rest. As one enters a Gothic cathedral, the eye goes forward and upward irresistibly. Religiously speaking, they created a sense of a living God inviting His people into a militant church. Classic temples had been built as sanctuaries for the gods. Medieval churches and cathedrals were built for the reception and edification of the people.

Sculpture and Painting

Medieval architecture evolved from Mediterranean models, but medieval sculpture and painting incorporated more northern influences. Germanic and Scandinavian invaders had brought with them only portable objects, as was natural. The Celtic or more primitive peoples that they had found in western Europe had never been great builders in stone. The Celts had, however, carried to a high point the art of decoration of their weapons and other implements, and of manuscripts after they became literate. The invaders brought with them their own skills in decoration. The forms they used were mainly abstract, derived from animal and plant forms in nature. In the early Middle Ages there occurred a creative interaction between these northern traditions and late classical styles. Northern artists converted to Christianity recognized the need for pictures and sculpture to tell stories and educate Christians in their faith. They imitated classical forms adapting their native style to new purposes. Something was lost and something gained in the process.

Romanesque sculpture and painting were, then, new syntheses of differing, if not conflicting, artistic ideas. They were both enlisted in the service of Christianity—to teach, preach, and illustrate. Sculpture was used chiefly in the decoration of churches and cathedrals, painting in the illumination of psalters, devotional books, and chronicles compiled in monasteries and in derivative fashion in the creation of stained glass windows. An elaborate symbolism had developed as an aid in the ambitious program of educating the illiterate. For example, a nimbus or halo behind the head of a human figure indicated sanctity. A nimbus with a cross indicated divinity. Size and relative position of figures expressed hierarchy. Order and meaning were more important than representation. Lions, wherever they appear, are conventionalized rather than real beasts of the veldt or the jungle. They are intended to convey to the viewer the dignity and power of the king of beasts, or to represent Mark the gospel writer, or to symbolize the resurrection—not to teach zoology or anatomy. Perspective and realistic proportion are sacrificed to architectural or decorative necessity. Medieval art transcended the merely real because of its religious purpose.

On the other hand, before the end of the thirteenth century, it became more humanistic, more expressive of love and respect for mankind. A thirteenth-century figure of Christ teaching in the sculpture of the south portal of Chartres Cathedral, in contrast to the judging Christ of the west portal (twelfth century), is identified not just by his crossed nimbus and his central position in the portal but also by his transcendently loving expression.

Painting of illuminations in manuscripts seems to have been less dedicated to the task of education, perhaps because the written words themselves could be trusted to convey the message while the artist indulged his fantasy or his humor in decorating the margins and the capital letters. Great diversity of styles in illuminating manuscripts were found in different parts of Europe, even in forming the letters of the alphabet. There were also distinct changes from one age to the next. Byzantine influence was strong in Charlemagne's time. Western European writing and illumination developed more independently in the High Middle Ages. In general, painting was livelier than sculpture and less bound by rigid conventions passed on from one generation to the next.

One aspect of medieval sculpture and painting that should not be overlooked is the humor that characterized it. From the top of the towers of Laon Cathedral, sculptured bulls or oxen look out over the landscape with amazed stupidity. There is a legend about the bovine contribution to the building of the cathedral, but no one puts cows in belfry towers without some humorous intent. Outside the upper doorway of the Sainte-Chapelle Cathedral a medallion showing Adam and Eve in the garden depicts with touching playfulness their meeting with God in the cool of the evening. In Lincoln Cathedral the ceiling bosses and the carvings on the underside of the hinged choir seats convey the comic relief essential in medieval life. (For example, a dead monkey is carried on a bier by two others; or a woman holds a man by his beard while she prepares to strike him with a sword.) Medieval illuminators paint initial letters of pages that are elaborate visual puzzles, or they present simple jokes like that in the Luttrell Psalter about the trials of the medieval peasant. (While the peasant sows his field, a crow behind his back is eating the seed from the sack while other crows steal the seed from the ground despite the frantic attacks of the peasant's dog.) These are only scattered examples. A medieval cathedral, from its foundations to its spires, was a kind of synthesis of life. The emphasis was on spiritual aspiration, the search for contact with God.

Philosophy and Theology

Medieval philosophy may seem to minds not trained to its methods rather sterile in comparison to the creativity of art and architecture. Yet, here, too, medieval men came to grips with fundamentals. The basic problems were epistemological. Twelfth- and thirteenth-century thinkers wanted to know how we know what we know. There were two schools of thought on the subject—what may be called the Reason school and the Revelation school. The latter took off from St. Augustine's *dictum* that we believe in order that we may know; that is, we cannot fully know until we have performed the act of will or love of believing in God. The Reason school held that the true road to truth and to God was through the intellect. In this particular aspect of their thinking, Christian philosophers could find little help from classical philosophers. The Greeks never really had to face the problem of reconciling philosophy and science on the one hand with theology and religion on the other. They had no dogmatic theology and cannot be said to have had a faith in the sense of a body of revealed truth that had to be systematically reconciled with the findings of reason. Aristotle rejected divine providence and the immortality of the soul. Plato was closer to Christian thinkers in that he believed in a transcendent deity, in the immortality of the soul, and in the possibility of mystical communion between man and God. For Christians, therefore, the problem was to reconcile their own body of revealed truth with their inheritance from the Greeks in philosophy and science.

The Muslims saw and tackled the problem of reconciling revealed truth with the findings of reason. They had translated and absorbed the works of Aristotle and of the neo-Platonists. The reconciliations of Avicenna (Ibn Sina, 980–1037) and Averroës (Ibn Rochd, 1126–1198), among others, circulated in the Christian West even after the Crusades against the "infidel" had transformed the authors into "the enemy." Avicenna, a Persian by birth and residence, proved that God is a necessary being, that "He is One in every respect, that He is exalted above all causes." He then went on to state "that He is Knowing, Living, Willing, Omnipotent, Speaking, Seeing, Hearing, and Possessed of all the other Loveliest Attributes"[5] as He is revealed in the Koran. However, Avicenna concerned himself very little with that specific body of revelation. Averroës, a Spanith Muslim, answering Avicenna's chief critic, Algazel (Al-Ghazzali, 1058–1111), posited a twofold truth. Revelation positively prescribes philosophical speculation, but speculation sometimes leads to conclusions different from revealed truth. This need not trouble us. Revelation is for those who reach truth through their imagination and emotions. Rational speculation is only for those few who are fit for it. In between there are those who need to have the truths of revelation logically demonstrated to them, although they are not capable of the highest level of thinking. From medieval Jewish philosophers, also, the Christian West learned something about how to tackle the problems.

Among Christian thinkers of the twelfth and thirteenth centuries, Anselm of Bec, who became the archbishop of Canterbury, is the first to deserve our attention. He, like Augustine, thought that faith is an essential prerequisite to understanding. But he sought also a conclusive logical proof for the existence of God. He became so obsessed with the question that he forgot food, prayer, and sleep. Ultimately, he found the answer in the comforting thought that man could not conceive of "that than which nothing greater can be conceived" if that, identified with God in the argument, did not exist. Therefore, God exists "both in the understanding and in reality." Abelard, the most famous of all twelfth-century scholars and teachers, belonged entirely to the Reason school. For him, nothing was to be taken on faith. The culminating resolution of this argument about faith and reason is to be found in the *Summa Theologica* of St. Thomas Aquinas (1225–1274):

> . . . it is impossible that one and the same thing should be believed and seen by the same person. Hence, it is equally impossible for one and the same thing to be an object of science and of belief for the same person. . . . It may also happen that what is an object of vision or scientific knowledge for one man . . . is, for another man, an object of faith, because he does not know it by demonstration. Nevertheless, that which is proposed to be believed equally by all is equally unknown by all as an object of science. Consequently, faith and science are not about the same things.[6]

But there are not two truths. There are simply two modes of approach to truth. Reason and faith operate in different spheres, but we need not fear that reason will lead us to conclusions that contradict revelation, not if the findings of reason and the matter of revelation are properly understood.

The most hotly debated question in the schools of the twelfth century was that of universals. This problem about the nature of knowledge is fundamental to philosophy and is still a subject of debate and research. "Universals" were categories of things like men, horses, roses, and the like. Somewhat simplified, the questions raised in the twelfth century were as follows: (1) Do we identify objects in extramental reality such as roses, desks, and horses by means of models existing in our minds? or (2) Do universals exist outside the mind in individual roses, desks, and horses? or (3) Do they exist independently of individual examples? Anselm of Bec was consistent with his proof of the existence of God and contended that roses exist in the mind and also as essences in things. Man recognizes them independently of his senses by relating them to the models in his mind that come to him as an irradiation from God. Roscelin of Compiegne, in opposition, contended that universals do not exist anywhere. In reality there are only individual roses, each one different from the other. Man uses names like rose for arbitrary collections of objects that he makes for his own convenience. This position was called Nominalism, in contrast to Anselm's teaching of Realism—that is, that universals have a "real" existence apart from and beyond particular examples.

Roscelin's younger contemporary, Abelard, a young nobleman from Brittany, studied with Roscelin long enough to master his technique of argument; then, in the tradition of the bright student throughout history, he proceeded to make a "monkey" of his teacher. He went on to work out his own solution to the problem. Universals, Abelard said, are neither objects nor mere names. They are conceptions developed in the mind through observation of particular objects and through generalization of relationships that man sees between things. He knows a horse is a horse because he has observed a number of four-footed beasts and distinguished among them certain ones who have hooves, elongated heads, eat grass, carry burdens, pull carts, and sleep standing up, not because there exists any such thing in the external universe as "horseyness." Man can do this with images (that is, with things in his mind), as well as with external reality.

St. Thomas Aquinas produced a resolution of the nominalist-realist argument that commands the respect of a whole school of thought in the twentieth century. It is impossible to do justice to his analysis either by lifting a quotation out of context or by summarizing. The central point, however, is that knowing and being are not essentially different. Abstraction, or formulation of universals, therefore, is a consideration by the mind of the essential elements within the actuality of things, a bringing into relationship of the knowing in the mind with being in external reality. Being and knowing are both incarnation, a consequence of God's original creation.

Many other scholars participated in these controversies, and lesser controversies revolved around the major ones. Because students sometimes think of these conflicts as rebellions against the authority of the Church, it should be said that they took place within, not outside the Church. The scholars were churchmen—some of them priests or bishops, some monks or friars, some canons of cathedrals. There were no outsiders except the Muslim and Jewish scholars and the heretics. Even Muslims and Jews were not treated as outsiders in the world of learning. Aquinas cites them frequently in his works. The centers of argumentation were cathedral schools and ultimately universities. These were fostered by the Church and peopled by clergy. The University of Paris won its autonomy with papal assistance.

Universities

The medieval university was a "community of scholars" with the authority to confer degrees. The origins of the earliest universities are obscure. The university at Bologna seems to have evolved from an eleventh-century center for the study of Roman law. Irnerius (1060–1125), its most distinguished teacher, attracted students from all over Europe. The University of Paris grew out of the schools originally situated on the Ile de la Cité around the Cathedral of Notre Dame but began to achieve its independence when teachers and students withdrew to the left bank of the Seine River to the Street of Straw in the near vicinity of the Church of Ste. Genevieve. Oxford was allegedly founded by a group of scholars who seceded from Paris; Cambridge, in turn, by a group that seceded from Oxford. The first university to be founded by a secular ruler was Naples (1224). Frederick II, King of Sicily and Germany and Emperor of the Holy Roman Empire, wanted trained judges and other administrators. He organized the university to provide the essential training.

At Bologna, student associations were the first to receive recognition under the term *universitas*. They negotiated with the teachers' gilds concerning fees and set up the rules for teaching. Teachers seem to have had a not unfamiliar difficulty in getting through the course in the prescribed time:

The form, moreover, to be observed by the Doctors as to the section is this: Let the division of the book into sections be determined, and then let him be notified. (And if any Doctor fails to reach any section on the specified date he shall be fined five pounds, and for a third and each succeeding violation of the rule, ten pounds.) . . . .

We decree also that no Doctor shall hereafter exceed one section in one lecture. . . .

We add that at the end of a section the Doctors must announce to the scholars at what section they are to begin afterwards. . . .

Since topics not read by the Doctors are completely neglected and consequently are not known to the scholars, we have decreed that no Doctor shall omit from his sections any chapter, decretal, law or paragraph. If he does this he shall be obliged to read it within the following section. We have also decreed that no decretal or decree or law or difficult paragraph shall be reserved to be read at the end of the lecture, if, through such reservation, promptness of exit at the sound of the appointed bell is likely to be prevented.[7]

Many of the southern universities followed the Bologna pattern of student rule with respect to fees and classroom methods. Related to this no doubt was the fact that they were, more than the northern universities, centers for higher professional training: in law, in medicine, in theology.

In the north the masters made the rules and the basic liberal arts subjects were taught: the *trivium,* consisting of grammar, rhetoric, and logic; and the *quadrivium,* consisting of arithmetic, geometry, astronomy, and music. Satisfactory completion of study in these subjects tested by oral examination, entitled the student to become a master and, if he chose, to go on to study for a doctoral degree in one of the higher branches of learning. Paris was the great center for theology. Control by the masters of the license to teach was not won without a struggle in the emerging universities. In Paris, when the schools had clustered around Notre Dame on the Ile de la Cité, the chancellor of the cathedral controlled the licensing. Then, as the result of a threeway struggle between city authorities, the bishop and the masters and scholars, the university finally won the power to regulate student life and to determine the criteria for the degree. The king conferred a charter on the masters and scholars in 1200 protecting them in relation to the townsmen; and the pope, by a bull of 1231 often called the Magna Carta of the universities, insured their right to control examinations and licensing of teachers.

"Colleges" (groups of students living together for protection and convenience in getting food and lodging) were first founded in Paris in the late twelfth century. The most famous college in Paris was the Sorbonne, founded about 1257. Some of the rules regulating student life illustrate familiar student problems:

> Also, no one shall eat in his room except for cause. If anyone has a guest, he shall eat in hall. . . .
>
> Also, the rule does not apply to the sick. If anyone eats in a private room because of sickness, he may have a fellow with him, if he wishes, to entertain and wait on him, who also shall have his due portion. . . .
>
> Also, all shall wear closed outer garments, nor shall they have trimmings of vair or grise or of red or green silk on the outer garments or hood.
>
> Also, no one shall have loud shoes or clothing by which scandal may be generated in any way.
>
> Also, no one shall be received in the house unless he shall be willing to leave off such and to observe the aforesaid rules. . . .
>
> Also, no women of any sort shall eat in the private rooms. If anyone violates this rule, he shall pay the assessed penalty, namely, sixpence. . . .
>
> Also, if anyone has spoken opprobrious words or shameful to a fellow, provided it is established by two fellows of the house, he shall pay a purse which ought to belong to the society.
>
> Also, if one of the fellows shall have insulted, jostled or severely beaten one of the servants, he shall pay a sextarium of wine to the fellows, and this wine ought to be *vin superieur* to boot. . . .[8]

It is not surprising that discipline was often a problem or that there were conflicts with the inhabitants of towns. Students were sent to university at a much younger age than is now customary—boys at thirteen or fourteen. Girls did not attend. Nor will it be a surprise to modern undergraduates that one of the chief problems of medieval students was money. They were drawn from all walks of life, but perhaps mainly from among the poorer families of knights, or from among townspeople who were ambitious for their children. They were perpetually short of cash, and their letters beg piteously for more money from home to pay fees, to buy books, of course.

Peter Abelard (1079–1142) taught at Paris before the university was fully organized, when it was still possible for an irrepressible rebel like him to set himself up as a rival to his teachers without asking anyone's leave. His "calamities," both professional and personal that he tells us about in an autobiographical *History* of them, were tragic, the more so since he brought them on himself through his intractibility and passionate intensity.[9] Twice tried for heresies, he taught and wrote nothing against the doctrine of the Church. His enemies were mainly men whom he had offended with his contempt or the indifference of his superiority. The exception was St. Bernard of Clairvaux. St. Bernard was his implacable enemy because he recognized in Abelard a man who acknowledged no power in Heaven or on earth that he would submit to except the inexorable power of the mind. This to Bernard was dangerous in a teacher, especially a rival teacher. But it must have been exciting to students and probably accounted more than the dialectical method he used or the substance of what he taught for the hordes who gathered to hear his lectures in Paris and who followed him into the wilderness when he tried to leave the world. It is worth remembering that the Athenians put Socrates to death for leading their youth astray in the fashion of Abelard. Peter Abelard was only silenced by the authority of the Church on certain subjects and never wholly effectively.

Thomas Aquinas taught at Paris in its most distinguished period. He was a Dominican in the period when the Dominicans and Franciscans dominated the thought of Europe. He had his conflicts with authority too, but he did not allow them to interfere with his work. Just before his death he completed his *Summa Theologica,* the definitive reconciliation of Christian and Greek thought and the most complete synthesis of the learning of his age—however, not the final one. His work was assailed not only in his own lifetime but continually throughout the last medieval centuries.

Science

Science in the Middle Ages was backward. While their minds were still open to Muslim learning, Europeans did acquire much knowledge from the Muslims, especially in mathematics, medicine, and chemistry. The Muslims, in turn, had learned and borrowed from Byzantium, from Persia, from India, and from the Greeks. Both Muslims and Christians dabbled in alchemy, the pseudoscientific search for a method of changing base metals into gold. This search was not as fruitless as the objective. It led to discovery of new chemical substances and new processes such as evaporation and distillation. Research was unsystematic and tended to stop at mere compilation of information or misinformation from the past. Those who asked questions were handicapped by scientific traditions of long standing. Adelard of Bath, a contemporary of Henry I of England (1100–1135), for example, set down for a nephew a long list of questions to be used as chapter headings of a book, among them:

1. Why plants are produced without the sowing of seed
4. Why they are not produced from water, or air, or even from fire as they are from the earth
7. Why certain beasts chew the cud, and certain others do not at all
13. Whether beasts have souls
38. Why men cannot walk when they are born, as animals do
50. How the earth moves
51. Why the waters of the sea are salty
52. Whence the ebb and flow of the tides come[10]

Most people would agree that except for 13 these are legitimate scientific questions, although randomly set forth. The nephew rejected them as childish and said that he wanted to "advance to the nature of animals in itself" (universals again). Adelard answered impatiently:

It is difficult for me to discuss animals with you, for I have learned from the Arab masters by the guidance of reason, while you, deceived by the picture of authority, follow a halter. For what else should authority be called but a halter? Indeed, just as brute beasts are led by any kind of halter, and know neither where nor how they are led, and only follow the rope by which they are held, so the authority of your writers leads into danger not a few who have been seized and bound by animal credulity.[11]

Adelard is tactful in his manner of telling his student he is a donkey, and he has the right spirit for the pursuit of scientific truth.

In the thirteenth century Robert Grosseteste, Bishop of Lincoln, made some interesting investigations into optics and the properties of light. The fact that Grosseteste believed that light was the means of operation of grace through free will (the soul being the transformer of light) does not impair the validity or importance of his experiments. His younger and better-known contemporary, Roger Bacon, continued Grosseteste's studies and went off on some tracks of his own. He did encounter trouble with the rulers of his order, but he and other Franciscans, by questioning and challenging Aristotle's physics, prepared the way for the scientific revolution of the sixteenth century.

Literature

Students in the universities produced a genre of Latin poetry of their own, usually called Goliardic, meaning Satanic. Bawdy, wistful, and full of yearning sentimentality about the shortness of life, the permanence of death and eternity, the enticing hazards of sin, these poems are hard to translate into modern English that will do justice to their succinctness and pungency in the original Latin. Here is one:

> Let's away with study
>   Folly's sweet
> Treasure all the pleasure
>   Of our youth:
> Time enough for age
>   To think on Truth

So short a day
And life so quickly hasting,
And in study wasting
   Youth that would be gay

'Tis our spring that's slipping
   Winter draweth near.
Life itself we're losing,
   And this sorry cheer
Drives the blood and chills the heart
   Shrivels all delight.
Age and all its crowd of ills
   Terrifies our sight.
So short a day . . . .

Let us as the gods do,
   'Tis the wiser part:
Leisure and love's pleasure
   Seek the young in heart
Follow the old fashion,
   Down into the street!
Down among the maidens
   And the dancing feet!
So short a day . . . .

There for the seeing
   Is all loveliness,
White limbs moving
   Light in wantonness
Gay go the dancers,
   I stand and see,
Gaze, till their glances
   Steal myself from me.
So short a day . . . .[12]

No one would presume to build a sociological description of student life in the Middle Ages from these verses any more than from the poetry of some of the more advanced undergraduate literary magazines of today. But it is evident from them that students were just as young in heart then as they are now.

The greatest literature of the Middle Ages was written in the native languages that emerged out of Latin or German or both in the early centuries of the period. It is in these native languages that medieval poets most fully expressed the feelings that still compel our listening, especially if we can make the effort to read them in the original language.

In the north of France in the tenth and eleventh centuries epic poems, usually called *chansons de geste,* began to be written down in the form in which they have come down to us. The *Chanson de Roland* is the best known and most attractive example. It is the story, much altered by time, of a rear-guard action fought by a portion of Charlemagne's army at Roncevalles in the Pyrenees, on his retreat from Spain in 778. The poem was not written down until the twelfth century, but it had probably been given shape by some unknown Homer considerably earlier. The value of the poem lies not so much in the narrative as in the expression of early feudal ideals of courage and loyalty to one's lord and one's brother-in-arms.

A new genre grew up among the feudal class of Aquitaine and Provence as a medium of expression for the courtly love game described in Chapter II. Many scholarly explanations have been offered to account for this brilliant growth. Southern France was particularly well situated to be influenced by Spain, by Byzantium, and by the north. Whatever the literary origins of the romantic tale and of romantic poetry, it would seem that an essential impetus came from the rebellion of Eleanor of Aquitaine and her daughter, Marie, Countess of Champagne, against the tyranny of feudal men. Women in feudal society were normally left at home when their men went off on their interesting expeditions to the Holy Land, to tournaments, or to wars nearer at hand. Sometimes they had to take charge of the defense of the castle. More often they languished in boredom in the company of other women, children, old people, and very young men. In this atmosphere the literature of courtly love developed. In it the young lover is nearly always frustrated or the victim of tragic consequences because of loving a lady who is inaccessible or forbidden. His beloved is often the lady who rules the castle and is already married. He cannot aspire to marriage, and he should not aspire to the comforts and pleasures of her bed. Bernart de Ventadorn rails against the pains and chains of love:

> Alas! I who thought I knew love
> Barely do know love at all!
> For I cannot keep from loving
> One whose gifts I'll never share:
> She has stolen from me my self,
> My heart, and my whole world;
> When she smote me thus she left
> But my longing and desire.[13]

And so, a convention grew up of a love that was bound to be unfulfilled or to end in tragedy. The women used this convention as an instrument for civilizing their absent spouses and the attendant young men, to make them more attentive and considerate. The convention spread to northern France and to Germany.

Poets and writers of romantic tales used it to create poetry and prose that, though some of it is sentimental and tawdry, can be in the works of Chrétien de Troyes and Wolfram von Eschenbach great literature. Townspeople were inevitably struck by the ridiculousness of the supposedly tough and well-armed knight pining for the love of an unattainable lady, especially perhaps because they were deliberately excluded from the strict rules of courtly treatment. Some burgher of low birth was probably the author of *Aucassin and Nicolette,* a delightful tale in which the lady takes all the initiative, rescuing her hero again and again from the direst perils, and in which we are finally asked to believe in a country where the king lies in bed preparing to give birth to a baby while his lady is out fighting a war in which roasted apples and cheeses are the weapons. Chaucer carried this ambiguous spirit into late fourteenth-century England. He read his poetry to the nobility and included in it many courtly tales, but he also knew the bawdy ribaldry of the tavern.

Medieval drama ranges all the way from *tropes*—or dramatic interludes interpolated in the mass—to fertility rites performed to celebrate surviving pagan festivals. The liturgical drama best known in America is the *Play of Daniel,* a twelfth-century opera intended for performance in churches. May-Day celebrations and Christmas revels carried the strongest survivals of old pagan ritual dances and drama. The popular and ecclesiastical traditions were brought together in some sort of synthesis when Urban IV, in 1264, instituted the festival of Corpus Christi in honor of Holy Communion. It was celebrated on the Thursday after Trinity Sunday, the eighth Sunday after Easter, and thus came usually in June. Miracle plays based on stories from the Bible, including the Old Testament or Hebrew Scriptures as well as the gospel narratives of the life and passion of Christ, were performed on carts in the streets as part of the processional to the churches for celebration of the mass. The craft gilds were assigned parts of the cycle of plays. In Chester, for example, the temptation of Eve was assigned to the drapers (a medieval joke?). A mixture of popular vernacular and Latin language was used in these performances. About the popular secular drama celebrating pagan festivals, we know only what survived in practice in modern times, as, for example, the Morris dances in England.

The greatest volume of prose writing of the period is history or biography. Historical writing after the time of Bede (see Chapter I), in spite of the efforts of rulers like Charlemagne and Alfred the Great of England, tended to degenerate in the ninth and tenth centuries into mere annals. But the sense of history and the feeling of responsibility of the historian revived, and in the work of Matthew Paris, an English monk, and Otto of Freisung, a German bishop, there is an awareness of the sweep of history and concern for its meaning. The chronicler historians, like Matthew and Otto, were mainly churchmen, and they show an ecclesiastical bias. They all borrowed without guilt from their predecessors. Each is valuable, therefore, not only for his original contributions about his own times, but sometimes also for his reproduction of material from manuscripts of which the original has not come down to us. The Crusades gave a new impetus to historical writing. Narratives of events by eyewitnesses and biographies were written. Among these are Villehardouin's account of the Fourth Crusade and Joinville's life of St. Louis, both written by laymen of the feudal class. Medieval historians took the view that history was God-directed and that success or failure in human enterprise was determined by God's favor rather than by human capability or weakness.

The greatest of all medieval writers was Dante Alighieri (1265–1321). He wrote in Latin a treatise *On Monarchy,* in which he offered a practical program of statesmanship to the Holy Roman emperor based on his own political experience and on Roman, Muslim, and earlier medieval political thought. His greatest work, the *Divine Comedy,* was written in an Italian that became standard for centuries. This was the truest and most complete of all medieval syntheses. Modeled on Vergil's *Aeneid,* but transcending it in intensity of feeling and vigor of language, this poem, if studied with sufficient dedication, will yield most of the secrets of the Middle Ages. Dante was a Florentine, but his "world" included far more of Europe than he experienced directly.

Political Thought and Law

Its classical heritage handicapped political thought. Medieval men read about monarchy in the Scriptures or as it was conceived and described by Greeks and Romans at their highest level of civilization. They tried to find in their own institutions the analogues of the classical statement. But medieval political institutions and relationships were nearer to Homer's Greece or Tarquin's Rome than to Aristotle's Athens or Cicero's Republic. John of Salisbury, a younger contemporary of Abelard, compared a Christian state ruled by a king to an organism, in which each part of the society was analagous to a part of the human body. The clergy were the soul; the king, the head; officials and soldiers, the hands; and so on down to the husbandmen or peasants who were like the feet in cleaving the soil and needing the "care and foresight" of the head. The metaphor becomes unreal in medieval terms when John states that "the place of the heart is filled by the senate, from which proceeds the initiation of good works and ill."[14] Where would one find the senate in England or France of the twelfth century? Yet John was a thoughtful student and a man concerned with moral purpose in the universe. His *Policraticus* expresses his concern for the betterment of human life through the moral use of power that God gives to kings. A tyrant may be overthrown or killed, but John does not say clearly who is to judge him or who is to execute the sentence.

With respect to law as well as to political thought, medieval men had difficulty in reconciling their daily practice with their inheritance from the Mediterranean past. Emperor Justinian (527–565) had set jurists to compiling and systematizing the vast body of Roman law and jurisprudence in a synthesis called the *Corpus Juris Civilis* (527–534). Its study, as has already been indicated, was revived in the twelfth century. Germanic law was customary law, and where codes had been compiled, they had been rather unsystematic. Church law, always strongly influenced by Roman law, had similarly been collected rather than systematically codified. In the twelfth century Gratian gathered together and systematized ecclesiastical law in what is called the *Corpus Juris Canonici* (*ca.* 1140). Experts on secular law began to write textbooks of local law. Glanvill, one of Henry II's officials, wrote a book about the common law of England. His more ambitious successor, Bracton, one of Henry III's judges, learned something about Roman law and worked it into his account of the common law. Beaumanoir, inspired by these English lawbooks, compiled a book about the law and custom of northern France. The one clearly original contribution of medieval lawyers to legal concepts was that of *dominium,* the keystone of feudal law. It is something between ownership and rulership combining elements of both. In feudal society no one fully owned land or power. Everyone held land and power from his lord. Even the king held his *regnum* from God, as did the priest his *sacerdotium.*

Music

Medieval men made inventive contributions to music. Early medieval music had been monophonic and modal, based on ancient Hebrew and Greek music. Gregorian and Ambrosian chants are the chief examples that have come down through the ages. Since there was no complete system of musical notation, it is not absolutely certain how they were sung at the time. In the eleventh century, however, an ingenious Italian thought of putting notes on lines like those of a stringed instrument. Soon after this French musicians began experimenting with polyphony, both in secular and sacred music. The chief examples that have survived from the High Middle Ages are sacred music. In addition, there are the poems that the troubadours, trouvères, and minnesinger (names given to the musical performers) sang at the festivities in the medieval castles for the nobles, ladies, and gentlemen. It is possible for musicologists to reproduce the musical accompaniment. Dances, too, have survived from the period. They are lively and rhythmic.

Of musical instruments there was a great variety. Ancestors of modern violins, of guitars and other plucked instruments, organs, primitive woodwinds, horns, harps, bells, bagpipes, hurdy-gurdies, and especially drums existed in profusion and variety. They were used both in the production of secular and religious music. Solemnity and sobriety had not yet become the musical setting for sacred proceedings to the extent that they have in modern times.

The main instrument a twentieth-century student needs in approaching the wealth of medieval thought and feeling is spontaneity of response and the imagination to think the thoughts of his medieval forefathers without imposing or insinuating his own more sophisticated or more pretentious values or demanding his own sense of order. Only by so clearing his mind of today's standards will he be able to fully appreciate and understand the culture of the Middle Ages.

VIII
Europe and the Wider World

Western Europe's most ambitious common enterprise and its most conspicuous failure was the attempt to bring together all mankind in Christian unity under the leadership of the bishop of Rome, St. Peter's successor, the pope. The most intense part of this enterprise and the one that enlisted the most widespread support in Europe from all levels of society was the Crusades. The Crusades in the narrow sense of the expeditions to conquer and hold the Holy Land for the West began at the end of the eleventh century and lasted throughout the remainder of the medieval period. In a more inclusive sense, the Crusades include the reconquest of Spain and Sicily from the Muslims and the extension of the Christian frontier in the Baltic region to take in Lithuanians, Estonians, Prussians, and Finns. Related to and concurrent with the Crusades was the effort to convert or eliminate the Jews within Europe that led ultimately to their expulsion from many parts of the West. Related also were Christian missions to convert the Mongols and other Eastern peoples. The Crusades inspired the most dedicated valor, the most bloodthirsty cruelty, and the greediest vandalism of medieval men. They offered the fullest opportunity for combined fulfillment of Germanic heroic aspirations and Christian ideals of brotherhood and self-sacrifice.

Catholic and Orthodox Christendom

The West's unity, such as it was, depended on Catholic Christianity. The Catholic clergy were a Europe-wide hierarchy under the leadership of the pope, and the language of Christianity—not just written and spoken church Latin, but also the artistic language of Christian symbols—was the one universal language. The religious character of the West's unity affected Europe's relations with all other peoples, Christian and non-Christian. In the early Middle Ages Christianity had succeeded everywhere in superseding, if not entirely overcoming, primitive paganism. The Germans, the Irish, the Scandinavians, and the Hungarians all gave up their primitive gods for the one great God whom the Christians preached. On the other hand, Catholic Christianity failed in relation to major rival religions. The Jewish communities in western Europe, in general, yielded neither to persuasion nor to force. The Muslims were pushed out of Spain and Sicily to the southern shores of the Mediterranean. But neither the prolonged warfare against them in the centuries from 1100 to the end of the Middle Ages nor such attempts as were made to convert them led them to accept Rome's leadership.

Rome was unable to establish or to maintain its leadership even over the whole of Christendom. Serious conflicts had developed between the Western Catholic and the Eastern Orthodox Christian worlds, and by 1100 there was already little chance of peacefully resolving these conflicts, although the effort continued throughout the medieval period. Since most of the Slavs of Russia and the West had been converted by Eastern Orthodox missionaries, this schism created a split between eastern and western Europe, which has continued to be important in modern times. The main factors in the breakdown between East and West were not profound differences in interpretation of the teachings of Christ. They were on the surface simply matters of organization and discipline. Below the surface were deep-seated cultural differences. The eastern Roman Empire was more Hellenistic than Roman. That is, essential ideas and values were Greek or Persian, or a combination of both, rather than Roman. Although the Byzantines considered themselves part of "Romania," the Latin language was not spoken nor often written. Justinian's *Corpus Juris*

Civilis had been compiled originally in Latin because Latin was the language of the leading Roman jurists. For everyday purposes, for theological discussion, and for worship the language was Greek. More important, the ideas were Greek.

Emperor Constantine's acceptance of Christianity and his transfer in 330 of the capital of the Roman Empire to Constantinople, a new city that he founded near the site of ancient Greek Byzantium, was an indication that, from the imperial point of view, the centers both of Christianity and of secular power were in the East. In an effort to effect both religious and political unity, Constantine had in 325 called a great council of the Christian clergy at Nicaea on the Asian shore across from Constantinople. He presided at the council that resolved conflicts among the clergy. This precedent and the rivalry among the bishops or patriarchs of the leading cities of the East (Alexandria, Antioch, Damascus, and Constantinople) had led to an acceptance in the East of the emperor's final authority in religious matters.

The bishops of Rome, committed as they were to the doctrine of the Petrine Succession, could not accept imperial intervention in religious matters. When Byzantine political and military power was strong in Italy, popes might be cooperative or submissive, but they did not thereby abandon their claims to leadership of the whole Christian Church. The first serious break occurred in 751 when Byzantine power in northern Italy collapsed in the face of Lombard attacks. The popes then turned west to the rulers of the Franks. In return for papal sanction of their seizure of power from the last of the Merovingians, the Carolingian kings gave their support to the papacy against the Lombards and their sanction to the pope's temporal rule of central Italy. From this time onward the power of Rome was turned to the West. Communication with the East became increasingly difficult. Disagreement over the wording of the creed adopted at Nicaea, over the use of images in churches in the eighth and ninth centuries, and over other lesser matters finally led to mutual condemnation and schism in 1054. On both sides those who sympathized with the other side were condemned as "fellow travelers," and each demanded of the other full surrender on all important issues before the restoration of Christian unity could be fruitfully discussed.

Yet it was to the pope that the Byzantine Emperor appealed when attacks of the Seljuks in Asia Minor and the Patzinaks in the Balkans threatened his frontiers. Seljuks and Patzinaks were both Turkic peoples pushing westward from central Asia. The Seljuks had conquered Baghdad by 1055 and had adopted Islam, including the Muslim policy of toleration toward Christians. But they had defeated a Byzantine imperial army and captured an emperor in 1071 at Manzikert near Lake Van. Since Asia Minor was the breadbasket and also the main source of recruits for the imperial army, any threat to this stronghold of the Byzantine Empire was viewed with dismay. The Patzinaks were pagans who for a long time had constituted a threat to the main route of trade between Kiev in Russia and Constantinople. Their incursion into the Balkans, even as far as Salonika in 1065, was another cause for alarm.

The first appeal to the West failed. Pope Gregory VII, to whom the Emperor Michael wrote, was too deeply involved in his conflict with Henry IV of Germany to respond as he would have liked to have done. Later, in 1094, when Alexius appealed to Urban II, conditions were more favorable.

The West's response to Alexius' call for help was threefold. Pope Urban II called on the knighthood of the West, particularly the French, to organize a military expedition for the relief of Constantinople and the Holy Land. Peter the Hermit, a propagandist for the Crusade, traveled through northern France and the Rhineland calling on Christians to go forth in the cause of Christianity. He won a large following of poor men who proved to be more of an impediment to the success of the Crusade than a help. Starting out without money, without supplies, and without arms, they roused hostility in Hungary and the Balkans by their depredations. Reaching Constantinople in a destitute condition, they were persuaded to move on into Asia Minor where they were the first victims of the Seljuks. Independent expeditions organized by various German knights tended to degenerate into Jew-killing operations at home.

Attempts at military cooperation between the Crusaders and the Byzantine emperor bred mutual distrust and contempt rather than better understanding between East and West. The emperor had hoped to use the Western Christians who came in response to his call for the protection and defense of his Christian empire. He was unprepared for their independent aspiration to recover the holy places in Bethlehem and Jerusalem from Muslim rule and to set up independent Christian states in the Holy Land. The Byzantines found the Western Christians crude, undisciplined, and uneducated in the amenities of civilized behavior. Worse still, the Westerners lacked food and equipment, and they optimistically expected the Byzantines to supply them. Anna Comnena, daughter of Alexius, describes the growing horror with which the Byzantine court viewed the coming of the Westerners:

> Now the Frankish counts are naturally shameless and violent, naturally greedy of money too, and immoderate in everything they wish, and possess a flow of language greater than any other human race . . . Now, as this was their character, and their speech very long-winded, and as they had no reverence for the emperor, nor took heed of the lapse of time nor suspected the indignation of the onlookers, not one of them gave place to those who came after them, but kept on unceasingly with their talk and requests.[1]

They even pursued the emperor into his private apartments, an unheard-of insolence according to Byzantine protocol. The Westerners, for their part, found the Byzantines shifty and treacherous, unfaithful to the simplest of promises, and weak, corrupt, and effeminate. A French Crusader's chronicle of 1148 gives the following report of them:

> And then the Greeks degenerated entirely into women; putting aside all manly vigour, both of words and of spirit, they lightly swore whatever they thought would please us, but they neither kept faith with us nor maintained respect for themselves. In gen-

eral they really have the opinion that anything which is done for the holy empire cannot be considered perjury.[2]

A French bishop made a critical survey of Constantinople's defenses and recommended its capture for the West. Byzantines, he said, were Christian only in name and need not be respected as allies. Frederick Barbarossa, later in the twelfth century, responded to an eastern emperor's threat to destroy his Holy Roman Empire with a counterthreat to destroy Byzantium and restore Roman imperial unity from the West. Mounting hostilities and recriminations made it easy for the Venetians, in 1203, to deflect 12,000 men gathered for embarkation at Venice to Zara, a Hungarian port on the Adriatic coast, instead of shipping directly to Palestine. Venice had long coveted this port as a base for her far-flung commercial empire. Then the son of a deposed Byzantine emperor persuaded the Crusaders to capture Constantinople on his promise to restore the East to Rome's allegiance. The great city fell with unexpected speed. The Crusaders entered the city. Their leaders sacked the palaces, and their followers were allowed to plunder the rest of the city. In the words of a French chronicler who was there and saw it all for himself:

> The rest of the army, scattered throughout the city, also gained much booty; so much indeed, that no one could estimate its amount or its value. It included gold and silver, table-services and precious stones, satin and silk, mantles of squirrel fur, ermine and miniver, and every choicest thing to be found on this earth. Geoffrey de Villehardouin here declares that, to his knowledge, so much booty had never been gained in any city since the creation of the world.[3]

Relations between the Crusaders and the would-be emperor broke down. The Crusaders decided that the solution to the Greek problem was to destroy the Byzantine Empire and set up a Latin Kingdom of Constantinople, a feudal state with an elected monarch. They never succeeded in controlling more than the European portion of the Byzantine Empire, and they lost even that by 1261. Byzantine power was restored, but the Byzantine Empire never fully recovered from the Latin conquest. The Crusaders lost a valuable though difficult ally in the fight against the Muslims and weakened the empire as a buffer between Europe and invaders from the East. Not until 1453 did Constantinople finally succumb to attack from the Ottoman Turks, but the empire had long before that date ceased to be of primary significance as a force in the balance of power between the Christian and the non-Christian world.

Jews in Christian Europe

Christianity owed Judaism a profound debt for the Scriptures, for basic moral teachings, and for liturgical music. For the Christian West the Jews presented what was, in many ways, its most difficult identity problem. Roman rulers had not at first distinguished between Christians and Jews. After the triumph of Christianity in the Roman Empire at the end of the fourth century, the Council of Chalcedon, in 451, legislated that Christians must not feast with Jews, marry Jews, nor even patronize Jewish physicians. Jews were not allowed to hold office nor to own Christian slaves. These rules were very likely more honored in the breach than the observance in the early centuries. There is some reason to believe that a Jew was chosen bishop of Paris in the sixth century, simply because he was popular and reputed to be a just man. Gregory the Great (590–604) protected Jewish freedom of worship while, at the same time, he condemned Jewish "insolence" in refusing to accept the Christian revelation. It may be hard for a twentieth-century secular-minded American to see the importance of the theological problems. It does not help to pretend that they did not exist. Each side obviously thought the other wrong. More important in human terms were such matters as circumcision and food laws. The charge that the Jews "killed Christ" was probably not very important in these early centuries. It became so only after other antagonisms had developed.

Jews became very useful to the Christian West, even though they did not fit into the feudal pattern of relationships. Oaths of fealty were protected by religious sanction. Jews would not take them, nor would their oaths have been accepted by Christians. They had never, in the West, been farmers. Medieval farming involved a kind of rural isolation that would have made hard the perpetuation of Judaism. Jews in the West were traders and moneylenders. Christian prohibitions on money-lending, like many other Christian rules, were laxly enforced until the twelfth century and after that largely evaded. But the Jews, through accumulation of cash surpluses from trade, had already become bankers and moneylenders to the Christians.

Sporadic outbreaks against moneylenders had occurred before the Crusades, but during the Crusades they gathered intensity and were widespread. With European territorial expansion in the eleventh century and with the Crusades beginning at the end of the same century, Jewish credit facilities became trag-ically important. Members of the feudal class departing on Crusade mortgaged their estates to Jews in a society that knew little about investment and profit, leaving wives and chil-dren to make the best they could of the situation. Peasants had always been resentful of those who had ready capital, and now with the Jews managing the estates of numerous noblemen resentment mounted. With the beginning of the long war against the "infidels" on the frontiers, there also began a persecution of the Jews in Europe. Old charges of ritual murder were revived and new charges of desecration of the sacred bread used in the Eucharist were circulated. Ghettos were established by official order, not just as formerly by Jews for their own convenience and protection. Jews were required to wear distinguishing badges or hats to "protect" the Christian population from the perils of social intercourse. In Belitz, near Berlin, the entire Jewish population in 1243 was put to death on a charge of desecration of the consecrated bread of the Eucharist. In England massacres began in the twelfth century and reached a climax after the alleged ritual murder of "Little St. Hugh" of Lincoln in 1255. Jews were rounded up and imprisoned, and during the next twenty years bloody massacres were common. It is impossible to say just how many Jews were killed in these massacres. Throughout the Crusade years the attacks on the Jews were widespread and frequent.

Official papal policy sanctioned neither the charges against the Jews nor the local attacks on them, although the Third and Fourth Lateran Councils of 1179 and 1215 had strengthened both the prohibitions against usury by Christians and the restrictions against intermarriage and other social intercourse. In Rome the Jewish community was protected and did survive the medieval period. Gregory X, in 1272, codified the papal legislation of several centuries including the following provisions:

> We decree moreover that no Christian shall compel them or any one of their group to come to baptism unwillingly. But if any one of them shall take refuge of his own accord with Christians, because of conviction, then, after his intention shall have been manifest, he shall be made a Christian without any intrigue. . . .
>
> Since it happens occasionally that some Christians lose their Christian children, the Jews are accused by their enemies of secretly carrying off and killing these same Christian children and of making sacrifices of the heart and blood of these very children. It happens, too, that the parents of these children, or some other Christian enemies of these Jews, secretly hide these very children in order that they may be able to extort from them a certain amount of money by redeeming them from their straits. . . . And most falsely do these Christians claim that the Jews have secretly and furtively carried away these children and killed them, and that the Jews offer sacrifice from the heart and blood of these children, since their law in this matter precisely and expressly forbids Jews to sacrifice, eat, or drink the blood, or to eat the flesh of animals having claws. This has been demonstrated many times at our court by Jews converted to the Christian faith: nevertheless very many Jews are often seized and detained unjustly because of this. We decree, therefore, that Christians need not be obeyed against Jews in a case or situation of this type, and we order that Jews seized under such a silly pretext be freed from imprisonment. . . .[4]

Although Gregory X here asserts some negative knowledge of Jewish religious belief and practice, in general there was neither much curiosity nor much desire to comprehend contemporary Judaism. The Christian West, engaged as it was in war with the infidel on its Mediterranean frontier and war against heretics at home, had little generosity to expend on stubborn dissidents within its society. The Dominicans engaged in disputations from time to time with Jewish opponents to convince both Jews and Christians of the errors of the Jewish faith. Jewish defenders risked condemnation for blasphemy, and the point of the disputations, like the point of burning heretics, was to strengthen Christians in their faith—not to examine the merits of Judaism.

The policy of secular rulers toward the Jews in this period was one of ruthless exploitation in return for some degree of protection. Jewish communities were treated in England as special vassals of the king. An Exchequer of the Jews was set up with some Jewish judges to deal with their finances and other problems. Jews were subjected to tallage as were serfs and townsmen. When they died without heirs, debts owed them by Christians became the property of the king as creditor. In 1201 King John sold them a charter of privilege protecting their right to fair trial, to inheritance from father to son, to travel without tolls in England and Normandy. For about £3000 John made sure that no one should be able to exploit their wealth but himself. Edward I increased the pressure on them. Finally, in 1290, he expelled them from England, as he had done a year earlier from Gascony. The French kings in their domains alternately expelled them and invited them back until, in 1306, Philip IV arrested them, confiscated their property and all their claims as creditors, and finally condemned them to exile. The recall of some Jews to Gascony and to France after these expulsions had more to do with rival financial needs of French and English kings in their wars with one another than with any genuine friendliness toward Jews. In Germany the expulsions were more sporadic, more a matter of local policy. Many Jews fled eastward to escape from brutal attacks by peasants and organized vigilantes calling themselves "Jewbeaters."

Their expulsion from Spain came late. Jews in that peninsula had achieved great prosperity and great usefulness, first under Muslim protection, then, as the Reconquista progressed, under Christian rulers. They were physicians, diplomats, translators and interpreters, tax collectors, merchants, and craftsmen. But, by 1391, the mounting tide of accusation against them for, allegedly, spreading the infection of the Black Death and a Europe-wide xenophobic hysteria about them led to massacres, forced conversions, and expulsion from Spain, too. Nothing commends to us medieval policies and practices toward the Jews. In explanation, it can only be said that the Jews were victims of Christendom's search for its identity.

Western Christendom and the Muslims

Early relations with the Muslims were relatively simple. They were mainly military. When the Muslims moved westward along the north African coast after the death of Muhammad, western European Christians were too absorbed in their own internal conflicts to be greatly disturbed. When they defeated the Visigothic rulers of Spain in 711 and pushed the Christians up into the mountains in the north, they became a more immediate problem. When they began to raid the Mediterranean coast of the Frankish kingdom and to extend their power north of the Pyrenees, Charles Martel, the Frankish ruler, collected his forces south of the Loire and in 732 defeated a Muslim band so decisively that they retreated. Nonetheless, Muslims continued to raid the Frankish seacoast on the Mediterranean. To stop these raids and to protect his frontier, Charlemagne carried the war beyond the Pyrenees to the south.

From Charlemagne's time to the beginning of the eleventh century, relations between the Muslims and European Christians were mainly commercial and intellectual. There developed a flourishing trade in slaves and northern products such as honey, amber, and furs. Muslims wanted slaves. Christian teaching forbade Christians to enslave other Christians, but there were always Finns, Slavs, and other pagan peoples to be captured, and commerce with Islam was profitable. Some of this traffic went down through central Europe to the Muslim world through the channels of Byzantine trade. Some of it went through Spain. A great center of pilgrimage for Christians was St. James of Compostella in Muslim Spanish Galicia. Commercial contacts and pilgrimage led to awareness of Muslim learning, not to mention Muslim wealth and luxury. The Muslims had absorbed Greek learning as well as lore from Persia and India. They had produced a rich synthesis of their own. Some northerners, like Gerbert of Aurillac, who died Pope Sylvester II in 1103, did try to gain some knowledge from the Muslims, particularly of science. Cordova and Toledo in Spain in the tenth century and Sicily in the eleventh century could have been centers for transmission of Muslim culture to the West. But Western Christians did not take advantage of these offerings, and they remained ignorant and indifferent with respect to Islam, the Muslim religion, and Muslim culture in general. In the *Song of Roland,* for example, the Muslims are credited with a trinity of pagan deities,—Tervagan, Mahomet, and Apollo—"gods of stone," whose idols they carry with them to war. Christians preferred not to know of a rival and more rigorous monotheism. Muslims could be credited with chivalry, as they often are in the literature of the twelfth and thirteenth centuries, but they could not be credited with acceptable religious ideas. For their part, the Muslims, before the Crusades, generally extended courteous hospitality to Christian pilgrims visiting the holy places in their realm. To them the Europeans from the West seemed crude and barbaric compared to themselves. They did not, any more than Greek Christians, think that Latin Christians held the future in their hands.

Beginning of the Crusades

The causes of the long war between Western Christians and the Muslims are many and difficult to assess. In Spain the intensive phase of the Reconquista, which began in the eleventh century, was mainly a matter of seizing opportunity. The caliphate of Cordova, which had included all of Muslim Spain since the eighth century, began to break up into small states warring with one another. In Sicily and southern Italy Norman adventurers who had passed through on pilgrimage to the Holy Land saw an opportunity to create a unified Christian state from the remnants of Byzantine power there and from Muslim Sicily. The main factor in bringing about the Crusades (defined narrowly as the long series of expeditions—roughly 1100–1300 —for the conquest and defense of the Holy Land), was the weakness of the eastern section of the Empire in relation to the Seljuk Turks. The Byzantines had just endured a "time of troubles" in which the succession had been in dispute and the state system had collapsed. Alexius' appeal to the West acknowledged the weakness. Ecclesiastical leaders in western Europe had long been troubled about internecine war among Christian nobles and knights. Gregory VII had wanted to divert this energy to war against the "infidel," but he had had neither the time nor the resources to spare for the task. Alexius' appeal in 1095 seemed to offer a great opportunity. Urban II met with leaders among the French nobility at Clermont and delivered a rousing call. This is in part what he said:

> Frenchmen! You who come from across the Alps; you who have been singled out by God and who are loved by Him—as is shown by your many accomplishments; you who are set apart from all other peoples by the location of your country, by your Catholic faith, and by the honor of the Holy Church; we address these words, this sermon to you! . . .
>
> Distressing news has come to us (as has often happened) from the region in Jerusalem and from the city of Constantinople; news that the people of the Persian kingdom, an alien people, a race completely foreign to God . . . has invaded Christian territory and has invaded this territory with pillage, fire, and the sword. The Persians have taken some of these Christians as captives to their own country; they have destroyed others with cruel tortures. They have completely destroyed some of God's churches and have converted others to the uses of their own cult. They ruin the altars with filth and defilement. They circumcize Christians and smear the blood from the circumcision over the altars or throw it in the baptismal fonts. They are pleased to kill others by cutting open their bellies, extracting the ends of their intestines, and tying it to a stake. . . .[5]

And so on with more atrocities listed including the "shocking rape of women." No doubt atrocities did occur. They do constantly in human affairs, especially in the midst of wars. Urban II was less concerned to establish the truth about the Seljuks (Persians, he calls them) than to rouse the Franks. A skilled propagandist, he told them that they fought each other because their land was poor. Let them just put aside their local hatreds and conflicts and go to the Holy Land (as the Scriptures said, the land flowed with milk and honey) to put down the infidels who threatened their brethren and the holy places of Christendom. Thus war to seize the land from the infidel became a "good thing."

The Crusaders surprised themselves and others by winning, by medieval standards, a quick initial victory. Despite the disastrous failure of a people's Crusade led by Peter the Hermit, the diversion of a number of German bands to the more immediate rewards of Jew-killing in Germany, and the difficulties the Frankish lords encountered in their relations with Byzantine Emperor Alexius, a western army entered Jerusalem on July 15, 1099. A blood bath ensued with the Crusaders cutting down all before them. A few Muslims escaped by buying their safe exit from the city. The Jews took refuge in their chief synagogue and were all burnt within it. Muslims were killed as long as the blood lust lasted. In the words of a Christian witness:

> Our men followed [the city's defenders], killing and beheading them all the way to the Temple of Solomon. There was such slaughter there that our men waded in blood up to their ankles. . . . Soon our men were running all around the city, seizing gold and silver, horses and mules, and houses filled with all kinds of goods. Rejoicing and weeping for joy, our people came to the sepulcher of Jesus our Savior to worship and pay their debt. . . . Our men then took counsel and decided that everyone should pray and give alms so that God might choose for them whomever he pleased to rule over the others and govern the city. . . . The living Saracens dragged the dead outside the gates and made heaps of them as large as houses. No one ever saw or heard of such a slaughter of pagan peoples, for funeral pyres were formed of them like pyramids and no one knows their number save God alone.[6]

The massacre impressed the world. Many even among the Christians who participated were sickened and shamed by the brutality. When more humane and sane counsels did prevail in Christian circles, the Muslims remained justifiably distrustful and suspicious. Having destroyed Muslim power, the Crusaders had to set up a state. They took counsel as to who should be chosen to rule in the Holy Land. After much intrigue, Godfrey of Bouillon, Duke of Lower Lorraine, was offered the title of king. He chose instead to be called the Defender of the Holy Sepulcher, saying that he could not wear a crown of gold in the city where his Savior had worn a crown of thorns.

The Crusading Movement

This was the catastrophic beginning of the long series of wars that marked the Crusade period. It does not much matter that the families of Outremer, as the permanent settlers from the West in the Holy Land were called, learned of necessity a great deal about Islamic material culture. The Holy Land did not flow with milk and honey and could not be made to support the Latin principalities there without commerce. Westerners had to learn from the Muslims how to live in a climate different from that of England or northern France. Commerce with the enemy and adoption of Islamic foods, clothes, sanitary precautions as well as marriage with Muslim wives brought on the Latin Christians of Outremer charges of betrayal of the Christian cause. Individual friendships between Muslims and Christians did develop, but these had no effect on the precarious nature of Christian rule in the land. Rivalries existed among the rulers of the Crusader states, and distrust between them and new arrivals was commonplace. Thus unity against the enemy was difficult to maintain. In 1154 Damascus fell to Nureddin, the Seljuk ruler of Mesopotamia. In 1187 Saladin, who had overthrown the Fatimid caliphate in Egypt, expanded his power into Palestine and seized Jerusalem. The Crusaders were left holding only a narrow strip of coastal plain from Acre to Antioch. This remnant of the Latin kingdom they lost in the course of the next century. In 1291, when Acre fell, Christian rule in the Holy Land ceased to be a matter of practical politics. There were Crusades after 1300, but having no secure base from which to operate, they had no chance of success.

Christendom and Islamic Culture

Rather curiously it was during the twelfth century, in which the Christians were most actively engaged in war against the Muslims, that Islamic philosophy and religion attracted the most intelligent attention in the West. This was an effect not of direct exchange between Crusaders or people of Outremer and Muslims so much as of traditions of scholarship already established or of objective reflection on events by some of the wiser men of the West. Peter the Venerable, abbot of Cluny, hired an English scholar to translate the Koran into Latin. This project marks the climax of fifty years or so of more rational interest in Islam. Peter's aim was neither understanding nor toleration of Islam. It was conversion:

> I attack you, not as some of us often do by arms, but by words; not by force, but by reason; not in hatred, but in love. I love you; loving you, I write to you; writing to you, I invite you to salvation.[7]

But the Muslims never heard this voice of love, if it was indeed love, and it is doubtful how seriously they could have taken it if they had. The year after the Latin version of the Koran was finished (1143), they captured Edessa. St. Bernard of Clairvaux, who advocated a more military policy in dealing with the Muslim menace, organized the Second Crusade, a bigger and better-organized expedition than the first. Two kings led this Crusade: Louis VII of France and Conrad III of Germany. Eleanor of Aquitaine (wife of Louis VII, who later divorced her) went along for the "ride," dressed with her attendant ladies in the costume of Amazon princesses. The result was a fiasco of the first magnitude, one from which the Muslims derived the encouragement to go forward to throw the Westerners out. But this did not deter scholars from the West in their pursuit of Muslim scholarship. A century later, after the Fourth and Fifth Crusades had also failed, Avicenna's and Averroës' philosophical concepts were still debated at the University of Paris, and the Muslim translations of Aristotle's scientific works became a subject of avid study throughout the West.

The Mongol Invasions

The Mongols resisted Christian efforts at conversion as successfully as the Arabs, Turks and other Muslims. They attacked Europe and the Middle East in the thirteenth century. The Mongols descended from the steppe regions in the upper Amur valley, swept across northern China, central Asia, and the Middle East, and conquered between 1205 and 1258 the largest territorial empire that has existed in the world's history. Genghis Khan (title meaning ruler of the world), the orphaned son of one of the Mongol tribal chieftains, began the Mongol expansion by uniting the tribes of the steppes. By the time he died in 1227, he had conquered much of north China and all of central Asia as far as the Caspian Sea. Under his sons and grandsons, the Mongols conquered south China, Russia, Mesopotamia, and north Syria. They were stopped at the borders of Sinai by the Muslim rulers of Egypt. Near Vienna in Austria and at Spalato on the Adriatic Sea they stopped only because Ogodai, son of Genghis, died in far-off Mongolia. Batu, grandson of Genghis, commander of the forces in Europe, returned to Mongolia for the election of his uncle's successor.

When Genghis Khan first appeared on the frontiers of Islam, the Christians had welcomed him as an instrument of God and an ally in their fight against the infidel. Pope Honorius wrote to the archbishop of Trier in 1221:

King David, vulgarly called Prester John, a Catholic and god-fearing man, has entered Persia with a powerful army, has defeated the Sultan of Persia in a pitched battle, has penetrated twenty days' march into his kingdom and has occupied it. He holds therein many cities and castles. His army is only ten days' march from Baghdad, a great and famous city, and special seat of the Caliph, whom the Saracens call their chief priest and bishop. The fear of these events has caused the Sultan of Aleppo, brother of the Sultans of Damascus and Cairo, to turn his arms, with which he was preparing to attack the Christian army at Damietta, against this king. Our legate, moreover, has sent messengers to the Georgians, themselves Catholic men and powerful in arms, asking and beseeching them to make war on the Saracen on their side. Whence we hope that, if our army at Damietta has the help which it hopes for this summer, it will with God's help easily occupy the land of Egypt, while the forces of the Saracens, which had been gathered from all parts to defend it, are dispersed to defend the frontiers of their land.[8]

King David, alias Prester John, was a legendary ruler of a Christian state in Asia, a distorted eponymous image, perhaps, of Nestorian Christians who had taken refuge there after their heretical views on the nature of Christ had been condemned by a fifth-century council of bishops. About Genghis Khan, the pope was misinformed. The great khan was an unregenerate pagan, although he was undoubtedly familiar with Christian teachings. The Uighurs and Kereits, whom he had conquered early in his career, were Nestorians. He had married a niece of the Christian Ong Khan of the Kereits. At his court were representatives of all major religions—Christians, Muslims, Buddhists, Taoists. His policy was one of toleration but at the same time of independence. His son and grandsons were converted, some to Islam, some to Buddhism, and some to Nestorian Christianity. None accepted Western Christianity in spite of missions from the pope and western kings to convert them.

The order and stability that the Mongols established in Asia and maintained for a hundred years (*ca.* 1250–1350) made possible a more extensive interchange of East and West than had been possible for centuries. But first came the "terror." Batu, grandson of Genghis, leader of the Golden Horde, crossed the Volga River in 1237 and swept across the steppes of Russia into central Europe, winning field battles by sheer mobility and spreading terror by destroying cities and their inhabitants. In 1241 the Mongols withdrew to the Volga basin, and whether because of internal rivalries among the descendants of Genghis or because of awareness of the problems of holding Europe once conquered, they did not again return to the West. Batu and his descendants continued to levy tribute from the Russians for several centuries; they maintained friendly relations with traders and missionaries from the West. Dawning recognition of the vast numbers of non-Christians beyond the frontiers of Europe led Pope Innocent IV to send a mission to the Mongolian court at Karakorum in 1245. Three Franciscan friars led by John of Plano Carpini, a fat and fearless Italian of sixty-five, traveled across Poland, the steppes of Russia, and on through the mountains of central Asia to the distant Mongolian capital on the Orkhon River to deliver the pope's letters. Innocent addressed the Mongol ruler in these terms:

> We, therefore, following the example of the King of Peace, and desiring that all men should live united in concord in the fear of God, do admonish, beg and earnestly beseech all of you that for the future you desist entirely from assaults of this kind and especially from the persecution of Christians, and that after so many and such grievous offences you conciliate by a fitting penance and the wrath of Divine Majesty, which without doubt you have seriously aroused by such provocation. . . .[9]

What Kuyuk, the newly elected successor to Genghis Khan, made of this appeal is not known, but he did give the friars safe conduct to pass along the Mongol roads and a letter addressed to the pope. When they got back to Kiev two years after the start of their mission, and "when the inhabitants of Kiev became aware of our arrival, they all came to meet us rejoicing and they congratulated us as if we were risen from the dead."[10] By the time they reached Rome, they had completed a round trip of some 8,000 miles, but neither they nor subsequent missions sent by Louis IX of France or the pope convinced the Mongol khans to become Catholic Christians or to assist the West either in the conversion or destruction of Islam. Just after the death of Khublai Khan, Mongol emperor of China (1260–1294), and the greatest of Genghis Khan's descendants, John of Montecorvino, a second Italian Franciscan missionary, was permitted to build a Catholic church in Peking and to baptize 6,000 converts. Little is known about these converts.

The trade contacts established with the East were probably more directly profitable to the West. The main record about the East in this period from the West's viewpoint is that left by Marco Polo, the great Venetian traveler of the thirteenth century. His father and uncle had gone to the court of Khublai Khan in 1260 and returned in 1269 with a letter requesting the pope to send Christian scholars and technicians. The Polos returned to the East in 1270 without the scholars and technicians but, this time, taking young Marco, son of Niccolo, with them. Marco joined the Khan's civil service and saw a great part of the East. He describes it in one of the world's great travel books. The Polos did not return to Venice until 1295. Even before the Mongol empire broke up into rival khanates, land routes to the East were unduly expensive for Western merchants. It was not until western Europeans discovered sea routes that trade with the Far East became really profitable.

Conclusion

The Crusades illustrate both the weaknesses and the strengths of western Europe in coming to terms with itself and the rest of the world. The Westerners of the period were ignorant; they did not know enough about their Christian and non-Christian neighbors to establish any sort of Christian concord, even if such concord had been acceptable from alien points of view. They failed in both their immediate and their ultimate objectives in relation to the Muslims. The infidels were neither conquered nor converted to Christianity. The Latin Christians were neither able to maintain their hold on the Holy

Land nor to take over permanently the Byzantine Empire. They greatly weakened the latter as a defense against invasion from the East. On the other hand, the Crusades did stimulate trade with the Eastern Mediterranean and bring the West into more direct contact with the more distant parts of Asia. They did give to the West the intellectual curiosity, the economic demands, and the missionary aspirations that made them seek and find ocean routes to the East when the land routes were finally cut off by the Ottoman Turks.

IX

Change in the Later
Middle Ages

Where to end the Middle Ages is a far more difficult problem than where to begin them. History is a continuum. Birth and death of individuals are real and can be established by medical science. Birth and death as applied to civilization are metaphors. No civilization has ever died at any given point of time that could be precisely established by a great coroner-historian. Yet historians are always looking for ways of dividing past time into manageable portions. The beginning of the Middle Ages is relatively easy. New peoples had entered the west European part of the Roman Empire in the fifth century bringing with them important new cultural elements to mix with the Greco-Roman traditions. These "aliens" had clearly taken over control by 800. No one would try to argue that the civilization of western Europe in 800 was still Greco-Roman, as it had been in the fourth century. Charlemagne's coronation as emperor in the West in 800 merely makes real for us the great power of the Roman imperial tradition. Between 1300 and 1500 no new cultural elements of importance were mixed in. Some had been picked up and assimilated by Europeans in their contacts with a wider world.

The Concept of a Renaissance in European History

Fourteenth- and fifteenth-century Italians had a sense of turning their backs on a dark and superstitious past, recovering their ties with the ancient Mediterranean world, and forging ahead in a great new adventure of the mind and spirit. The concept of a "Renaissance" in Europe's history beginning in Italy about 1300 and spreading northward to reach northern France, the Netherlands, and England toward the end of the fifteenth century has had a long vogue in textbooks and seems likely to survive all efforts at revision. A nineteenth-century historian, Jacob Burckhardt, established a pattern of thought about the matter that is still compelling:

> In the Middle Ages both sides of human consciousness—that which was turned within as that which was turned without—lay dreaming or half awake beneath a common veil. The veil was woven of faith, illusion, and childish prepossession through which the world and history were seen clad in strange hues. Man was conscious of himself only as a member of a race, people, party, family, or corporation—only through some general category. In Italy this veil first melted into air; an *objective* treatment and consideration of the State and of all the things of this world became possible. The *subjective* side at the same time asserted itself with corresponding emphasis; man became a spiritual *individual,* and recognized himself as such.[1]

The political climate of Italy, Burckhardt says, was the chief factor in making possible this emergence of the individual, of the modern state, of skepticism, and of scientific curiosity. The revival of antiquity under the patronage of Italian rulers, the emergence of a humanist outlook, a more secular spirit, and a greater naturalism in arts made the Italian Quattrocento (the 1400s) comparable in its brilliance to Periclean Athens or Cicero's Rome.

Scholars immersed in the Middle Ages have always had difficulty in accepting this interpretation. Some have argued that, if there was a Renaissance, it must be considered to have come earlier when western Europe had first become more aware and more critical of its heritage from antiquity. Moreover, it is hard for a medievalist to think of Gregory VII, Henry IV of Germany, Abelard, or St. Bernard, Henry II, Eleanor of Aquitaine, or Thomas Becket as persons who had no individuality or to evaluate them as less spiritual individuals than Lorenzo dei Medici, Pico della Mirandola, Savonarola, or Michelangelo, to name just a few. It is hard also to overlook the medieval beginnings of naturalism and humanism in art, the emergent scientific curiosity, the playful irony, the cutting satire or passionate emotion of vernacular poetry. On the other hand, it is equally difficult to accept a current revision concerning the fourteenth and fifteenth centuries in which they are presumed to be centuries of decline and death, a time in which Europe lost its bearings and fell into chaos. In some interpretations this thesis has been carried so far as to speak in Freudian terms of a "death wish" and an ensuing "self-destruction" of the West.

The student should not be overimpressed by any of the more extreme points of view. In all important aspects of life in the West there was more continuity than discontinuity. The universal church continued to exist beyond 1500, and religion continued to be a dominant influence in European life, one important enough to die for in the religious wars of the sixteenth and seventeenth centuries. Philosophical and theological conflict continued in the schools and universities and about the same fundamental questions that had agitated the twelfth-century scholars. Sculpture and painting became more naturalistic and realistic following the tendencies established in the twelfth and thirteenth centuries. They were still mainly enlisted in the beautification of churches, tombs, psalters and other religious books, although public buildings and secular books were created in increasing numbers. In northern Europe Gothic architects continued to explore the possibilities of the new forms they had created. National monarchies in France, England, and Spain were the outgrowth of older feudal monarchies. Kings began to encourage and exploit national feeling as a means of gaining support for their policies; yet Edward III of England (1327–1377) and John II of France (1350–1364) were as feudal in their outlook as their predecessors a century earlier. The Hundred Years War, in its beginnings was in all essentials simply a continuation of earlier feudal warfare between the kings of France and England begun when the dukes of Normandy, having conquered England in 1066, became rivals to the French kings for allegiance of continental vassals.

The class structure remained what it had been in earlier centuries although there were some changes in economic organization and the wealthy townsmen became increasingly important. The feudal aristocracy continued to dominate society in spite of the fact that their direct power to rule had been much reduced by the growing strength of national monarchies. Commercial oligarchies continued to rule the towns and cities despite uprisings among the poorer townsmen. And, although the peasants won concessions for themselves, there was no profound reorganization of the agricultural life of western Europe or change in the hierarchical order of society.

Signs of Change

However, there were changes, and they were important, although not cataclysmic, enough to effect a break in continuity. Although religion remained dominant and the universal church survived, the authority of the ecclesiastical hierarchy diminished. New heresies disturbed the precarious unity won by the papal inquisition of the thirteenth century. Laymen became not necessarily less religious, but more independent of the Church hierarchy in seeking their salvation. Mystics challenged the Church widely, not by rebelling against it but by withdrawing into a spiritual communion with God in which they were not easily accessible to discipline. Criticism of the hierarchy became sharper and more satirical. Although the Crusades continued, they became increasingly defensive in character. No one except a few idealists thought it possible to win back the Holy Land or convert the Muslims to Christianity. The more immediate problem was to save western Europe from the Turks, and the burden of this task fell mainly on the kings of Hungary and Germany.

National monarchs began to levy taxes on all their subjects and to enlist laymen of all classes in their service. In the city-states of northern Italy despots took over the state power and used it without reference to medieval rules of morality. Feudalism changed its character markedly. Feudal nobles lost their power of direct government of vassals and peasants. They tried to compensate by exercising more power in relation to royal governments and by a more ostentatious display of the trappings of chivalry. Merchant oligarchies had to fight to maintain their dominant position in the towns against the demands of the poorer townsmen. Peasants began to ask for a greater share in the product of the land and to revolt against the vandalism and destructiveness that they had suffered in feudal warfare. They found some sympathy among the clergy and the poets. Laymen began to vie with the clergy in liberal education and in technical knowledge of the law. Seamen and cartographers became immersed in the unexplored mysteries of the Atlantic Ocean and began to amass the knowledge that ultimately led to the discoveries of the Portuguese seamen and of Columbus at the end of the fifteenth century.

In a brief book like this one in which the author is attempting only to evoke for the student a human society that historians have labeled "medieval," it is not possible to relate in detail the narrative history of the changes of the fourteenth and fifteenth centuries and to discuss whether they are termed a Renaissance or a decline or death of the Middle Ages. Only certain general points can be made. We shall now turn to these.

Demographic Tendencies

The rate of increase of the population of Europe, high between 1100 and 1300, began to decline at the end of the thirteenth century, and continued to fall until about the middle of the fifteenth century. Exact chronology and statistics are difficult to establish. Censuses of population were not taken regularly by medieval governments. Such statistics as do survive—tax records, estate records, lists of citizens of towns, and the like—do not furnish all the necessary evidence, such as the average size of families among the different classes, average life expectancy, and so on. War, famine, and plague appear to be the main factors in causing the decline. Declining productivity of agriculture had, before the end of the thirteenth century, begun to put a strain on the food supply and can be considered a contributing factor in the population decrease. Between 1315 and 1317 terrible floods occurred throughout western Europe. Crops were destroyed and people starved.

The Black Death, which struck Europe in 1347, entering along the trade routes from the East, was a far more severe calamity. There was an estimated 30 to 50 percent mortality rate, although the incidence of the plague was much heavier in some places and lighter in others. The bubonic form of the plague was carried by rats and struck where they congregated, more heavily in the overcrowded towns than in the countryside, more heavily also in the vermin-infested homes of the poor than in the castles and palaces of the rich. The pneumonic and more deadly form of the plague struck wherever a human carrier passed on the contagion. Governmental authorities were helpless in dealing with the problem in spite of attempts at quarantine. Few persons understood the plague medically. Some explained it as a judgment of God, others as the work of witches or of Jews who had poisoned the wells. A brilliant Italian writer, Boccaccio, introduced a collection of stories called *The Decameron* with the following description of the incidence of the plague in Florence:

> In the year then of our Lord 1348, there happened at Florence, the finest city in all Italy, a most terrible plague; which, whether owing to the influence of the planets, or that it was sent from God as a just punishment for our sins, had broken out some years before in the Levant, and after passing from place to place, and making incredible havoc all the way, had now reached the west. There, in spite of all the means that art and human foresight could suggest, such as keeping the city clear from filth, the exclusion of all suspected persons, and the publication of copious instructions for the preservation of health; and notwithstanding manifold humble sup-

plications offered to God in processions and otherwise; it began to show itself in the spring of the aforesaid year, in a sad and wonderful manner. Unlike what had been seen in the east, where bleeding from the nose is the fatal prognostic, here there appeared certain tumours in the groin or under the armpits, some as big as a small apple, others as an egg. . . . To the cure of this malady, neither medical knowledge nor the power of drugs was of any effect; whether because the disease was in its own nature mortal, or that the physicians (the number of whom, taking quacks and women pretenders into the account, was grown very great), could form no just idea of the cause, nor consequently devise a true method of cure; whichever was the reason, few escaped; but nearly all died the third day from the first appearance of the symptoms. What gave the more virulence to this plague was that, by being communicated from the sick to the hale, it spread daily, like fire when it comes in contact with large masses of combustibles.[2]

Men's reactions were various, Boccaccio says. Some withdrew into retreats where they lived soberly; others tried to pack their lives full of extravagant sensual pleasures. Whatever men did, the most important effect of the plague, in Boccaccio's opinion, was that men became selfish, callous, and indifferent toward one another.

Thus divided as they were in their views, neither did all die, nor all escape; but falling sick indifferently, as well those of one as of another opinion, they who first set the example by forsaking others now languished themselves without pity. I pass over the little regard that citizens and relations showed to each other, for their terror was such that a brother even fled from his brother, a wife from her husband, and, what is more uncommon, a parent from his own child. Hence, numbers that fell sick could have no help but what the charity of friends, who were very few, or the avarice of servants supplied. . . .[3]

Regardless of the more reliable conclusions that statisticians may eventually be able to establish about effects on the population, Boccaccio is surely right that the plague's most devastating effect was the undermining of people's faith in one another. Priests were reported to have refused the last rites, doctors to have refused their services, neighbors to have fattened on the misfortunes of neighbors. God, so far as anyone could see,

poured his wrath upon the just and the unjust, inflicting indiscriminately on all mankind punishment for their sins.

Warfare, too, took its toll in terms of population and productivity. The Hundred Years War between the English and
French kings was destructive to the agriculture of northern
France and to the cloth industry in Flanders. Wars over the
succession in Germany, wars among and within the city-states
of Italy, religious wars in Bohemia, all these devastated and
taxed resources of manpower and produce. The wars against
the Muslims in Spain and on the eastern frontier continued
endlessly. Wars cost increasingly more money as armies
became paid armies, and kings had to demand more and more
from their subjects in taxation.

Changing Feudalism

The "art" of war itself changed greatly in the later Middle
Ages, and feudal relationships changed responsively. Edward
III's armies for the French war fought on foot as English
armies had learned to do in the Welsh and Scottish wars of
Edward's grandfather. They depended heavily on bowmen and
men-at-arms as well as on knights. The men were paid from
funds raised by taxes, and they expected rewards in plunder.
Increasingly, on the French as well as the English side, men
were hired in companies led by a captain, who had contracted
with the king for their services. For example, a Richard Hastings received a receipt on April 12, 1419, for the employ of his
company in these terms:

> This indenture made on the xii day of April in the seventh year
> of our lord King Henry the fifth since the conquest witnesses that
> Richard Hastings, Knight, received from John Rochevale, war treas-
> urer of our said lord [king] xlii *li.* ix *s.* iii *d. ob.* [forty-two pounds,
> nine shillings, four pence and a farthing] for the wages and rewards
> of himself, five men-at-arms, and eighteen archers for a half quarter
> of a year. In witness of which fact the aforesaid parties have affixed
> their seals the said day and year.[4]

Feudal forms were followed in the agreements between war leaders and captains, but vassals now owed their own service with that of their retainers for a specified period in return for an agreed upon annual sum of money instead of land. This substitution of the money fee for the landed fief, itself resulting from the increasing strength of royal government, had, in turn, an impact on government. In feudal states nobles and knights had shared with kings the powers of government. They had administered justice and protection to their own vassals and to the peasants living on their lands. By the late Middle Ages royal governments had taken over most of these powers and functions, leaving to the feudal class power only to exploit the peasantry and to vie with one another for social and political prestige. The new money feudalism gave those who seized the opportunities the wherewithal to build up followings of retainers paid to serve them, wearing their badges or livery, and advertising their power and glory. These armed retainers could be used to intimidate the king's officers, attack their rivals' houses, families, and estates, and abuse the peasants. Where royal government was weak, as it was in France in the early fifteenth century under a mad old suffering king, or in England under that same king's grandson, the result was chaotic civil war on the upper level of society and danger for those below. The fact that new men rose into the aristocracy through plunder and prowess in war did not help matters. The newcomers brought with them more competitive energy than enlightened conformity to codes of chivalry.

As for chivalry, it reached heights of exaltation that took little note of men maimed by cannon fire, or dead of dysentery, or dead from the treacheries and cruelties of the men who professed the code. Chastellain may say that:

> Honour summons every noble nature
> To love all that is noble in his being
> Nobility also adds its rectitude[5]

Sir Thomas Malory may contend that the knight errant was courteous as well as valiant and that he cared for the poor and the weak as well as the rich and the strong. But this was not the case. War was perhaps as "joyous" a thing as it has ever been, to borrow the word of a medieval observer, in this time just before firearms began to be effective weapons, but its pleasures must have been reserved to the few who fought in successful armies or were of sufficient rank so that captors would find it more profitable to demand ransom than to kill. War offered opportunity for the ambitious. A man of prowess might rise to great fame and wealth though he was of humble origin.

As the war between the English and the French wore on to its weary close, men became more desperate and more cruel. Mercenary companies devastated large parts of France and were scarcely distinguishable in their treatment of noncombatants from the numerous bands of brigands who attacked undefended villages and towns as well as travelers on the roads. The general public reveled in spectacles of cruelty. The people of Mons, for example, bought a brigand for the pleasure of seeing him publicly quartered. Torture was publicly inflicted in the center of the Bruges marketplace on magistrates suspected of treason so that the citizens might "feast" on their sufferings. When the victims begged for the release of death, they were refused in order that the people's pleasure might be prolonged. Louis XI of France (1461–1483) shut his enemies in undersized cages in order to enjoy the sight of their sufferings. The Wars of the Roses, the internal wars that followed England's defeat in the war with France, were filled with incidents of bloodthirsty cruelty.

Italy, too, had its floating population of outlaws and was ruled by despots who could indulge their sensual enjoyment of suffering. A robber chief refused a papal offer of pardon on the ground that brigandage offered greater rewards and more security than any peaceful trade he might adopt. Condemned murderers were enlisted in the wars of city-state against city-state. Giovanni Maria Visconti, ruler of Milan (1403–1412), threw his enemies to his hunting dogs for the pleasure of watching their dismemberment. Alexander VI, the Borgia pope (1492–1503) and his son, Cesar, established an unparalleled reputation for sensuality and assassination.

Was this medieval or modern cruelty? It is hard to say without some better method than we have at present for distinguishing between medieval and modern. The point that many historians have made is that the times were "out of joint," that the harmony of the High Middle Ages had broken down. If this proposition is accepted, it should be recalled that the old harmony had never been the triumphant harmony of a medieval cathedral. Popes had been at loggerheads with emperors; English kings had fought French kings, Scottish kings, and Welsh princes; Catholic Crusaders had massacred Albigensians and Jews and had fought the infidel. What was new was perhaps a breakdown of trust between the established orders in a hierarchical society.

Peasant Uprisings

Most disturbing to the landowners of the period were peasant uprisings. Revolts of serious and frightening dimensions occurred in Flanders, France, and England in the fourteenth century and in central and eastern Europe in the fifteenth and sixteenth. The Black Death and Hundred Years War were catalysts of these uprisings in western Europe. The *Jacquerie* in northern France, in 1358, was a reaction of peasant rage against the depredations of English armies and French armed companies, against royal tax collectors, and against nobles demanding money to help pay their ransom from English captors after the English victory at Poitiers. The peasants pillaged castles and murdered their inhabitants. They were soon quelled, however. They had little chance against armed professional soldiers.

In England in 1381 the peasants of southeast England revolted in outraged frustration at practices and policies of the ruling classes that kept them from making the most of their opportunities after the Black Death. The plague had carried off a third to a half of the labor force. Enterprising landlords anxious to fill vacant holdings and to get wage labor for the demesne offered better terms and higher wages. More conservative landlords tried to reintroduce old labor services. The government, like other European governments in response to the same developments, adopted maximum wage legislation (the Statute of Laborers) aimed at keeping wages down to pre-plague levels. Efforts to enforce the Statute of Laborers failed but aggravated peasant grievances. When the government in 1377 and subsequent years tried to substitute a broad-based poll tax for the subsidies levied on property that had up to this time constituted the main source of extraordinary royal revenue, the peasants began to converge on London. Poor preachers had stirred the peasants to demand their rights. The following is from a sermon of John Ball, a Kentish preacher:

> Good people, things cannot go well in England, nor will they, until all goods shall be in common and when there shall be neither villeins nor gentles, but we all shall be one. Why should he, whom we call lord, be a greater master than us? . . . They have ease and beautiful manors, and we have hardship and work, and the rain and wind in the fields; and it is through us and our labour that they have the wherewithal to maintain their estate.[6]

The idea that all men were equal was not new in medieval thought. Medieval philosophers and poets had long held this view. What was new was that the peasants should hold it and that Wat Tyler, leader of the Kentish peasants, should shake King Richard's hand and demand of him that he give the peasants a charter of freedom under which all men save the king should be "free and of one condition" and the peasants should hold their land at a moderate rent.

This peasant revolt was put down too, but changing economic conditions in western Europe led to changed relationships between landlords and peasants. The changes were markedly different in different regions of Europe and did not everywhere mean improvement in the lot of the peasantry. In France and England demesne lands were leased widely to the peasants, and the landlords became *rentiers*. In England there was some conversion of arable land to pasture in response to the expanding demand for wool, but this "enclosure" movement did not gain much headway until the last quarter of the fifteenth century. In Spain the peasants were either subjected to more intensified labor service or were driven off the land, which was then converted to vast sheep pastures. In eastern Europe the seignorial system became more thoroughly entrenched than it had been in the days of the expanding frontier. Land in western Europe changed hands more rapidly in the late Middle Ages than earlier, and some enterprising new landlords managed to extract more profit from the soil than their predecessors. In general, however, the trend seems to have been toward declining productivity and depression. Peasant agriculture produced less for the market though it may conceivably have produced more for the peasants' stomachs.

Industry and Commerce: Worker Revolts

Europe's commerce and industry also went through a period of decline and depression resulting in part from declining population and production. Trade with the Far East, safe during the great period of the Mongol empire, became more difficult. Tamerlane carved out an ephemeral empire in India, Persia, and Mesopotamia in the latter part of the fourteenth century but showed no capacity for peaceful rule. His empire collapsed with his death in 1402. The Ottoman Turks expanded at the expense of the Byzantine Empire, already weakened by its conquest and occupation by the Crusaders. Venice and Genoa were weakened by their long contest with one another for dominance of the Eastern trade. When Constantinople fell to the Ottoman Turks in 1453, the centers of trade had already begun to shift westward. Sea routes to northern Europe had been opened up as Muslim power in Spain receded and as the old land routes through Champagne and Gascony became more difficult as the result of restrictive policies of the French kings and the war with England. Spanish Catalonia began to challenge Italian dominance of Mediterranean trade and to share in the trade with the north. Finally, by the second half of the fifteenth century, Portugal and Spain with the help of Genoese seamen and their maps and charts were beginning to explore the possibility of a westward all-sea route to the East.

Northern merchants—first the Germans, then the English—began to build up their strength at the expense of the Italians. Northern commerce was increasingly controlled by groups of merchants organized cooperatively in large companies. In England the Merchants of the Staple won a monopoly of the wool trade with the Netherlands in return for loans and other facilities to Edward III for the prosecution of the war in France. Heavy export duties, amounting to as much as 33 percent, had been granted by the wool merchants in the reign of Edward I (1275–1303) in return for protection and privilege. When in need of quick cash, he and his successors made a practice of borrowing on the expectations of these returns. In the fifteenth century the Merchant Adventurers were granted a comparable monopoly of the export trade in woolen cloth and imports of wine and other continental products. These companies received their privileges under royal charters and were national in scope, in contrast to the older local merchant gilds. The great German trading towns of the North Sea and Baltic coastal region organized the Hanseatic League and, under the leadership of Lubeck in 1370, won from the Danish king in the Treaty of Stralsund control of the "Sound," that is, the passage between Denmark and Sweden. They built up a network of routes through central Germany down into the Mediterranean. The treaty marked the culmination of a century of growth in the economic and political power of the League, a power that was to remain great throughout the rest of the medieval period.

Industrial growth was checked almost everywhere in the year immediately following the Black Death, and the towns of northern Italy, of northern France, and of Flanders suffered serious decline. Internal conflict within the towns and wars were additional important factors. Conflict in Italy between the *populo grasso* and the *populo minuto,* in the north between the *majores* and the *minores,* or the *grands* and the *petits,* broke out into open hostility and violence. Emperors, kings of England and France, dukes of Burgundy and Brabant, and counts of Flanders manipulated these conflicts in their own interest and the complexities were manifold. At the same time as the internal conflicts, an industrial revolution was underway, resulting from the application of water power to the fulling of cloth. In response to this, centers of the cloth industry shifted to rural regions that had swift running streams to run the mills. In England the villages of the West Riding in Yorkshire and the Cotswold Hills replaced the older cloth-producing centers. Flanders, a flat country in which water mills were impractical and also a country devastated by war and torn by internal conflict, lost out in the competition. The rest of the Netherlands began to steal away both her industry and her commerce. The Italian towns, especially Florence, recovered and survived for a while by specializing in the finishing of cloth. But, by the fifteenth century, the big Italian fortunes had been made and were being spent in conspicuous consumption on the works of Renaissance sculptors, painters, architects, poets, and philosophers—not on new capitalist enterprise. England showed the most marked signs of industrial growth in this period. By the fourteenth century she had begun to build up a substantial native cloth industry that consumed a considerable part of her large output of wool. Growth was by spurts and starts in the uncertain time after the great plague of 1347–1349, slower but steadier in the fifteenth century. By 1500 woolen cloths were England's largest export.

Capitalist entrepreneurs engineered and mainly profited from this growth and change. The artisans who did the work were at their mercy for supplies of raw materials and for sale of their finished products. The merchant oligarchies that controlled the older towns kept food prices up and wages down. They forbade strikes and cut down opportunities for journeymen to become masters in the gilds or for poorer craftsmen to share in the governments of towns. The oppressed journeymen in industrial areas revolted against this treatment. In Flanders the workers rose against the patricians; in 1302 an army gathered from the leading cloth towns led by a poor weaver of Bruges defeated the forces of the king of France at Courtrai. This victory was ephemeral, however, and social unrest became a chronic problem in Flanders in the fourteenth century. Many weavers emigrated to England and to Italy to find work and wages. In Florence, where the gild of woolen merchants dominated the city government, the *Ciompi,* primarily workers in the woolen industry, rose in revolt in 1378 and seized power briefly. They lost in the end because the moderates among them joined with the shopkeepers against the extremists. By 1382 the old oligarchy was back in power. England's labor troubles were less acute and clearly defined. Even so, the peasants found some support in London for their revolt in 1381, and, two years later, the lesser craft gilds attempted to assert themselves and to break the power of the greater gilds, particularly the victuallers, who held a monopoly of power in the city. The attempt failed in the end. The wealthy gildsmen recovered power and continued to dominate the city for the remainder of the medieval period. The new village cloth industry was controlled by the clothiers (the great cloth merchants). The cottagers who spun the thread and wove the cloth had small chance of organizing against them.

However, in the fourteenth century the poorer folk in town and country did make themselves heard for the first time. What they said was not ideologically profound nor even very practical in the contemporary social context. But it was an achievement that they spoke at all. Power remained in the hands of the prestigious feudal class and rich townsmen.

Schism and Change in the Church

The three centuries from 1300 to 1600 saw the breakdown of Christian unity in the West. It is hard to find in these centuries a diminution of the importance of religion in men's lives. In the fifteenth and sixteenth centuries men died as bravely for their religion at the stake or on the battlefield as they had in the twelfth and thirteenth centuries. On the other hand, there was perhaps a greater diversity than there had been of loyalties that a man had to balance against one another. National loyalties challenged religious and feudal loyalties. The English Parliament in 1362 attempted with somewhat incomplete success to change the language of government from French to English. To the French, led by St. Joan, the English were the "Goddams." Poets increasingly used national vernacular languages in which to write their verse. Meanwhile townsmen found their choice of loyalties diversified and complex. They had to choose among economic groupings within the towns and more distant loyalties outside. Italians of the northern city-states had to choose between the imperial party and the papal party. Flemings could adhere to the count of Flanders, the king of France, or the king of England, depending on the internal play of politics. Peasant loyalties probably remained elemental. The prime loyalty was to the family. Beyond that was the village. If one were stirred by the opportunities of the more remote world, there was the king, whom one might enlist, at least in one's imagination, against the local bailiff, sheriff, or tax collector. The Church, conceived as a universal institution headed by the pope, no longer commanded the loyalty shown in the early era of the Crusades.

The Church was itself divided by schism beginning in 1378. The college of cardinals in that year elected first Urban VI, who entrenched himself in Rome, then, regretting their choice, Clement VII, a Frenchman, who retreated to Avignon and maintained a rival court under protection of the French kings. Europe had survived periodic schisms in earlier medieval centuries. Now national loyalties complicated allegiances. The English would not accept a French pope and succeeded in winning to their view Flanders and Germany. The French won the support of Spain, Sicily, and Scotland. Both sides refused compromise. A council at Pisa in 1409 succeeded only in complicating the matter still further by choosing a third pope. Ultimately, the Council of Constance called in 1415 under the presidency of the Holy Roman Emperor resolved the problem by deposing all three popes and choosing a fourth. In the end the council's choice, Martin V, restored Catholic unity.

He did not win immediately. Serious damage had been done to the doctrine of reforming popes of the High Middle Ages. Under this doctrine the pope held the "plenitude of power" in Christendom. An alternative doctrine, advocated strongly by the French kings, was that the highest power in the Church should rest in a council of its clergy rather than in the bishop of Rome. Laymen took part in the church councils of the fifteenth century, and kings made the most of opportunities to negotiate, in return for recognition of the pope's power, greater autonomy in dealing with their national churches.

Some of the developments of the fourteenth and fifteenth centuries illustrate the success of the medieval Church in educating the laity in their religion. The heresies of these centuries were not, like the Albigensian heresy, rival religious systems of ancient origin. They were revolutionary attacks on Catholic Christianity from within. John Wycliffe and Jan Hus attacked the very foundations of ecclesiastical authority, the very power of the priesthood to administer the sacraments and the efficacy of the sacraments themselves as administered by and to those not in the grace of God. They did not reject Christian revelation. They demanded that it be made more fully available to the faithful in language that they understood. They were successful in finding wide-based popular support. Wycliffe's immediate disciples were his students at Oxford. The converts they won were knights and peasants in the countryside but, more numerously, journeymen artisans in the towns of the south and west central part of England. Hus found his followers among the students of the University of Prague and among the townsmen of Bohemia. No one can read the records of examination of Wycliffe's followers without being impressed by the grasp these relatively unlearned people had of Christian theology. In that respect, St. Joan's examination during her long trial also makes impressive reading. She was an illiterate peasant.

No major new monastic orders were founded in the late

Middle Ages, but all sorts of semimonastic orders of lay brothers and sisters were founded in the north of France, Flanders, and the Rhineland. The beguines and beghards, lay brothers and sisters who did not necessarily withdraw into conventual life but who engaged in works of charity, the Friends of Christ, the Brethren of the Common Life who founded schools, are just some among the many new organizations. Religious hysteria as a consequence of the Black Death produced an outcropping of groups like the Flagellants. They went about in bands flogging and beating themselves for their own salvation and for the edification of the populace. They lived by public charity.

Mysticism was on the increase, and it created serious problems for the ecclesiastical authorities. In general, the mystic did not reject the doctrines of the Church, or its sacraments, although he might consider them empty forms. He merely claimed through direct spiritual communion with God to receive his own revelation. Meister William Eckhart and his followers, Tauler and Suso, Dominicans of the Rhineland, greatly influenced Martin Luther. Mystics flourished also in the Netherlands and in England. Meister Eckhart acknowledges the problem for authority in saying, "I may err but I may not be a heretic—for the first has to do with the mind and the second with the will."[7] The intense individualism of the mystics endangered orthodoxy, particularly in a time of anticlericalism when any fresh personal religious experience attracted popular attention and devotion.

Anticlericalism and the attacks of William of Ockham, an English Franciscan, and Marsiglio of Padua on the papal office are, in a sense, a measure of the success of Gregory VII's movement to place the clergy above the laity in the hierarchy of the world and the pope in the plenitude of his power at the apex. Success inevitably brought reaction. Marsiglio returned to older definitions of *ecclesia,* insisting that:

the name church is applied to the whole body of the faithful believing in and calling upon the name of Christ, and this means all parts of this whole body in whatever community they may be and even in the home.[8]

Both William and Marsiglio insisted on Christ's ultimate headship of the Church in spiritual matters and the headship of lay rulers in temporal affairs. Popular anticlericalism produced no new or original criticism of the sins of the clergy. What was new was that the criticism was by the laity of the clergy and that it did not, in general, lead (as earlier) to a reform movement within the clergy. Monasteries, which in the early Middle Ages had been the vanguard of Christianity, fell into decline. They ceased even to be the good landlords they had been in the thirteenth century. Popular resentment at the neglect of good lands and the conservatism of monastic landlords who attempted to exact old labor services were added to criticism of worldliness and even corruption among the monastic clergy.

The failure of the Crusade movement, the greatest common enterprise of western Europe, and the Black Death, which so subtly undermined men's faith in one another, are the most important developments of the later Middle Ages. Western Europe, having discovered its identity through conflict with alien faiths and cultures, now was thrown back on self-examination and faced with the problems of internal coexistence. The ultimate solution was a kind of recharging of batteries from rediscovery of ancient sources of inspiration and an opening up of new frontiers. As far as "periodization" is concerned, the Middle Ages is a misnomer. But, if one has to end this formative period of European history anywhere, the third quarter of the fifteenth century is probably as good a time as any. Depending on which aspect of life or which part of Europe one examines, one sees a different cutoff point. The shift in the centers of economic life to the Atlantic seacoast and the spread and impact of Italian Renaissance culture on northern Europe are probably the most important criteria.

Epilogue

The Middle Ages have suffered greatly both from admirers and from detractors. Why a thousand years of human history should be either condemned wholesale as a period of delusion and superstition or treated as a period of romantic vacuity is hard to understand. Yet, every day, when one picks up a newspaper or watches television, one finds evidence of both points of view. A New York City official finds landlord-tenant relations in Harlem deplorable and condemns them as "medieval." They are worse than medieval. A teenager writing to Ann Landers about her parents' refusal to let her go out with boys complains that their outlook is "medieval." If she only knew, a medieval girl of almost any class had greater freedom than she but less privacy. A student signs up for a course on the Middle Ages because "they are so beautiful." The Gothic cathedrals of Europe attract undue concentration of attention from tourists simply because they are still there. Historical novelists wishing to let themselves go in descriptions of sadistic cruelty or man's inhumanity to man choose the Middle Ages as their setting. Popular psychiatrists treat the whole thousand years as a time when man's mind and spirit were in bondage.

None of this would be serious if it did not lead to the neglect of a long period of human history that, because it is formative in the creation of a new civilization, has meaning and relevance today in a time when Europe has lost its preeminent position in the world and new civilizations are in formation—on the continent of Africa, for example. Most of the romantic notions about the Middle Ages derive from the popular literature of the late medieval period. This is about as reliable a source for understanding medieval society as the English detective story is for English society in the twentieth century. Even serious historians have allowed their view of the period to be obscured for them by the criticism or ridicule of the "men of the Renais-

199

sance." These men rejected the immediate past, as the men of any creative period are likely to do. The important point for students of history to understand is that no time in which men lived, struggled with the problems of existence, thought about these problems, and tried to solve them is wholly without relevance for other men.

Finally, contributions of the Middle Ages to modern Western civilization are many and deserve study for their relevance in our own society. What were the main contributions of this new European civilization of the medieval period? In government, the main inheritance is the belief in the supremacy of law and the idea that government is based on a contract between the ruler and the ruled. In feudal society, as has been shown, governmental functions were mainly performed by kings and their vassals and the followers of those vassals. These men were bound to each other mutually by bonds of contract and by chivalric custom. Toward the mass of the people who produced the food, clothing, and shelter for this society, the rulers had a mixed attitude of contempt, compassion, and *noblesse oblige*. They exploited the peasant's labor on the one hand and cared for him on the other. When the lower orders began to find ways to improve their lot and to demand more of their share of the goods of the society, to develop new ways of increasing production, and to initiate rival activities in war and government, the ruling class reacted with the whole gamut of predictable human emotions: fear, greed for the proceeds, vision of the new possibilities, and determination to exploit them. The essential point, however, is that the man who worked for his living made a widespread bid for a share in the wealth and the power. Eventually, much later than the so-called "middle ages," this man came to share in the contract of government and to negotiate his share of economic power.

Moreover, we can credit the Middle Ages with a new ideal of the individual. The Greeks had had an ideal of the individual as a harmoniously adjusted citizen, a member of the elite *demos* (people of the right birth) thoroughly integrated into and taking his responsibility in the city-state. The Romans most admired in the individual the quality of *gravitas,* a sense of responsibility toward the "customs of the majority" in the society—meaning, of course, the customs accepted by the ruling class. The ideal medieval individual was a more romantic, untrammeled, less predictable, and rational person. Typically, he was vassal to a king toward whom he owed loyalty, service, and homage. Yet he might, either in revenge for injuries or merely out of Satanic impulse, commit the worst of treacheries. His "castle" was his home, and in the last resort, he protected and defended his own land, his own peasants, his own family, without depending on any resources but his own. He had no civic virtues or responsibilities.

Yet civic virtues and responsibilities—in the sense in which the ancients used it, for those obligations associated with the city-state—and "civilization" were renewed in the towns and cities of the Middle Ages. Townsmen rediscovered the values of cooperation in winning freedoms and in making economic progress. This was an important contribution to the early modern world.

To science, medieval men contributed little except a revival of scientific curiosity of the Greek sort. Medieval research, rudimentary though it was, did lay the foundations for the scientific revolution of the sixteenth and seventeenth centuries. Philosophy for medieval man was inseparable from theology, but this did not prevent him from grappling with fundamental problems like the nature of knowledge and being.

Gothic architecture, with its complementary sculpture, was the most brilliant success of medieval man. It expressed most fully his aspirations, his tensions, his grotesque humor, and his sadness. In medieval literature, especially the poetry, we find new principles at work. Rhythm and rhyme replace meter, and fantasy rather than fact and philosophy provide the content. Romantic love, a frustrated and essentially tragic conception of the relations between men and women, emerged from the repressiveness of Christian teaching and the subordination of women in feudal society. But the strained overrefinement of courtly love was balanced by a robust ribaldry of peasant common sense and bourgeois amusement at aristocratic pretension.

Medieval men's search for knowledge led to the organization of the universities, new educational institutions having a continuing importance in the world today. In the beginning they were not part of the establishment, and their faculty and students had to fight their way against the rulers of society. The medieval university was a "community of scholars." It was a different type of center of learning from the Academy of Plato. There was less emphasis on the great teacher, more on the process of learning together.

Warfare was a chronic feature of medieval society, as it has been of human society since its inception. Medieval warfare was more anarchic, less organized, and disciplined than Roman imperial warfare. It was also less destructive than modern warfare. Moreover, there was a modern sense of guilt about war arising both from the complexities of the Germanic system of loyalties and from the Christian ideal of peace.

But what of the Christian Church, the outstanding creation of the era? It became thoroughly institutionalized and, in the process of organizing and administering power, lost the pristine purity of the Christian message. Peace and brotherly love surrendered some of their force even as ideals in favor of militancy and asceticism. But there were many individuals who managed to love themselves and their fellow men as well as to love and to worship God. In the imagery of Christianity there were the merciful and loving Virgin Mother and her Child as well as Christ, the broken figure on the cross. Whatever the human failures of the Christianity of the Middle Ages, its successes contributed to modern Europe a faith in the essential equality and dignity of all men.

This book has attempted to describe the main features of medieval society in the High Middle Ages, that is mainly the twelfth and thirteenth centuries. It is hoped that the student has remained aware of change and diversity in the medieval world despite the broad generalizations necessary in a book of this scope. It is hoped also, and most of all, that he has made

the effort of imagination necessary to empathize with the people living in the times and has understood that the problems
of medieval men were the basic ones of all men in all ages.

Chronological Tables

Chronological Table of Events in Europe as a Whole

Political and Social	Thought, Arts, and Letters
4 B.C. Birth of Jesus Christ	

A.D. 1–1000

Political and Social	Thought, Arts, and Letters
	c. 55–118 Tacitus
100 98–117 Emperor Trajan	
200	
300 306–337 Emperor Constantine	c. 340–397 St. Ambrose of Milan
313 Edict of Milan	c. 347–419 St. Jerome
325 Council of Nicaea	354–430 St. Augustine of Hippo
379–395 Emperor Theodosius	
400 410 Death of Alaric, Visigoth chief	
	c. 450 Ireland converted to Christianity
451 Battle of Châlons	
476 Deposition of last Roman Emperor in the West	
500	
	529 The Benedictine Rule
	527–534 Compilation of Corpus Juris Civilis
600 590–604 Pope Gregory I, the Great	
	673–735 Bede
700 732 Charles Martel's victory at Tours over Muslims	

Political and Social	*Thought, Arts, and Letters*
768–814 Charlemagne	
	c. 780 Alcuin at Charlemagne's court; the Carolingian Renaissance
800 800 Coronation of Charlemagne as Emperor	
871–899 Alfred, the Great	
900 911 Count Rollo acquires Normandy	910 Foundation of Cluny
936–973 Otto I, the Great, Emperor	
955 Battle of Lechfeld	
987–996 Hugh Capet, King of France	
	980–1037 Avicenna

1000–1500

1000	
1050	
	1038–1109 Anselm of Bec and Canterbury
1071 Battle of Manzikert	1060–1125 Irnerius, Roman law at Bologna
1073–1085 Pope Gregory VII	1079–1142 Peter Abelard
1073 *Dictatus Papae*	1090–1153 St. Bernard of Clairvaux
1100 1096 First Crusade	
1122 Concordat of Worms	1126–1198 Averroës
	1136 Abbot Suger introduces Gothic
1150 1147 Second Crusade	
1159–1181 Pope Alexander III	1159 John of Salisbury's *Policraticus*
1187 Saladin's capture of Jerusalem	
1200 1198–1216 Pope Innocent III	
1208 Albigensian Crusade	

Chronological Table of Events in Europe as a Whole, Continued

Political and Social	*Thought, Arts, and Letters*
1215 Fourth Lateran Council	1225–1274 St. Thomas Aquinas
1215 Dominican order founded	
1223 Franciscan order; papal sanction	
1226 Mongol attack on Europe	

1250

	1265–1321 Dante
	1276–1337 Giotto
	c. 1280–1342 Marsiglio of Padua

1300

1294–1303 Pope Boniface VIII	c. 1300 Beginning of Italian Renaissance
1302 Bull *Unam Sanctam*	1304–1374 Petrarch
1302 Battle of Courtrai	1313–1375 Boccaccio
	c. 1320–1384 John Wycliffe
1337–1453 The Hundred Years War	c. 1340–1400 Geoffrey Chaucer
1347–1349 The Black Death	

1350

1378–1415 The Great Schism	

1400

1450

1453 Capture of Constantinople by Ottoman Turks	1450 Invention of movable type

II

Chronological Table of Events in the British Isles, Western Europe, and Central Europe, 1000–1500

	British Isles	Western Europe	Central Europe
1000	1016–1042 Rule of Canute and his sons 1042–1066 Edward the Confessor, King of England		1024–1125 Salian Emperors
1050	1066 Harold, King of England 1066 William of Normandy's conquest of England 1086 Domesday Book		1056–1106 Henry IV, King of Germany and Emperor 1073–1122 Investiture controversy
1100	1100–1135 Henry I, King of England 1107 Compromise of Bec 1135–1154 King Stephen and the Anarchy	1122–1204 Eleanor of Aquitaine 1137–1180 Louis VII, King of France	
1150	1154–1189 Henry II, King of England 1164 Constitutions of Clarendon Assize of Clarendon		1150–1254 Hohenstaufen Emperors 1152–1190 Frederick I, Barbarossa, King of Germany and Emperor

Chronological Table of Events in the British Isles, Western Europe, and Central Europe, 1000–1500, Continued

	British Isles	Western Europe	Central Europe
	1170 Murder of Thomas Becket		
	1189–1199 Richard I, King of England	1180–1223 Philip II, Augustus, King of France	1190–1197 Henry VI, King of Germany and Emperor
1200	1199–1216 John, King of England		1211–1250 Frederick II, King of Germany and Emperor
	1215 Magna Carta	1226–1270 Louis IX, King of France	
	1216–1272 Henry III, King of England		
1250	1272–1307 Edward I, King of England		1273–1291 Rudolf (Hapsburg), King of Germany and Emperor
		1285–1314 Philip IV, King of France	1282 Sicilian Vespers
1300	1300 Edward's confirmation of charters		
	1307–1327 Edward II, King of England		
	1327–1377 Edward III, King of England		
	1337 Beginning of Hundred Years War		

British Isles	Western Europe	Central Europe
	1350–1364 John II, King of France	
	1358 Jacquerie in France	
		1378 Revolt of Ciompi in Florence
1381 Peasants' revolt		
		1434–1464 Cosimo de' Medici dominates Florence
	1461–1483 Louis XI, King of France	1478–1492 Lorenzo de' Medici
1453 End of Hundred Years War		
1455–1485 Wars of the Roses		

1350

1400

1450

1500

209

Notes

Chapter I THE FORMATION OF EUROPE

1. *Aristotle's Politics,* translated by Benjamin Jowett (Oxford: Clarendon Press, 1923), 1327b, vii, 7.
2. Tenney Frank, "Race Mixture in the Roman Empire," *American Historical Review,* Vol. XXI (1915–1916), 689–708.
3. *Cambridge Medieval History,* 2nd ed. (New York: Cambridge University Press, 1924ff, 1967ff), Vol. I, pp. 399–400.
4. St. Orientus, "Deathroll of a World," in Jack Lindsay, *Song of a Falling World* (London: Dakers, 1948), pp. 200–201.
5. *The Complete Works of Tacitus,* edited by Moses Hadas, and translated by A. J. Church and W. J. Bodribb (New York: Random House, 1942), p. 714.
6. These illustrations are drawn from the laws of the Salian Franks.
7. In Paul Vinogradoff, *Roman Law in Medieval Europe* (New York: Harper and Row, 1908), p. 16.
8. C. W. Kennedy (ed. and tr.), *An Anthology of Old English Poetry* (New York: Oxford University Press, 1960), pp. 5–6.
9. Gregory, *History of the Franks,* translated by Ernest Brehaut (New York: Columbia University Press, 1916), p. 48.
10. "The Nicene Creed," in Henry Bettenson (ed.), *Documents of the Christian Church* (New York: Oxford University Press, 1947). p. 36.
11. Matt. 16:18–19.
12. "The Letter of the Churches of Vienne and Lyons, A.D. 177," quoted in R. H. Bainton, *Early Christianity* (Princeton, N.J.: D. Van Nostrand, 1960), p. 106.
13. "Trajan's Policy towards Christians," in Bettenson, *op. cit.,* p. 7.
14. "The Edict of Milan, March 313," in *ibid.,* pp. 22–23.
15. "Theodosius (379–395) on Catholic and Heretic," in *ibid.,* pp. 31–32.
16. "The Rule of St. Benedict," in *A Pax Book* (London: Society for Promoting Christian Knowledge, 1931), pp. 1–2, 5–6.
17. Kennedy, *op. cit.,* p. 145.
18. From Dudo of St. Quentin, translated and quoted in *Ideas and Institutions in European History, 800–1715,* edited by T. C. Mendenhall, B. D. Henning and A. S. Foord (New York: Holt, Rinehart and Winston, 1948).

Chapter II AGRARIAN ECONOMY AND PEASANT LIFE

1. From T. Madox, *Formulare Anglicanum,* quoted in G. G. Coulton, *Life in the Middle Ages* (Cambridge, Eng.: University Press, 1954), Vol. IV, pp. 203–204.
2. Georges Duby, *Rural Economy and Country Life in the Medieval West,* translated by Cynthia Postan (Columbia: University of South Carolina Press, 1968), p. 513.
3. Selections from manor court rolls in G. G. Coulton, *Social Life in Britain from the Conquest to the Reformation* (Cambridge, Eng.: University Press, 1919), pp. 306–308. Distraint was the taking of some piece of the defendant's property to induce him to come to court. Pledges were men who undertook to pay the fine if the defendant failed to do so. The Purification of the Virgin was celebrated on February 2.
4. *Here may a young man see how he should speak subtly in court,* translated by Helen M. Briggs (London: Sweet and Maxwell, 1936).
5. Shakespeare, *As You Like It,* Act V, Scene III, 1. 18.
6. From Thomas Tusser's "Five Hundred Points of Good Husbandry," quoted in G. C. Homans, *English Villagers of the Thirteenth Century* (Cambridge, Mass.: Harvard University Press, 1941).
7. "Medieval German Charm," translated and quoted in Eileen Power, *Medieval People* (Boston: Houghton Mifflin, 1927), pp. 12–13.

Chapter III FEUDAL SOCIETY

1. *Bracton on the Laws and Customs of England,* translated, with revisions and notes, by S. E. Thorne (Cambridge, Mass.: The Belknap Press, 1968), Vol. II, p. 232.
2. "Fulbert of Chartres on the Duties of a Vassal, 1020," translated and quoted in J. R. Strayer, *Feudalism* (Princeton, N.J.: D. Van Nostrand, 1968), p. 113.
3. Sir Frank Stenton, *The First Century of English Feudalism, 1066–1166,* 2nd ed. (Oxford: Clarendon Press, 1961), p. 272. This passage is translated into English by the present author.
4. "Multiple Homage in the Early Thirteenth Century," in Strayer, *op. cit.,* pp. 146–147.
5. Translated by F. B. Luquiens (New York: Macmillan, 1952), p. 52.
6. "The Church and Feudalism," in Strayer, *op. cit.,* pp. 99–100.
7. *The Statesman's Book of John of Salisbury,* translated and edited by John Dickinson (New York: Knopf, 1927), p. 199.

8. Sidney Painter, *William Marshal* (Baltimore: Johns Hopkins Press, 1933), pp. 285–286.

9. André le Capelain, *The Art of Courtly Love,* translated by J. J. Perry (New York: Columbia University Press, 1941), pp. 184–186.

Chapter IV   MEDIEVAL COMMERCE: TOWNS

1. The question of just when and where the Vikings reached "Vinland," or North America, is a highly controversial one.

2. From Abu al-Qasim, *The Book of Routes and Kingdoms,* quoted in R. S. Lopez and I. W. Raymond, *Medieval Trade in the Mediterranean World* (New York: Columbia University Press, 1955), pp. 31–33.

3. Otto of Freising, *Gesta Frederici,* quoted in J. B. Ross and M. M. McLaughlin (eds.), *The Portable Medieval Reader* (New York: Viking, 1959), pp. 281–283.

4. *The Autobiography of Guibert, Abbot of Nogent-sous-Coucy,* quoted in J. F. Scott, Albert Hyma, and A. H. Noyes (eds.), *Readings in Medieval History* (New York: Appleton-Century-Crofts, 1933), pp. 303–312.

5. Magna Carta, *ch.* 41.

6. Adolphus Ballard, *British Borough Charters, 1042–1216* (Cambridge, Eng.: University Press, 1913), p. 32.

7. From *Flowers of History,* Matthew Paris' additions, translated by J. A. Giles (London: Bohn, 1849), pp. 146–147.

8. From the customs of Avignon, translated and quoted in J. H. Mundy and Peter Riesenberg, *The Medieval Town* (Princeton, N.J.: D. Van Nostrand, 1958), pp. 157–158.

9. D. C. Douglas and G. W. Greenway (eds.), *English Historical Documents, 1042–1189* (New York: Oxford University Press, 1953), pp. 956–962.

10. B. Jarrett, *Social Theories of the Middle Ages, 1200–1500* (London: Ernest Benn, 1926), p. 156.

11. Translated and quoted in Iris Origo, *The Merchant of Prato* (London: Jonathan Cape, 1960), p. 319.

12. Translated and quoted in Lopez and Raymond, *op. cit.,* pp. 160–161.

Chapter V   FEUDAL MONARCHY: THE FORMATION OF TERRITORIAL STATES

1. *The Statesman's Book of John of Salisbury,* translated and edited by John Dickinson (New York: Knopf, 1927), p. 3.

2. G. B. Adams and H. M. Stephens (eds.), *Select Documents of English Constitutional History* (New York: Macmillan, 1919), p. 88.

3. *Statutes of the Realm,* Vol. I, p. 168.

4. *Bracton on the Laws and Customs of England,* translated with revisions and notes, by S. E. Thorne (Cambridge, Mass.: The Belknap Press, 1968), Vol. II, p. 305.

5. Robert Fawtier, *The Capetian Kings of France,* translated by Lionel Butler and R. J. Adam (London: Macmillan, 1960), p. 7. This passage is translated from Latin to English by the present author.

6. J. R. Strayer, *Feudalism* (Princeton, N.J.: D. Van Nostrand, 1965), pp. 159–160.

7. G. Barraclough, *The Origins of Modern Germany* (Oxford: Basil Blackwell, 1949), pp. 170–171, n. 1.

Chapter VI   CHRISTIANITY AND THE CHURCH

1. Bede, *A History of the English Church and People,* translated by Leo Sherley-Price (Baltimore: Penguin, 1955), Book I, Chapter 30, p. 87.

2. *The City of God* (New York: Dutton, 1945), Vol. II, p. 283.

3. The sacraments are the instruments of God's grace through which man is freed from sin. Man was conceived to have been born in sin because of the original sin of Adam and Eve. Baptism is the provisional induction of new members into the Church by sprinkling water on them for purification from sin. In medieval western Europe, it was normally administered to infants. Holy Communion (Eucharist) is the ceremonial taking of bread and wine conceived to be transformed into the body and blood of Christ by the miracle of transubstantiation. Penance is a multiple sacrament comprising the following steps: confession and repentance of sin by the penitent, assignment of penance and absolution by the priest, and finally, performance of the assigned penance (prayer, pilgrimage, charitable works, and so forth) by the penitent as a sign of his good faith in repentance. Confirmation is the strengthening of the baptized Christian in his membership in the Church after he has received instruction in his faith. Ordination is the induction of the priest into the priesthood. Marriage, a civil ceremony with the Romans, became a sacrament in Christianity. Extreme unction, or the last rites, is the final cleansing from sin administered for the comfort and consolation of the Christian at death to ease his passing.

4. Odo of Rigaud, in J. B. Ross and M. M. McLaughlin, (eds.), *The Portable Medieval Reader* (New York: Viking, 1949), pp. 78–79.
5. Quoted in Gerd Tellenbach, *Church, State and Christian Society at the Time of the Investiture Contest*, translated by R. F. Bennett (Oxford: Basil Blackwell, 1948), p. 126.
6. The diocese of Rome, like some other large and important dioceses, had more than one bishop. Assistant bishops were in most cases called suffragan bishops or cardinal bishops. Eventually, cardinal bishops, cardinal priests, cardinal archdeacons, and deacons of the diocese of Rome became in popular terminology simply "cardinals."
7. "Dictatus Papae," in J. H. Robinson (ed.), *Readings in European History* (New York: Ginn and Co., 1904), Vol. I, pp. 284–287.
8. Letter of Henry IV to the Pope, January 24, 1076, in T. C. Mendenhall, B. D. Henning, and A. S. Foord (eds.), *Ideas and Institutions in European History* (New York: Holt, Rinehart and Winston, 1948), p. 58.
9. "The Annals of Berchtold," in *ibid.*, p. 74.
10. "The Bull 'Unam Sanctam,' 1302," in Henry Bettenson (ed.), *Documents of the Christian Church* (New York: Oxford University Press, 1947), pp. 161–163.
11. *Life and Works of St. Bernard*, edited by J. Mabillon and translated by S. J. Eales (London: John Hodges, 1896), Vol. IV, pp. 316–317.
12. "On the Lord's Day," in Richard Morris (ed.), *Old English Homilies*, Early English Text Society, original series, 29 (London: Kegan Paul, 1867), pp. 40–46.

Chapter VII LEARNING AND THE ARTS

1. Chrétien de Troyes, quoted and translated by W. A. Nitze, "The So-Called Twelfth Century Renaissance," *Speculum*, Vol. XXIII (July 1948), p. 467.
2. Erwin Panofsky (ed. and tr.), *Abbot Suger on the Abbey Church of St. Denis and Its Art Treasures* (Princeton, N.J.: Princeton University Press, 1946), p. 49.
3. *Ibid.*, p. 51.
4. *Ibid.*, pp. 63–65.
5. *Avicenna on Theology*, translated by Arthur J. Arberry (London: John Murray, 1951), p. 32.
6. *Basic Writings of St. Thomas Aquinas*, edited and annotated with

an Introduction by Anton C. Pegis (New York: Random House, 1945), pp. 1061–1062.

7. "Lecturing in the Medieval Universities," in J. F. Scott, Albert Hyma, A. H. Noyes (eds.), *Readings in Medieval History* (New York: Appleton-Century-Crofts, 1933), pp. 353–354.

8. From the cartulary of the University of Paris, quoted in Lynn Thorndike (ed.), *University Records and Life in the Middle Ages* (New York: Columbia University Press, 1944), pp. 88–92.

9. Abelard's worst "calamities" arose from his love affair with Eloise. As a man approaching middle age with a reputation for chastity, he was retained by a canon of Notre Dame to teach his sixteen-year-old niece, a girl of exceptional intellectual abilities. They fell in love. Eloise gave birth to a son but tried to avoid marriage, thinking to save Abelard from disgrace in his professional field. The uncle insisted on marriage; then, in distrust of Abelard, he hired rowdies to take him unawares and castrate him. Both lovers withdrew into monastic life. Eloise became an abbess. Abelard ended his days at Cluny. Their letters and Abelard's own account of the calamities constitute our main source for this tragic story.

10. From Adelard's *Questiones Naturales,* quoted in J. B. Ross and M. M. McLaughlin (eds.), *The Portable Medieval Reader* (New York: Viking, 1959), pp. 620–626.

11. *Ibid.*

12. Helen Waddell, *Medieval Latin Lyrics* (London: Constable, 1929), pp. 203–205.

13. Second stanza of "When I Saw the Skylark Winging," by Bernard de Ventadorn, translated by Daisy Aldan, in Angel Flores (ed.), *An Anthology of Medieval Lyrics* (New York: Modern Library, 1962), pp. 31–32.

14. *The Statesman's Book of John of Salisbury,* translated and edited by John Dickinson (New York: Knopf, 1927), p. 65.

Chapter VIII   EUROPE AND THE WIDER WORLD

1. Princess Anna Comnena, *The Alexiad,* translated by E. Dawes (London: K. Paul, Trench, Trubner, 1925), pp. 372–373.

2. From *De Profectione Ludovici VII in Orientem,* translated by V. G. Berry (New York: Columbia University Press, 1948), p. 57.

3. Joinville and Villehardouin, *Chronicles of the Crusades,* translated by M. R. B. Shaw (Baltimore: Penguin, 1963), pp. 92–93.

4. J. R. Marcus (ed.), *The Jew in the Medieval World* (Cincinnati: Sinai Press, 1938), pp. 151–154.

5. Robert the Monk, *Historia Hiersolomitana*, Vol. I, pp. 1–3, translated and quoted in J. A. Brundage, *The Crusades: A Documentary Survey* (Milwaukee: Marquette University Press, 1962), pp. 17–20.

6. From *Gesta Francorum et Aliorum Hierosolimitanorum*, translated and quoted in Brundage, *op. cit.*, pp. 63–65.

7. Translated and quoted in R. W. Southern, *Western Views of Islam in the Middle Ages*. (Cambridge, Mass.: Harvard University Press, 1962), p. 39.

8. *Ibid.*, p. 45. The Georgians are a people of the Caucasus region.

9. Translated and quoted in Christopher Dawson (ed.), *The Mongol Mission* (New York: Sheed & Ward, 1955), pp. 75–76.

10. *Ibid.*, p. 70.

Chapter IX   CHANGE IN THE LATER MIDDLE AGES

1. Jacob Burckhardt, *The Civilization of the Renaissance in Italy*, translated by S. G. C. Middlemore (New York: Phaidon, 1951), p. 81.

2. Giovanni Boccaccio, *The Decameron*, as quoted in J. F. Scott, Albert Hyma and A. H. Noyes (eds.), *Readings in Medieval History* (New York: Appleton-Century-Crofts, 1933), pp. 495–496.

3. *Ibid.*

4. W. H. Dunham, "Lord Hastings' Indentured Retainers, 1461–1483," *Transactions of the Academy of Arts and Science* (New Haven, Conn.: Yale University Press, 1955), Vol. 39, p. 137.

5. J. Huizinga, *The Waning of the Middle Ages* (London: Edward Arnold, 1924), p. 58.

6. Quoted in Margaret Aston, *The Fifteenth Century* (New York: Harcourt, Brace & World, 1968), p. 144.

7. R. B. Blakney, *Meister Eckhart* (New York: Harper & Row, 1957), p. xxiii.

8. Translated by the present author in W. Y. Elliott and N. A. McDonald, *Western Political Heritage* (Englewood Cliffs, N.J.: Prentice-Hall), p. 315.

Suggested Readings

There are many good one-volume narrative histories of the Middle Ages. The latest and best is Brian Tierney and Sidney Painter, *Western Europe in the Middle Ages, 300–1475.* New York: Knopf, 1970. There is also a plethora of anthologies of sources. They are most effectively used conjointly with a textbook that refers to them. One anthology that deserves special mention for its readability is J. B. Ross and M. M. McLaughlin, *The Portable Medieval Reader.* New York: Viking, 1949.

In reading medieval European history the reader must have at hand a good historical atlas. Two are recommended. The first is E. W. Fox and H. S. Deighton, *Atlas of European History.* New York: Oxford University Press, 1957; the section of this atlas devoted to ancient and medieval history is published in a separate paperbound edition. The second is W. R. Shepherd, *Historical Atlas,* 8th ed. rev. New York: Barnes & Noble, 1956.

The standard general bibliography for medieval history is L. J. Paetow, *A Guide to the Study of Medieval History,* rev. ed. New York: Crofts, 1931. The main general work of reference is *The Cambridge Medieval History,* 2nd ed., 8 vols. New York: Cambridge University Press, 1924ff, 1967ff. For economic history, the general reference work is *The Cambridge Economic History.* Cambridge, Eng.: The University Press, 1941ff. This work was begun under the editorship of J. H. Clapham and Eileen Power. The first three volumes deal with medieval history.

In the following list of suggested readings, items are available in paperback unless indicated by *. The dates given are of the most recent editions available.

GENERAL WORKS

*Bettenson, Henry. *Documents of the Christian Church.* London: Oxford University Press, 1963.

Bloch, Marc. *Feudal Society.* L. A. Manyon (tr.). Chicago: Chicago University Press, 1964.

*Evans, Joan, (ed.). *The Flowering of the Middle Ages.* New York: McGraw-Hill, 1966.

Hay, Denys. *Europe: the Emergence of an Idea.* New York: Harper & Row, 1966.

_____. *The Medieval Centuries*. New York: Harper & Row, 1964.

Heer, Friedrich. *The Medieval World: Europe 1100–1350*. New York: New American Library, 1964.

Painter, Sidney. *Medieval Society*. Ithaca, N.Y.: Cornell University Press, 1951.

Power, Eileen. *Medieval People*. 10th ed. rev. New York: Barnes & Noble, 1963.

Southern, R. W. *The Making of the Middle Ages*. New Haven, Conn.: Yale University Press, 1953.

Trevor-Roper, Hugh. *The Rise of Christian Europe*. New York: Harcourt, Brace & World, 1966.

Chapter I   THE FORMATION OF EUROPE

Bainton, R. H. *Early Christianity*. Princeton, N.J.: D. Van Nostrand, 1960.

Bark, W. C. *Origins of the Medieval World*. Garden City, N.Y.: Doubleday, 1960.

Bede, the Venerable. *A History of the English Church and People*. Leo Sherley-Price (tr.). Baltimore: Penguin, 1955. With an introduction by Leo Sherley-Price.

Brøndsted, Johannes. *The Vikings*. Kalle Skov (tr.). Baltimore: Penguin, 1965.

*Duby, Georges. *Rural Economy and Country Life in the Medieval West*. Cynthia Postan (tr.). Columbia: University of South Carolina Press, 1968.

Duckett, Eleanor. *The Wandering Saints of the Early Middle Ages*. New York: Norton, 1964.

Einhard. *The Life of Charlemagne*. Ann Arbor: University of Michigan Press, 1960.

Fichtenau, Heinrich. *The Carolingian Empire*. New York: Harper & Row, 1963.

Easton, S. C. and Helene Wieruszowski. *The Era of Charlemagne*. Princeton, N.J.: D. Van Nostrand, 1961.

Latouche, Robert. *Birth of Western Economy*. E. M. Wilkinson (tr.). London: Methuen, 1957.

Laistner, M. L. W. *Thought and Letters in Western Europe, A.D. 500–900*. 2nd. ed. Ithaca, N.Y.: Cornell University Press, 1957.

Lewis, A. R. *Emerging Medieval Europe, A.D. 400–1000*. New York: Knopf, 1967.

Pirenne, Henri. *Mohammed and Charlemagne*. New York: Barnes & Noble, 1955.

Rand, E. K. *Founders of the Middle Ages*. New York: Dover, 1957.

Severus, Sulpicius, *et. al. The Western Fathers.* F. O. Hoare (ed., tr.). New York: Harper & Row, 1965.

Wallace-Hadrill, J. N. *The Barbarian West, A.D. 400–1000.* New York: Harper & Row, 1962.

*White, Lynn. *Medieval Technology and Social Change.* New York: Oxford University Press, 1962.

Winston, Richard. *Charlemagne: From the Hammer to the Cross.* New York: Random House, 1954.

Chapter II AGRARIAN ECONOMY AND PEASANT LIFE

Bennett, H. S. *Life on the English Manor: a Study of Peasant Conditions, 1150–1400.* New York: Cambridge University Press, 1960.

Boissonade, Prosper. *Life and Work in Medieval Europe.* Eileen Power (tr.). New York: Harper & Row, 1964.

*Bloch, Marc. *French Rural History: an Essay on its Basic Characteristics.* J. Sondheimer (tr.). Berkeley and Los Angeles: University of California Press, 1966.

Coulton, G. G. *Medieval Village, Manor and Monastery.* New York: Harper & Row, 1960.

*Duby, Georges. *Rural Economy in the Medieval West.* Cynthia Postan (tr.). Columbia: University of South Carolina Press, 1968.

*Homans, G. C. *English Villagers of the Thirteenth Century.* Cambridge, Mass.: Harvard University Press, 1960.

Chapter III FEUDAL SOCIETY

Ganshof, F. L. *Feudalism.* 2nd. ed. New York: Harper & Row, 1961.

Hoyt, R. S. *Feudal Institutions.* New York: Holt, Rinehart and Winston, 1961.

Oman, C. W. C. *The Art of War in the Middle Ages, A.D. 378–1515.* Ithaca, N.Y.: Cornell University Press, 1953.

*Painter, Sidney. *Feudalism and Liberty.* F. A. Cazel, Jr. (ed.). Baltimore: Johns Hopkins Press, 1961.

————. *French Chivalry.* Ithaca, N.Y.: Cornell University Press, 1957.

Stephenson, Carl. *Medieval Feudalism.* Ithaca, N.Y.: Cornell University Press, 1942.

Strayer, J. R. *Feudalism.* Princeton, N.J.: D. Van Nostrand, 1968.

Chapter IV   MEDIEVAL COMMERCE: TOWNS

Adelson, Howard L. *Medieval Commerce.* Princeton, N.J.: D. Van Nostrand, 1962.

*Beresford, Maurice. *New Towns of the Middle Ages.* New York: Praeger, 1967.

*Clarke, M. V. *The Medieval City-State.* New York: Barnes & Noble, 1966.

Lopez, R. S. and I. W. Raymond. *Medieval Trade in the Mediterranean World.* New York: Norton, 1967.

Mundy, J. H. and Peter Riesenberg. *The Medieval Town.* Princeton, N.J.: D. Van Nostrand, 1958.

Pirenne, Henri. *Medieval Cities.* Frank D. Halsey (tr.). Garden City, N.Y.: Doubleday, 1956.

Rörig, Fritz. *The Medieval Town.* Berkeley and Los Angeles: University of California Press, 1967.

Chapter V   FEUDAL MONARCHY: THE FORMATION OF TERRITORIAL STATES

*Barraclough, Geoffrey. *Medieval Germany, 911–1250.* 2 vols. New York: Barnes & Noble, 1961.

*————. *Origins of Modern Germany.* New York: Putnam, 1963.

Fawtier, Robert. *The Capetian Kings of France.* New York: St. Martin's, 1960.

*Kantorowicz, E. H. *The King's Two Bodies: A Study of Medieval Political Theology.* Princeton, N.J.: Princeton University Press, 1957.

*Kern, Fritz. *Kingship and Law in the Middle Ages.* S. B. Chrimes (tr.). Oxford: Blackwell, 1948. With an introduction by S. B. Chrimes.

*McIlwain, C. H. *The Growth of Political Thought in the West.* New York: Macmillan, 1932.

Painter, Sidney. *The Rise of the Feudal Monarchies.* Ithaca, N.Y.: Cornell University Press, 1951.

Petit-Dutaillis, Charles. *The Feudal Monarchy in France and England, from the Tenth to the Thirteenth Century.* New York: Harper & Row, 1964.

*Ullmann, Walter. *Principles of Government and Politics in the Middle Ages.* New York: Barnes & Noble, 1961.

Chapter VI CHRISTIANITY AND THE CHURCH

Bainton, R. H. *The Medieval Church.* Princeton, N.J.: D. Van Nostrand, 1962.

Barraclough, Geoffrey. *The Medieval Papacy.* New York: Harcourt Brace & World, 1968.

*Deanesly, Margaret. *History of the Medieval Church, 590–1500.* New York: Barnes & Noble, 1965.

*Lea, H. C. *The Inquisition of the Middle Ages.* New York: Citadel, 1954. Chapters from his three volume history.

Runciman, Steven. *The Medieval Manichee.* New York: Viking, 1961.

Russell, J. B. *A History of Medieval Christianity: Prophecy and Order.* New York: Crowell, 1968.

*Tellenbach, Gerd. *Church, State and Christian Society at the Time of the Investiture Contest.* New York: Humanities, 1959.

Tierney, Brian. *The Crisis of Church and State, 1050–1300.* Englewood Cliffs, N.J.: Prentice-Hall, 1964.

Ullmann, Walter. *Growth of Papal Government in the Middle Ages.* 2nd. ed. New York: Barnes & Noble, 1962.

Chapter VII LEARNING AND THE ARTS

Adams, Henry. *Mont-Saint-Michel and Chartres.* New York: Doubleday, 1959.

Crombie, A. C. *Medieval and Early Modern Science.* 2 vols. New York: Doubleday, 1959.

*Flores, Angel. *An Anthology of Medieval Lyrics.* New York: Modern Library, 1962.

Fremantle, Anne, (ed.). *The Age of Belief.* New York: New American Library, 1965.

*Gilson, Etienne. *History of Christian Philosophy in the Middle Ages.* New York: Random House, 1955.

————. *Reason and Revelation in the Middle Ages.* New York: Scribners, 1952.

Haskins, C. H. *The Renaissance of the Twelfth Century.* Cleveland: World Publishing, 1957.

————. *Rise of the Universities.* Ithaca, N.Y.: Cornell University Press, 1957.

Henderson, George. *Gothic Style and Civilization.* Baltimore: Penguin, 1967.

Holmes, U. T. *Daily Living in the Twelfth Century.* Madison: University of Wisconsin Press, 1952.

Knowles, David. *The Evolution of Medieval Thought.* New York: Random House, 1962.

*Lewis, C. S. *The Allegory of Love: A Study in Medieval Tradition.* New York: Oxford University Press, 1936.

Mâle, Emile. *The Gothic Image.* New York: Harper & Row, 1958.

Mason, Eugene. *Aucassin and Nicolette and other Medieval Romances and Legends.* New York: Dutton, 1958.

McKeon, Richard. *Selections from Medieval Philosophers.* 2 vols. New York: Scribners, 1959.

Panofsky, Erwin. *Gothic Architecture and Scholasticism.* Cleveland: World Publishing, 1957.

Simson, Otto von. *The Gothic Cathedral.* New York: Harper & Row, 1962.

*Thorndike, Lynn, (ed.). *University Records and Life in the Middle Ages.* New York: Octagon, 1967.

Ullmann, Walter. *History of Political Thought: The Middle Ages.* Baltimore: Penguin, 1965.

Waddell, Helen. *Medieval Latin Lyrics.* Baltimore: Penguin, 1963.

_____. *Peter Abelard.* New York: Viking, 1959.

_____. *The Wandering Scholars.* Garden City, N.Y.: Doubleday, 1955.

Chapter VIII   EUROPE AND THE WIDER WORLD

Andrae, Tor. *Mohammed, the Man and His Faith.* New York: Harper & Row, 1960.

Atiya, A. S. *Crusade, Commerce and Culture.* New York: Wiley, 1962.

Baynes, N. H. and H. St. L. B. Moss. (eds.). *Byzantium: Introduction to East Roman Civilization.* New York: Oxford University Press, 1948.

*Dawson, Christopher. *The Mongol Mission.* New York: Sheed & Ward, 1955.

Gibb, H. A. R. *Mohammedanism: An Historical Survey.* New York: Oxford University Press, 1953.

Joinville and Villehardouin. *Chronicles of the Crusades.* M. R. B. Shaw (tr.). Baltimore: Penguin, 1963. With an introduction by M. R. B. Shaw.

Lamb, Harold. *Genghis Khan: Emperor of All Men.* New York: Doubleday, 1927.

Lewis, Bernard. *The Arabs in History.* New York: Harper & Row, 1960.

Marcus, J. R. *The Jew in the Medieval World.* New York: Atheneum, 1969.

Newhall, R. A. *The Crusades*. Rev. ed. New York: Harper & Row, 1963.

Polo, Marco. *Travels of Marco Polo*. R. E. Latham (tr.). Baltimore: Penguin, 1958.

Oldenbourg, Zoe. *The Crusades*. New York: Ballantine, 1967.

*Ostrogorsky, George. *History of the Byzantine State*. New Brunswick, N.J.: Rutgers University Press, 1957.

Roth, Cecil. *History of the Jews*. New York: Schocken, 1964.

Runciman, Steven. *History of the Crusades*. 3 vols. New York: Harper & Row, 1964–1967.

Southern, R. W. *Western Views of Islam in the Middle Ages*. Cambridge, Mass.: Harvard University Press, 1962.

Chapter IX   CHANGE IN THE LATER MIDDLE AGES

Aston, Margaret. *The Fifteenth Century: The Prospect of Europe*. New York: Harcourt, Brace & World, 1968.

Burckhardt, Jacob. *Civilization of the Renaissance in Italy*. S. G. C. Middlemore (tr.). New York: New American Library, 1961.

Cheyney, E. P. *The Dawn of a New Era, 1250–1453*. New York: Harper & Row, 1936.

*Ferguson, W. K. *Europe in Transition, 1300–1520*. Boston: Houghton Mifflin, 1963.

Gilmore, M. P. *The World of Humanism, 1453–1517*. New York: Harper & Row, 1952.

Hay, Denys. *Europe in the Fourteenth and Fifteenth Centuries*. New York: Holt, Rinehart and Winston, 1967.

Huizinga, Johan. *The Waning of the Middle Ages*. New York: Doubleday, 1956.

Lerner, R. E. *The Age of Adversity*. Ithaca, N.Y.: Cornell University Press, 1968.

Parry J. H. *The Age of Reconnaissance*. New York: New American Library, 1969.

Perroy, Edouard. *The Hundred Years War*. New York: Putnam, 1965.

Smith, Preserved. *Age of the Reformation*. 2 vols. New York: Collier-Macmillan, 1962.

Schevill, Ferdinand. *Medieval and Renaissance Florence*. 2 vols. New York: Harper & Row, 1963.

Index

225

About the Author

Margaret Hastings is Professor of History at Douglass College, Rutgers, the State University of New Jersey. She received her B.A. and M.A. from Mount Holyoke College and her Ph.D. from Bryn Mawr College. Professor Hastings, a specialist in late medieval and early modern British history, has received a Fulbright Research grant, a Guggenheim Fellowship Award, and an American Council of Learned Societies Faculty fellowship. She is the author of *The Court of Common Pleas in Fifteenth Century England* and a regular reviewer for the *American Historical Review*.